The Fundamentals of Coaching Football

The Fundamentals of Coaching Football

Second Edition

George C. Kraft
Hope College
Holland, Michigan

Wm. C. Brown Publishers

Wm. C. Brown Publishers Trade and Direct Group

Vice President, Publisher *Thomas E. Doran*
Executive Managing Editor *Edward E. Bartell*
Senior Editor *Chris Rogers*
Media Assistant *Karla Blaser*
Production Coordinator *Deborah Donner*

Cover and interior design by Kay D. Fulton

Cover photo by Jim Shaffer

Library of Congress Catalog Card Number: 90–85734

ISBN 0–697–13112–2

Printed in the United States of America by Wm. C. Brown Publishers, 2460 Kerper Boulevard, Dubuque, IA 52001

10 9 8 7 6 5 4 3 2 1

Contents

Part 5
The Kicking Game

Preface

HOW DOES THIS EDITION DIFFER FROM THE FIRST?

As is true in all professions, football is constantly changing. This edition incorporates several new ideas in blocking techniques, and offensive and defensive schemes. The chapter on offensive systems has been expanded to allow for greater development and integrity in presenting the historical development of American football. It is now in paperback, which has brought down the cost. No book on the market is more suited as a textbook for an introductory football course.

WHAT APPROACH DOES THIS BOOK TAKE?

This book attempts to cover everything a coach needs to know to establish a successful football program. The book begins where any coach must begin—personal considerations. What are my motives for going into the profession? What value system will I adopt? How will I assess success? How will I treat others? Unfortunately, many coaches never take the time to analyze these fundamental issues.

A coach can have his personal philosophy and interpersonal relationships clearly established and still never get a program off the ground. He must consider such practical items as playing fields, equipment, training rules, safety, and the like. Closely tied to these practical considerations is organization and planning. A thorough knowledge of all the Xs and Os of offensive and defensive football will be wasted if a coach cannot organize and plan in a systematic, coherent manner.

Only after all of these areas have been covered, does the author get into the key ingredients of building an offense and defense, and the kicking game. No one system is presented at the expense of another. Instead, the emphasis is on why systems evolved as they did, both offensively and defensively, and what coaches can do to meet changes when they evolve.

WHO CAN BENEFIT FROM THIS BOOK?

This book is written for both the experienced and inexperienced coach. It will be especially beneficial to the young coach who, in all likelihood, only knows what his high school and college coaches taught to him or modeled for him. Young coaches especially must evaluate themselves, their philosophies, ethics, and interpersonal skills before entering the intense arena of athletic competition. It is also necessary for the young coach to have at least a rudimentary knowledge of a variety of blocking schemes, offensive systems, and defensive strategies. If a coach only knows what he was taught as an athlete, he will be of little help to a staff that runs a different system. This book will provide the young coach with the basic knowledge necessary to contribute to any coaching staff.

The experienced coach can also benefit from this book. The book is written in an almost checklist style. The experienced coach can go through the headings in each chapter and check items he has or hasn't considered. An analysis of each topic is presented to stimulate further thinking. A summary is presented of all blocking schemes, offensive and defensive systems, and the kicking game.

Even the "armchair quarterback" can receive valuable information from this book. The chapters on offensive and defensive terminology, for example, provide as complete a verbal and diagrammatic guide to the terminology used by coaches and announcers as can be found anywhere. No assumptions on previous knowledge are made. Each section logically builds upon previous sections.

WHAT MAKES THIS BOOK UNIQUE?

All the basic fundamentals that the beginning coach needs to know are objectively and fairly presented. Virtually every other football book on the market presents its material from the point of view of a successful coach, a successful system, or a "winners" platform. In this book, no single system is advocated, but a number are discussed.

The historical development of offensive systems, beginning with soccer and rugby and continuing through the I, Pro, Veer, and Wishbone attacks of today, is unique to this book. Defensive systems developed to meet changing offensive strategies. The 7–1, 6–2, 4–3, 4–4, and four-deep secondaries are presented not only as isolated defenses but also as necessary adaptations to changing offensive concepts. The reader is encouraged to understand basic offensive and defensive alignments and plays as necessary evolutions in the exciting game of American football.

The author deliberately avoids telling the reader what he does, or what he thinks is necessary for a successful program. Instead, he has pulled together the best information from many sources and presents a balanced perspective.

The book constructively challenges traditional thinking. The coach who continues to teach and use the offensive and defensive systems he learned in college because it is the only system he knows, will not be successful for long. This book encourages the coach to make a preliminary exploration of various offenses, defenses, and blocking schemes.

COACH'S (INSTRUCTOR'S) MANUAL

A coach's manual is available to accompany this text. It includes an extended section on offensive and defensive drills, potential course outlines, bibliographies, daily lecture and discussion materials, group learning projects, and a complete bank of carefully written test questions. Write the publisher for your copy.

ACKNOWLEDGMENTS

The author wishes to acknowledge the contributions of Joyce McPherson, Office Manager of the Dow Center at Hope College, who supervised the typing and editing for this edition. Finally, I wish to thank my best friend and wife Roberta who has encouraged me throughout the project. Successful completion of the second edition would not have been possible without her support.

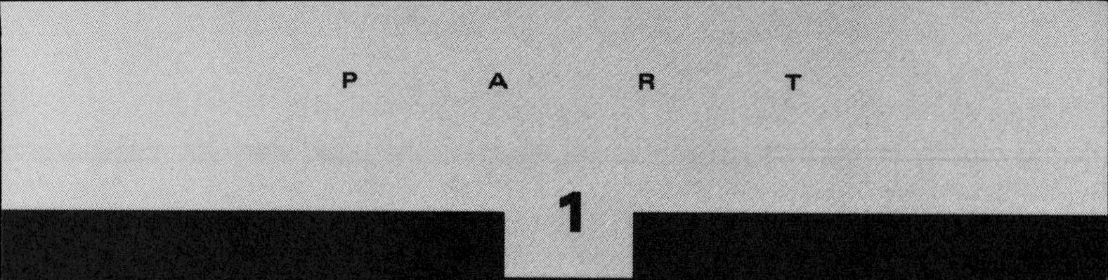

PART 1

1

Personal Considerations

WHY COACH?

Young men enter the profession of coaching for different reasons. An ancient Chinese proverb expresses an eternal truth.

> Those who want to leave an impression for one
> year should plant corn.
> Those who want to leave an impression for ten
> years should plant a tree.
> Those who want to leave an impression for 100
> years should educate a human being.

The most frequent reason given for wanting to coach is success and enjoyment as an athlete and a desire to continue this positive association with sport. People enjoy doing what they do well and this motivation for entering the profession is a worthy one. The potential danger is that, although actually playing the game is a key experience for the prospective coach, it is no guarantee of success.

Young men interested in coaching should begin exploring the field prior to graduation from college. Summer camps, little leagues, churches, and schools are looking for enthusiastic men to help them with coaching responsibilities. Even if there is no pay, assisting will give a young man opportunities to explore whether he is really interested in coaching and if he possesses the necessary qualifications.

Often a college student will declare physical education as his college major because of his physical skills and aptitudes. Most physical education majors prepare for employment in both coaching and teaching.

Admiration for a particular coach and a desire to influence young people in the way he influenced them is a worthy goal and is often mentioned as a motivating reason for entering the profession. With the increase in single-parent families and working mothers, the stability and image that a coach can present may very well be a crucial dimension in the development of a young man's life.

Young people that are enthused and eager to learn are fun to be around, and it can be very rewarding to work with them.

The following reasons are also cited and, although not inherently bad, will not carry any coach through very many years of coaching.

The first is the extra money that is paid to a coach. To a young teacher in junior or senior high school it may seem like a nice additional income, but it doesn't take long before almost every coach, except a few at the top, realizes that his salary doesn't begin to pay for the time, effort, and energy expended. If money is the primary motivation, a young man won't be coaching very long.

Prestige is another factor that draws many young men into coaching. It is certainly true that coaches get their names in the paper more frequently than most of their colleagues, but fame is fleeting and fans are fickle. "You're about as good as your last ball game" is an often-quoted phrase that every coach soon discovers to be true! Fans have notoriously short memories and many armchair quarterbacks can turn from being loyal to critical after surprisingly few losses. Even in junior and senior high school settings, many administrators place won-loss records above other, more worthy goals when determining the fate of coaches.

Closely allied with prestige is ego satisfaction. Egotistical people are self-centered and need continuous positive affirmation. This need can drive a person to great lengths to insure positive feedback. A willingness to work hard with great intensity is necessary for success in coaching, but a person who is excessively self-centered will run into difficulty before too many seasons have passed. Some coaches behave in such a manner that one would think the game was invented so they could coach it! The game was developed so that the players could play it and in the experience, have fun. Egotistical coaches often fail to respect the dignity of every player and will utilize coaching techniques that humiliate, ridicule, or demean. This robs the athlete of the joy in sport and has no place in any coaching style. It is rewarding to see a marked trend away from these coaching techniques.

Most coaches are also teachers in the school system. Since athletic teams are in the public eye and the classroom is not, too many coaches make the mistake of shirking their classroom responsibilities and devoting all their energies to their coaching assignment. This is unfortunate. It gives the profession of physical education a bad name with the majority of the students and faculty in the school. An interscholastic sports experience is frosting on the cake for physically gifted students. When it becomes the primary motivating force for the teacher/coach, or when the coach suggests that it should be this for the student/athlete, he does a great disservice to the athletes as well as to himself. If he is also a teacher, a coach's first responsibility is in the classroom.

Coaching provides opportunities for unique relationships with players. Emotions run high and situations surface during a season that aren't experienced in a typical classroom. Concerned coaches must seize these "teachable moments" and use them to develop positive character traits and attitudes in the players.

Coaches must wear many hats. They are not only teachers but often are called upon to be substitute parents, guidance counselors, public relations officers, and public speakers. It requires a lot more than a prescribed series of coaching courses to adequately prepare oneself for this demanding profession. Courses in the sociological and psychological dimensions of sport, public speaking, and administration are also necessary.

QUALITIES POSSESSED BY SUCCESSFUL COACHES

Many qualities are possessed by successful coaches. Every coach isn't born with them; they must be developed. The degree to which a coach can build on his strengths and correct his weaknesses will determine to a great extent his success.

Successful coaches have the ability to motivate players to peak performances. Webster's dictionary defines the word *motive* as "some inner drive, impulse, intention, etc. that causes a person to do something or act in a certain way. . . ." In the following paragraphs several motivational techniques are noted.

Winning coaches are effective salesmen. The best salesmen exhibit all the traits noted in this section, but it must originate from a wholehearted, enthusiastic endorsement of the great game of American football. If a coach possesses this total commitment to the sport, it will enable him to remain upbeat during the trying times that confront every athletic team. Coaches must model, in their life-styles, the behavior that they expect their players to exhibit. The most important behavior is a buoyant, positive attitude.

Certain individuals have the ability to block out distractions and totally focus on the task at hand. A variety of techniques are used to assist athletes in this. One is the development of a positive self-image. Athletes are encouraged to mentally picture themselves as always succeeding. Linemen can run one-on-one blocks through their minds and always visualize the opponent on his back or well removed from the hole. Ball carriers can visualize themselves as running for touchdowns every time they carry the ball. If their minds start to wander, they can force themselves back to the task at hand with another mental image of a successful performance. Mental practice should be done before the game, during the game, and often when away from the football field. In many ways this is taking the notion of positive thinking and directing it at specific activities at certain points in time. On the value of concentration there can be no disagreement; on the value of always visualizing a successful performance there is still debate.

It is an obvious understatement that nothing succeeds like success. Successful athletes, like successful people, begin to see themselves in a more positive light and this attitude becomes contagious.

Closely associated with this concept of positive self-image is the coach's utilization of praise versus reproof as a motivator. There are coaches who subscribe to the theory that fear is the best motivator. Such coaches attempt to keep the athletes off balance and edgy by belittling and humiliating them, reasoning that they will perform more effectively. They rationalize that the ability to subtly "inflict pain" produces the best results. Research does not support this view. All humans have basic needs and the degree to which the coach can satisfy these needs will provide the stimulus for increased effort. Some of these basic needs are recognition, love, security, status, and self-esteem. The old adage to "accentuate the positive, eliminate the negative" is true. The evidence does suggest, however, that either reproof or praise is better than indifference. Nothing is worse than not being noticed by the coaching staff at all.

Coaches need to look at their vocabulary.[1] Some examples of phrases used by coaches that negatively reinforce are: "Get your head in the game," "You're a sissy," "Don't be a crybaby," "Your sister could block better than that," "You're worthless," "Shut up and listen," and "They cheated, you really won." These phrases are usually uttered in a hostile tone accompanied by frowning facial expressions and an overall attitude of disgust.

The following positive phrases are generally said in an enthusiastic manner: "Way to go," "Even though the offensive drive stalled, look at the great field position we gave the defense," "Good hustle," "Great kick," "Tremendous hit," "Great gang tackling," "Good pursuit," "Forget it," and "Heads up play." Whenever possible, look for opportunities to positively reinforce every player.

Recruiting skills, charm, and a winsome personality are no substitute for a thorough knowledge of all the technical aspects of the game. Coaches at all levels of coaching and experience must attend clinics, read books, and discuss strategies and techniques with fellow coaches. Effective communication originates from a thorough knowledge base.

It is also true, however, that all the knowledge in the world is no guarantee of success. The coach must be able to communicate that knowledge and the athlete must be willing to be taught. As was stated, a climate must be established between coaches and players that makes learning possible. There is truth to the adage that players would really rather *know* that you *care* than *care* that you *know*.

Mike Bobo, *Principles of Coaching Football* (Dubuque, IA: Wm. C. Brown Publishers, 1987), 219.

In addition to caring for the athlete and gaining his respect, a coach must understand the background of each athlete. A player from the ghetto in New York thinks and talks differently than a player from a farm in Kansas. Interviews, team meetings, and questionnaires can assist in this process.

Two additional criteria for effective communication are logical thinking and clarity of expression. A person who doesn't think clearly can't express himself clearly. Hopefully, the whole process of education encourages people to critically analyze what is said and not merely memorize the statements of others. Once thoughts have been formulated, they must be spoken so that they can be understood. Courses in speech can help.

How to motivate players that don't play regularly is a major concern for any coach. Their enthusiastic support can go a long way toward determining the outcome of a season. Team goals must never be at their expense. An example of this is a goal of shutting out an opponent. This goal discourages substitution since it discourages a coach from playing athletes of lesser skill even when, for all practical purposes, the game is won. Every coach realizes the value of a good scout team. Conscientious substitutes who will run the opponent's offense and defense every week provide a valuable service.

Coaches must constantly be looking for legitimate ways to give substitutes recognition. If a substitute gets into a ball game and makes a key tackle or pass interception, mention it at a team meeting and to the press. As a general rule, coaches should stress the fact that wins are team wins. Everyone on the team contributes to the win regardless of whether or not he got into the game. Losses are never the fault of one player or assistant coach. Substitutes must feel that the coaches are interested in what they have to say. They provide a perspective that should be heard, and there should be periodic, private meetings with the substitutes to indicate interest and concern. Whenever possible, adjust the lineup so they have a chance to play. In many cases this year's substitutes will be next year's regulars, so keep their morale high. Even if an athlete doesn't appear to possess the necessary skills to contribute to the program, it is a mistake to adopt a philosophy that says "Don't spend time with people that can't help you."

A successful coach must realize that what motivates each athlete to peak performance varies. He must be ready to provide the correct stimulus at the proper time in order to maximize results. Some players play for ego satisfaction. Others have a real fear of failure that can almost paralyze them at times. For others the motivation is the prospect of material gain some time in the future.

Successful coaches are goal oriented. They establish both personal and team goals. A person can't go anywhere if he doesn't know where he's going. Goals should be clearly spelled out. It is an excellent idea to write goals down and share them with a trusted friend who will assist in evaluating progress. For example, if one of your goals is to make football a rewarding experience for every member of the team, it could be pushed aside in the heat of a league championship or close ball game. Being accountable to a friend periodically might help keep this in focus. Other goals might be to: (1) have fun together as coaches and players, (2) develop each player as a person, (3) build camaraderie among team members, and (4) keep sport in its proper perspective.

Goals must be both realistic and capable of assessment. The four goals noted in the previous paragraph need to be spelled out in more clearly definable terms. A post-season questionnaire, meetings with the captains, or individual conferences with the players might be ways of determining how much fun the players are having. The social, emotional, and spiritual growth of the players is more difficult to objectively assess than physical and intellectual growth, but writing them down, reading them, and discussing them periodically helps a coach keep these goals in perspective during a season.

More specific goals or objectives, like running to and from practice, attaining a certain won-loss record, not sitting on helmets, keeping shirt tails tucked in, running at a certain speed, and bench pressing a certain amount of weight, can be assessed more readily.

Successful coaches have clearly thought through their philosophy of coaching and are consistent in the practical applications of that philosophy. Consistency in the application of one's philosophy is as important as the philosophy itself. Athletes resent partial treatment.

The single most important ingredient of any successful program, if success is defined by a won-loss record, is personnel. Without good material no coach will win very often. In most high school situations the coaching staff can't do anything about this and judicious use of available personnel becomes the key to success. Some coaches instinctively seem to know where to place players to maximize their contribution to the team. It's embarrassing when a player is positioned wrongly or rides the bench and isn't discovered until well into the season. Successful coaching staffs spend many hours evaluating the position and productivity of all players.

Successful coaches possess leadership skills. Athletes look up to them because they have earned their respect, not demanded it. They most often lead by example, not command. "Follow me" not "get going" is their motto. True leaders make subordinates feel that they are working with them and not for them, and they are constantly looking for the *best* way to accomplish things, not necessarily their way. Successful coaches are authoritative but not necessarily authoritarian.

Successful coaches are constantly evaluating themselves and their program. It was Socrates who said that "the unexamined life is not worth living." They examine themselves before someone else does and finds them wanting. After every season an evaluation form should be filled out by the players. One form that could be used is shown on the next page.

Evaluation of Coaching Performance by Athletic Squad Members

The purpose of this evaluation is to aid the coach in becoming a more effective coach. A candid appraisal on your part of his strengths and weaknesses will assist in this process. A space for additional comment or elaboration is provided at the end of the form.

Name of coach being evaluated ______________________________

Sport ______________________________

Instructions to rater:

1. Do not put your name on this form.
2. Make sure your assessment of the coach's performance applies only to the season just completed—this is the period of present evaluation.
3. Rate the coach's ability on each item 1 through 5 as follows or circle no. 6, which indicates that the item does not apply in the sport being dealt with:

   1 = excellent
   2 = good
   3 = average
   4 = below average
   5 = poor
   6 = item does not apply

4. Indicate your year in school:

   Fr. _____ Soph. _____ Jr. _____ Sr. _____

5. Check your squad status:

   _____ Regular
   _____ Starter part-time
   _____ Substitute

Category I: *Character and Ethical Conduct*

1 2 3 4 5 6 — 1. Holds to ethical beliefs and makes genuine attempt to apply them in treatment of his players.

1 2 3 4 5 6 — 2. Sets a good example in terms of personal behavior and habits.

1 2 3 4 5 6 — 3. Is a person of principle without leaving a "holier than thou" impression.

Category II: *Rapport with Players*

1 2 3 4 5 6 — 1. Makes decisions with welfare of entire team in mind; makes genuine attempt to be impartial and fair.

1 2 3 4 5 6 — 2. Is able to motivate players to play hard and practice diligently.

1 2 3 4 5 6 — 3. Inspires confidence in his system and his ability to teach it.

1 2 3 4 5 6 4. Is able to exercise discipline without being overly authoritarian.

1 2 3 4 5 6 5. Has ability to resolve differences between players.

1 2 3 4 5 6 6. Is open to player criticism of his procedures—listens.

1 2 3 4 5 6 7. Changes procedures (at least on occasion) as a result of players' suggestions.

1 2 3 4 5 6 8. Displays sense of humor and serious-mindedness in proper proportions.

1 2 3 4 5 6 9. Has enthusiasm for the program.

1 2 3 4 5 6 10. Is unselfish.

1 2 3 4 5 6 11. Presents a professional appearance.

Category III: *Knowledge of Sport and Ability to Communicate Same*

1 2 3 4 5 6 1. Shows evidence of continuing study and examination of his sport.

1 2 3 4 5 6 2. Is innovative, imaginative, and realistic in choosing systems of operation (offense, defense, etc.).

1 2 3 4 5 6 3. Is able to demonstrate or provide for proper demonstration of various techniques.

1 2 3 4 5 6 4. Is able to effectively detect flaws in his players' technique.

1 2 3 4 5 6 5. Is positive in suggestions for improving a players' technique.

1 2 3 4 5 6 6. Is generous in praise of good performance and genuine effort.

1 2 3 4 5 6 7. Explains clearly and convincingly his reasons for advocating a given procedure.

1 2 3 4 5 6 8. Is patient in repeating explanations.

1 2 3 4 5 6 9. Displays insight in placing personnel effectively as to position.

1 2 3 4 5 6 10. Receives useful information from his scouting system.

1 2 3 4 5 6 11. Makes effective use of films or other similar aids in teaching.

Category IV: *Organization and Administration of Program*

1 2 3 4 5 6 1. Shows evidence that program for the season has been organized well in advance of the season.

1 2 3 4 5 6 2. Practice sessions follow a logical progression and are meaningful.

1 2 3 4 5 6 3. Practice sessions are generally kept at a reasonable length.

1 2 3 4 5 6 4. Team trips are well planned.

1 2 3 4 5 6 5. Responsibility is exercised in providing equipment and caring for same.

Category V: *Stability and Performance Under Pressure*

1 2 3 4 5 6 1. Keeps a clear head in game situations.

1 2 3 4 5 6 2. Displays a manner that includes courtesy, confidence, and firmness.

1 2 3 4 5 6 3. Can see and understand what the opposing team is doing or attempting to do.

1 2 3 4 5 6 4. Is adept at adjusting his team's effort to counter unexpected moves by the opposition.

1 2 3 4 5 6 5. Has his players and substitutes under control in terms of behavior during the game situation and immediately following.

Additional Comment: (Use this space to elaborate or speak to an area not covered by the specific items above.)

Coaches must be open enough to evaluate and critique themselves. If they are weak in certain areas, the weakness must be rectified. Coaches should also solicit an evaluation from the athletic director. He will be making an evaluation anyway, so it is a good idea to ask him for it.

Truly successful coaches realize that they are models for youth. They can't speak to the value of physical activity if they aren't physically active themselves. It does no good to speak of character development through sport at a postseason banquet if everyone knows that questionable tactics are used to win contests. Some coaches will actually deplore the use of profanity when talking with parents and then swear continuously during practice and in ball games. Actions always speak louder than words. Coaches must model those traits in their life-styles that they want their athletes to exhibit.

Genuine enthusiasm is contagious. Everyone enjoys being around people who are wholeheartedly involved in what they are doing. Enthusiastic people are usually positive, quick to see the good in a situation, and ready to affirm others.

Most successful coaches have been former players. It isn't necessary to have been a "star," but many lessons can only be learned from actually having been on a team. Even if a player never gets into a game or serves as the team manager, valuable insights will be acquired that can later be used in coaching.

Reference has been made to academic preparation. A solid major in physical education from a reputable college is the best degree to pursue. It must include more than the traditional skills, methods, and coaching courses. As has been mentioned, courses in the sociology and psychology of sport, mechanical and kinesiological aspects of movement, and physiology of exercise must also be included.

Football coaches who have been successful over a number of years list flexibility high on their list of elements that have led to their continued success. A coach who doggedly persists to coach the way he played and was coached will soon become obsolete. Abilities change, times change, and offenses and defenses change. What worked in previous years cannot automatically be transported into the present.

Flexible coaches also have an open mind. They listen to others—assistant coaches, athletes, knowledgeable associates, and friends. To continue to pursue a course of action when a majority of competent friends and associates think otherwise is dangerous.

Successful coaches continue to learn. The coach who does not go to clinics and conventions and ceases to read contemporary literature on football will not be in the profession very long. A tenured faculty member may dust off twenty-year-old notes and continue to pretend that he is teaching. Coaches with this mentality don't last.

Coaches must be good listeners. This is more difficult for some than others. A lot of coaching time is spent giving directions and instructions. Learning, however, takes place when the ears are open and the mouth closed.

Without organization no coach can be successful. That is why Part Two of this book is devoted to this topic.

Other qualities of successful coaches that have been noted in the literature are: (1) outgoingness, (2) willingness to accept blame, (3) emotional maturity, (4) stick-to-itiveness, and (5) dependability.

Above all, successful coaches have the ability to keep sport in proper perspective. Football is a game to be played for fun. Yogi Berra's famous line "it ain't over till it's over" is certainly true, but equally true is that "when it's over, it's over." Coaches who can't leave the game behind them and make life miserable for everyone the following week will not last long in the coaching profession. Faith, family, and football are all important, and football must never have top priority. Grantland Rice's famous quatrain still holds true today.

> For when the one great scorer comes
> To write against your name,
> He marks—not that you won or lost—
> But how you played the game.

ETHICS IN COACHING

Webster's dictionary offers the following definition for *ethics*. It is "the study of standards of conduct and moral judgment; moral philosophy."

Every coach must carefully think through the set of moral principles and values that will govern his actions. To assume that good sportsmanship and favorable character traits develop automatically through participation in sport is ridiculous. The potential is present for positive or negative development. Factors that will determine the direction of growth are: (1) qualities exhibited by the coach, (2) affirmation or lack thereof by the player's peer group, (3) time involvement (a year-round relationship possesses greater potential for influence than one of brief duration), and (4) the player's home environment. Sport itself doesn't make the difference or cause any change; it is the interaction with people that are admired, and identification with peers in their interests and activities through the potentially powerful medium of sport that will change behaviors.

Unique pressures are placed on coaches from players, parents, administrators, and fans. If the coach hasn't clearly defined his guiding rules for action, temptations to compromise his convictions will be great.

In sport there is generally a winner and a loser at the end of the contest. Every player and coach knows that it is more fun to win, and a person without that competitive drive will not become a successful athlete or coach. But the extent to which coaches will go to insure victory varies. Coaches interested solely in the outcome of a game often read the rule book more to devise devious means for circumventing the rules than to insure conformity to them. Many rule changes and clarifications are a result of coaches being technically correct in their actions but violating the intent of a rule. After using a questionable tactic to gain an advantage, many coaches will sanctimoniously claim that they did not violate any rule and only did what any conscientious coach would do.

The quote attributed to Vince Lombardi that "winning isn't everything, it's the only thing" comes dangerously close to saying that the end justifies the means. All too often coaches that adopt this ethic find people expendable, view the opponent as the enemy, tolerate dehumanizing tactics, and submerge individual freedoms and dignity to rigid, authoritarian structures.

Other coaches are equally desirous of victory but refuse to place outcome ahead of process. For them, the means by which excellence is achieved is as important as the excellence itself. Opponents are not viewed as enemies or as objects to hate, but as persons to be held in genuine respect. Without their presence neither team would be able to achieve their maximum potential.

Coaches who view process to be as important as product tend to encourage participatory democracy in contrast to rigid authoritarianism in decision making. Athletes are encouraged to speak out and become involved in the process of learning. Blind adherence to the dictates of an authoritarian figure is not considered a trait to be praised. These coaches would encourage athletes to develop their own moral ideology and not simply accept that of the coach.

Sport provides a natural setting for coaches to teach standards of conduct and demonstrate moral judgments. Actions speak louder than words, however, and no amount of talk extolling integrity and honesty can undo a single dishonest act done in the heat of an athletic contest.

The American Football Coaches Association has a Code of Ethics. Articles one through eight of the Code are printed here so that every aspiring and practicing coach who has not read them will become familiar with their content.

ARTICLE ONE
Responsibilities to Players

1. In his relationship with players under his care, the coach should always be aware of the tremendous influence he wields, for good or bad. Parents entrust their dearest possession to the coach's charge, and the coach, through his own example, must always be sure that the boys who have played under him are finer and more decent men for having done so. The coach should never place the value of a win above that of instilling the highest desirable ideals and character traits in his players. The safety and welfare of his players should always be uppermost in his mind, and they must never be sacrificed for any personal prestige or selfish glory.

2. In teaching the game of football, the coach must realize that there are certain rules designed to protect the player and provide common standards for determining a winner and loser. Any attempts to beat these rules, to take unfair advantage of an opponent, or to teach deliberate unsportsmanlike conduct, have no place in the game of football, nor has any coach guilty of such teaching any right to call himself a coach. The coach should set the example for winning without boasting and losing without bitterness. A coach who conducts himself according to these principles need have no fear of failure, for in the final analysis, the success of a coach can be measured in terms of the respect he has earned from his own players and from his opponents.

3. The diagnosis and treatment of injuries is a medical problem and should, under no circumstances, be considered a province of the coach. A coach's responsibility is to see that injured players are given prompt and competent medical attention and that the most minute detail of a physician's orders are carried out.

4. Under no circumstances should a coach authorize the use of drugs. Medicants, stimulants, or drugs should be used only when authorized and supervised by a physician.

5. A player's future should not be jeopardized by any circumvention of eligibility rules.

6. A coach should not make demands on his players that will interfere with the player's opportunities for achieving academic success.

ARTICLE TWO
Responsibility to the Institution

1. The function of the coach is to educate students through participation in the game of football. This primary and basic function must never be disregarded.

2. A coach shall conduct himself so as to maintain the principles, integrity, and dignity of his institution.

3. A coach should not exert pressure on faculty members to give players consideration they do not deserve.

4. A coach should not exert pressure on the admissions office to admit players not qualified.

5. A coach should discuss his problems with his athletic director and/or faculty chairman in a friendly manner and then accept and support the decisions that have been reached.

6. Official student records and transcripts should never pass through the coach's office.

7. The coach should constantly be alert to see his program is being conducted and promoted properly. The coach should lend his experience and training to the governing body of the school's athletic program in the solution of football problems. Where differences of opinion arise, and the council overrides the coach's judgment, discretion should be exercised in airing such differences outside the council meeting.

8. It is highly important that a coach support the administration in all policies, rules, and regulations regarding football.

9. A coach's immediate superior, or supervisor, should be notified immediately of a possible position transfer.

ARTICLE THREE
Rules of the Game

1. The Football Code which appears in the Official Football Rule Book shall be considered an integral part of the Code of Ethics and should be carefully read and observed.

2. Each coach should be acquainted thoroughly with the rules of the game. He is responsible for having the rules taught and interpreted for his players.

3. Both the letter and the spirit of the rules must be adhered to by the coaches.

4. To gain an advantage by circumvention or disregard for the rules brands a coach or player as unfit to be associated with football.

5. A coach is responsible for flagrant roughing tactics. He is responsible for illegal substitutions. He shall not permit faking of injuries in order to stop the clock. He shall not permit an illegal shift with the intent of drawing an opponent offside.

6. A coach must remember always that IT IS NOT the purpose of football to hurt or injure an opponent by legal or illegal methods.

7. GOOD SPORTSMANSHIP. Habit formation is developed on the practice field.

Where coaches permit, encourage or condone performance which is dangerous to an opponent, they are derelict in their responsibility to teach fair play and good sportsmanship. This aspect of coaching must be attacked just as vigorously as the teaching of offense and defense, and to the players it is far more important than all the technical aspects of the game combined. Any coach who fails to stress this point, or who permits, encourages, or defends the use of unsportsmanlike tactics shall be considered guilty of the most serious breach of football coaching ethics.

ARTICLE FOUR
Officials

1. No competitive contest can be played satisfactorily without impartial, competent officials. Officials must have the respect and support of coaches and players. On and off-the-record criticism of officials to players or to the public shall be considered unethical.

2. Officials Associations. There should be a cooperative relationship between coaches and officials associations, with frequent interchange of ideas and suggestions. Coaches should, whenever possible, accept invitations to attend officials' rules meetings. Similarly, coaches should extend officials invitations to discuss rules interpretations with their squads, and, on occasion, to officiate at scrimmages, for mutual benefits.

3. Treatment of Officials. On the day of a game officials should be treated in a courteous manner. They should be provided with a private room in which to meet and dress for the game. Conferences between coaches and officials shall always be conducted according to procedures established by the governing Conference or Officials Association. In every respect the official Rule Book shall be followed in coach-official relationships, on the field and during and following a game. Any criticisms which the coach may have to make concerning officiating should be made in writing to the office which assigned the official to the game. For a coach to address, or permit anyone on his bench to address, uncomplimentary remarks to any official during the progress of a game, or to indulge in conduct which might incite players or spectators against the officials, is a violation of the rules of the game and must likewise be considered conduct unworthy of a member of the coaching profession.

4. Use of Movies in Checking Officials. It should be recognized that slow motion study of controversial decisions by officials is far different from on-the-spot decisions which must be made during the course of a game. To show critical plays to sportswriters, sportscasters, alumni and the public, which may incite them to label officials as incompetents, must be considered unethical conduct.

ARTICLE FIVE
Public Relations

1. Members of the news media should be treated with courtesy, honesty, and respect. Derogatory and misleading statements should be avoided. Direct questions should be answered honestly, or not at all. If good judgment indicates an honest answer would be prejudicial to the best interests of the game, ethical procedure demands that it not be answered. In such instances, "No comment" is justifiable.

2. Coaches should assume the responsibility of teaching their players how to conduct themselves in interviews in the best interests of football.

3. The Association recommends that the media be admitted to dressing rooms as soon as practicable after games.

4. Coaches should not stress injuries, disciplinary measures, academic difficulties, eligibility problems, and similar personal matters. Disciplinary problems should be a "family affair" to be solved between the coach and players. Scholastic eligibility is a province of the Dean's or Registrar's office, injuries are essentially the province of the team physician or trainer. No good purpose can be served by emphasizing such matters.

5. Coaches should avoid talking in public about unethical recruiting and use of illegal formations.

6. Any statements that tend to portray football in any light other than being part of the educational process is detrimental to the future of the profession.

7. Falsifying weights is a bad educational process.

8. Coaches should not predict game winners.

9. It shall be unethical for coaches to use alumni, booster, and quarterback club organizations in an attempt to defeat or obstruct institutional athletic controls, or to encourage violation of established rules. It shall be unethical for coaches to make demands, financial or otherwise, upon such groups which are not in keeping with the letter and spirit of existing controls or in any other manner misuse such strength and power in violation of accepted rules and regulations.

10. Accepting money or goods for endorsement of any product or commodity not in keeping with the traditions of the coaching profession is unethical. It is the coach's responsibility to be certain the wording and sense of any testimonial does not bring discredit. Endorsement, directly or indirectly, by active members of the Association, of alcoholic beverages and/or tobacco products is unethical.

11. Solution of professional problems should be within the profession and not in the press. Newspaper columns and magazine articles over the signature of a coach are his responsibility exclusively.

12. Coaches should not be associated in any way with professional gamblers and should not be present where gambling on team sports is encouraged or permitted.

ARTICLE SIX
Scouting

1. It is unethical under any circumstances to scout any team, by any means whatsoever, except in regularly scheduled games. The head coach shall be held responsible for all scouting. This includes the use of motion pictures.

2. It is unethical conduct to violate conference rules on the exchange of film.

3. Direct exchange of film is urged by the Association.

ARTICLE SEVEN
Recruiting

1. All institutional, conference, and national regulatory body rules pertaining to recruiting shall be observed strictly.

2. It is a breach of ethics to recruit a player enrolled at another school (or to recruit a prospective freshman who has avowed his intention to enroll at another school and who has taken residence therein) for the purpose of participating in regularly organized fall practice.

3. A student-athlete should not be recruited during his participation in another sport so that he misses, or is late for, practices and games.

4. In discussing the advantages of his institution, the coach must confine his statements to an honest and forthright presentation of the facts. He shall refrain from making derogatory statements about other institutions and their officials.

5. It is unethical for any coach to make statements to any prospective student which cannot be fulfilled.

ARTICLE EIGHT
Game Day and Other Responsibilities

1. It is vitally important a coach's actions and behavior at all times bring credit to himself, his institution, and the game of football.

2. Before and after a game, rival coaches should meet and exchange friendly greetings.

3. During a game a coach should be as inconspicuous as possible. Coaches are encouraged to demonstrate a friendly and kindly attitude toward their players. The attitude of coaches towards officials should be controlled and undemonstrative.

4. After the game, visitors should not be permitted in team dressing room until coaches have completed their post-game responsibilities, including a careful check of player injuries.

5. Coaches should use their influence to upgrade levels of sportsmanship by rooting sections by working closely with cheerleaders and leaders of card sections.

6. A coach should do all he can to prevent scalping of tickets by players.

7. A coach shall not receive compensation from professional teams for talent scouting of or negotiating for his players.

ASSESSING SUCCESS

Coaches must be constantly evaluating their performance. One thing is certain—others are evaluting you! The yardstick of success that the public uses is the won-loss record of the team. If the person has a son on the team, his success and playing time are also factors. Every coach must know what additional objectives he is seeking to accomplish and communicate these to his players, the administration, and the public.

Won-Loss Record

The typical football fan equates excellence with superior scoreboard scores and generally little more. Many alumni take great pride in the ego satisfaction they can obtain via identification with a winner. Pride in the quality programs of one's alma mater is desirable but must be kept in perspective.

No player or coach enters a contest without a commitment to win. To do otherwise is to cheat your opponent. It's what happens behind the scenes that determines whether true satisfaction can and should be derived from the victory. If dehumanizing tactics, illegal recruiting practices, and rule violations have assisted in the victory, no satisfaction can be gained from it. Most fans can't see these, but the coach and the players know how victory is achieved.

Effect on the Coach and His Family

Every coach must evaluate the extent of his involvement in coaching and its effect on himself and his family. When an unthinking public equates success strictly in terms of a won-loss record, and a coach knows that he will be evaluated in these terms, the pressure to compromise his principles becomes intense. Many coaches spend more time than is necessary organizing and planning. This may sound like a surprising thing to say. The pressures to win force many coaches into beginning full-time planning sessions from early morning until late at night a full month before practices start. All day Sunday is spent viewing films and every evening is spent with the staff. This is not necessary to insure success at any level, and it can have a devastating effect on the coach's family life. Every coach is looking for that winning edge, but the price of success must also be considered.

Effect on the Players

No coach can keep all the players happy all the time. Some coaches don't spend time with the players who, in their opinion, won't help them. Other coaches feel a commitment to every player on the team regardless of whether he is a star, starter, or substitute. The opinion of the athletes in various categories can be determined through the use of the questionnaire presented earlier. Coaches should use a form like this after every season.

The coach can have periodic meetings with the players during the season and in the off-season. In these meetings the players should be encouraged to express their opinions on a variety of topics such as practice organization, personal aspirations, how the programs can be improved, their contribution to the team effort, and so forth.

Coaches must be constantly evaluating their programs. This provides one of the most effective means for improvement.

RELATIONSHIPS WITH OTHERS

The coach's relationships with his players are crucial. Motivation, communication, enthusiasm, flexibility, listening, praise versus reproof, and positive self-image—all items noted in the previous two sections have a direct bearing on this relationship. The coach must constantly evaluate himself in these areas if he hopes to improve his relationships.

Relationships between members of the coaching staff will go a long way toward determining the success of a program. The staff should not be like-minded in all aspects of football, but there must be a basic philosophical agreement on foundational issues or disharmony will develop. Foundational issues include: Sunday preparation and practice time, use of profanity, training rules and their enforcement, and responsibility given to assistants.

There must be mutual respect between coaches. This doesn't mean that they all have similar interests and abilities. Some head coaches frustrate able assistants by insisting that they adopt their life-style. No one life-style has proven to be best for a coach, so no coach should be forced to do things that run against his beliefs.

One word crops up in the literature repeatedly when discussing staff relationships—loyalty. This does not mean that an assistant coach is a "yes" man; it does mean that disagreements are fully discussed at staff meetings and not continued with the players after a decision has been made. If an assistant coach finds himself consistently in disagreement with the rest of the staff on important issues, he should resign.

A coach's family and the personal dynamics of this relationship will greatly affect a coach's effectiveness. It has even been suggested that a head coach can learn more by interviewing a prospective assistant's wife than the prospective coach!

Skip Stogsdill reported the results of a questionnaire that he administered to 100 wives at a Fellowship of Christian Athletes Conference in *The Christian Athlete*. The responses, although made some years ago, provide excellent insights into the reactions and involvement of spouses in the coaching experience.

Ninety-five percent responded favorably when told that many outsiders felt it must be "exciting" to be the wife of a coach. Nevertheless, a significant portion of the wives resented: (1) having their husbands gone so much, especially in the evenings and at times of crisis; (2) bearing the bulk of the responsibility for children's discipline; (3) having to be both parents during the season; (4) contending with late suppers; (5) putting up wth their husband's tensions; (6) conflicts with special plans and special days; and (7) keeping quiet whenever fans or the press criticized their husbands.

When asked if they felt it was essential to be a sports fan, especially in their husband's sport, the wives were evenly divided in their responses, but all felt that it was important to enthusiastically support their husbands in their effort.

When asked if they felt that coaches made better fathers, 20 percent said "no," 25 percent said "yes," and 55 percent said "not necessarily." Most felt that it depended on the individual, but that coaching did provide opportunities to see and cope with the problems facing young people.

Some of the rewards of being a coach's wife were: (1) opportunities to meet people, (2) "staying young" through the associations with wholesome young men and boys, (3) hearing from former athletes either by mail, phone, or in person, (4) being married to someone who loves what he's doing, and even (5) watching all those football games on New Year's Day!

How can coaches' wives fill the long hours that their spouses are away from home? Finding outside interests was the most frequently given suggestion, but others admitted that they hadn't learned to cope with it. One enterprising spouse said, "I'm learning how to scout!"

Coaches must be careful that they don't automatically expect their sons to become interested in the sports they coach. Children should be allowed to explore all avenues of worthy endeavor and to deprive children of this opportunity is unfair.

It's a mistake for a coach to marry a person who has no interest in sports, but it doesn't mean that the marriage is destined to be a failure. If the wife of a coach is not sports-minded, it is crucial that she explore outside interests. If she sits around at home devoting herself to the sole chore of raising the kids, anger and resentment will inevitably develop. Her education should not cease just because she married a coach. Babysitter funds must be squeezed into the budget, since the father won't have the time or the energy to give as much attention to the children.

It is as important for a coach to continually evaluate his family life as it is for him to evaluate his coaching effectiveness. Ineffectiveness in either area can have disastrous effects.

The players' parents are another group that influences a coach. Some coaches adopt the attitude that parents are nothing more than a potential source of trouble and, therefore, avoid them completely. Other coaches more realistically build relationships with the players' parents and attempt to make them positively disposed to the program. One excellent way of getting to meet parents and creating a friendly environment in which they can get to know each other, is to invite them to a preseason scrimmage that is followed by a coffee or brunch. At the brunch, name tags should be worn by everyone. The head coach should introduce his staff and other key people in the program, including the coaches' wives! Players can introduce themselves and their parents. Following the formal portion of the program, a climate must be created that encourages parents to interact with each other. Friendships can begin this way and a loyal rooting section can be developed for both home and away games.

The major concern of all parents is that their son have a positive experience. This is obviously made easier if their son is playing regularly. If he isn't a regular, it becomes more of a challenge, especially if the family's life totally revolves around football. This is why getting parents involved with the total team effort and introduced to other players and parents is so crucial. In this way they can contribute, even if their son isn't playing. Parents will appreciate the attention and concern that the coaching staff gives to their son, even if he isn't playing.

Coaches must treat officials with the dignity and respect that they deserve. To attempt to intimidate officials by threatening not to rehire them (if the coach has a say in this), or by attempting to make them look foolish is indefensible. If a coach genuinely feels that an error has been made, he owes it to himself and the team to obtain an explanation, but this should be done in an orderly fashion. To incite the crowd by questioning calls in an overt, provocative manner cannot be tolerated. A coach who deliberately resorts to this tactic is unprofessional. It is an official's responsibility to be in the right place at the right time to make a call. If he is on top of the play and makes an unfortunate judgment call, a certain amount of frustration is natural. But to continually blame losses on this at post-game press conferences, and to be always questioning the officials' decisions when viewing film, is a sign of an immature coach.

A coach can't escape interactions with the media, and it is essential that he court that relationship. It is foolhardy to unnecessarily antagonize reporters. They don't report to you and are responsible to the public, so don't argue with them. It has been said, "The only way you can argue with a newspaper is to start a publication of your own!"

Most conferences have a preseason press day to which local representatives of the media are invited. If your conference doesn't have such an event, the coaches should attempt to organize one. Several activities can be conducted on this day. The veteran coaches can meet and introduce any new coaches to the conference, rules and policies can be clarified, formal speeches can be made, a time for interviews can be set aside, and often a golf outing is planned where coaches and media can interact in an informal setting. The time, effort, and even out-of-pocket expense for such an occasion can be worthwhile in terms of favorable coverage.

The school's alumni can be a valuable source of support. If they appreciate sports, they enjoy the pride that comes via identification with a winner. It is the coach's job to sell them on himself, his team, and his program. One excellent means of accomplishing this is through the development of a "Quarterback Club." It can meet over a lunch hour or some evening during the week. One logical format for the club could be: (1) a meal or dessert, (2) introductions by the head coach (assistant coaches and key players could be invited each week), (3) viewing a portion of the previous week's game, (4) analysis of an upcoming opponent, and (5) a time for questions. This is also an excellent opportunity for the head coach to educate the alumni and faithful fans on his personal philosophy of life and football.

Every coach needs to develop good relations with his faculty colleagues. In most instances, the coach is a formal part of the academic community. If the football program is perceived as constantly wanting special favors, resentments develop. Much misunderstanding can be alleviated through communication. Coaches should not be isolated in a "football complex." If the physical arrangement of the campus places the coaches away from their colleagues, it is essential that they go to the faculty. The faculty lounge should be frequented and the coaches should be open to questions. Football should not dominate the conversation, however. Coaches should be knowledgeable in other areas and demonstrate an interest in discussions on a variety of topics.

If a particular faculty member is especially hostile to the program, one of the coaches could go out to lunch with him to discuss the problem. Faculty could be invited to join the squad for a pregame meal or be on the sidelines or in the press box during a game.

A supportive student body goes a long way in lifting the morale of the team. Coaches should not pass up invitations to speak at pep rallies or other student functions. A student body will be more supportive of athletes that they know personally and admire. For this reason, it is a mistake to house athletes in a separate dormitory.

The trainer, if a school is fortunate enough to have one, must be treated with dignity and respect. His professional decisions cannot be questioned. If he is viewed as being a puppet of the management, the players will not trust his decisions. He can also serve as a valuable link between the players and the coaches.

A final individual that should be recognized and given enough authority to function effectively is the equipment manager. His responsibilities are covered in the next chapter.

2

Practical Considerations

FIELDS AND EQUIPMENT

The amount of available practice space varies greatly from school to school. If the practice area is the regulation field, it should be properly lined. If another area is available, it should also be lined every five yards with hash marks for whatever length is possible. Offensive and defensive linemen must immediately establish the habit of getting lined up squarely and this should be done during all the phases of practice. Clear, straight lines are necessary. Quarterbacks, receivers, and defensive backs need to become familiar with the boundaries of the regulation field and, therefore, must practice on one. A reliable lining machine is a necessary part of the maintenance equipment. Also, an additional set of goal posts should be located at the end of this practice area so that the place kickers can continue to practice when the regular practice field is in use.

It is especially crucial when space is limited to insure proper maintenance. Fields must be watered during two-a-day practices, especially if the weather is hot and dry. Coaches must immediately check with the maintenance department if this is not happening. Coaches should rotate practice locations on the field and not always do agility drills on the yard lines.

A seven-man sled is a valuable piece of equipment. Sleds that include the T-bar striking surface are ideal for teams that use a forearm lift (palm punch) blocking technique, but they are more expensive. This sled provides an ideal teaching station for instruction in blocking and tackling techniques. Many drills noted in the Coach's Manual incorporate use of this sled.

A two-man sled can be moved more easily and can be effectively used in observing two blockers' actions. If one strikes sooner than the other or at an incorrect angle, the sled will spin.

Standing dummies are becoming obsolete. Defenses are constantly shifting and a standing dummy presents an unrealistic picture. They can be used in the early practices for instruction in form blocking if sleds are unavailable. The newer dummies are filled with foam and are much lighter than the canvas dummies that were filled with kapok.

Hand dummies (light air bags) are necessary pieces of equipment. The person holding one can still react to the situation, thus making it more realistic, but at the same time protect himself from unnecessary injury.

Several boards that are ten feet long and eighteen inches wide can be excellent for blocking instruction. Several drills noted in later chapters utilize them.

A simple long piece of rope with a knot tied at each location where a lineman's head should be can serve as an excellent device to teach correct spacing and alignment. A knot could be included for a split end or flanker at a specified distance, so that they can begin to measure the precise distance from the quarterback.

Chutes are not as popular as they used to be, but can be constructed to assist linemen in staying low as they come off the football.

Rubber tires or a grid system of rope is often created. Football players practice high stepping through them. The actual function of this setup and drill has been questioned by some coaches.

Some schools have put a net behind the goal posts and hung a tire in front of it. Quarterbacks can practice throwing through the tire, while the net saves unnecessary shagging of footballs.

Pullover jerseys or vests are necessary to slip over the practice jerseys of players as they practice with the scout team. It is very expensive to outfit a football player, but football is a high-risk sport and safety must be a major consideration. The coaches must familiarize themselves with the Rule Book and make sure that their equipment conforms to these standards. Reputable sporting goods salesmen will be able to assist in this regard.

Blisters can hobble an athlete, especially in the early practices. Be sure that the players' shoes fit properly and that petroleum jelly is used by every athlete early in the season.

Many coaches know very little about fitting helmets and shoulder pads properly. The determining factors on shoulder pad selection are the position the athlete plays and the width of his shoulders. Linemen's shoulder pads are cut square and come down farther. Pads must cover the shoulders and sternum. All shoulder pads should have a strap arch support and a foam arch support with air pockets between them. Helmets must be snug but not constricting and must conform to current standards. The skin should move with the helmet as it is twisted laterally. If it doesn't, it is too loose. Depending on the position the athlete plays, he may want OPO (oral protection only), NOPO (nose and oral protection only), NJOPO (nose, jaw, and oral protection only), or JOPO (jaw and oral protection only). All helmets must be NOCSAE (National Operating Committee on Standards for Athletic Equipment) approved.

Mouth protectors must be fitted properly, ideally checked by a dentist, and examined regularly for possible breaks. The coaching staff should personally fit the helmets and shoulder pads. This immediately demonstrates to the players concern for their safety, and it provides a relaxed environment for the coaches to either meet or reacquaint themselves with the athletes. Hip or girdle pads must be worn by all athletes, and the pants must fit in such a way that the thigh and knee pads protect the thigh and knee.

The locker room and lockers must provide for good ventilation. If ventilation is poor, large fans can be used. A regular schedule of laundry must be established. During two-a-day practices, it is ideal if the players can have clean socks, jock, and a T-shirt for each afternoon practice.

In the off-season equipment must be stored in good condition. Items that need repair must be identified and reconditioned. The equipment manager must keep an accurate record of all equipment that includes its age, condition, and size.

A suggested card that can be used to keep track of the equipment checked out to each player is presented in Figure 2.1.

Coaches need to consider their attire. Uniformity in their dress, although not necessary, looks sharp. The coach responsible for the kicking game should bring a stopwatch with him. Each coach should also have a whistle, since he can lose his voice quickly if he doesn't use one. Legitimate budget items include shorts, long pants, hat, shirt, and jacket.

KNOWLEDGE OF THE RULES

Coaches are notoriously unfamiliar with the official rules of football and the code of officials' signals. Many arguments between coaches and officials stem from ignorance on the coach's part. Every coach must have a copy of the current rules and have read it prior to the season. In addition, he should attend a meeting where an official explains the latest rule changes. Better yet, he should have an official come to an early scull session of the entire team and go over rule changes. Figure 2.2 presents 47 official football signals.

Locker No. Combination	Date
Name	Lock No.
College Address	Sport

No.	Phys. Ed.	No.	Equipment
	Shirt		
	Shorts		
	Socks		
	Towel		
	Supporter		Football
No.	**Equipment**	**No.**	**Equipment**
	"T" Shirt		Helmet
	Shorts		Shoulder Pads
	Towel		Girdle Pads
	Socks		Thigh Pads
	Supporter		Knee Pads
	Bag No.		Pants–Football
			Jersey–Football
	Sweat Shirt		Knee Brace
	Sweat Pants		
	Parka		
	Basketball Shoes		
	Football Cleats		
	Signature Check Out		Signature Check In

▶ **Figure 2.1** Equipment Check-Out Card

Official Football Signals

▶ **Figure 2.2** Official Football Signals

SAFETY

Football is a contact sport and injuries will occur. However, it is the responsibility of everyone associated with the program to do everything possible to minimize the risks. For many years manufacturing companies were the target of mammoth law suits. Recently, allegations of negligence have fallen into the following two areas: failure to properly instruct and failure to warn sufficiently.

The importance of coaches warning the athletes of potential dangers is a spin-off from product-liability cases. All equipment now has warnings of the potential hazards clearly affixed to it. Coaches *must* intensively and extensively warn players about inherent dangers in the execution of various techniques.

Warning procedures and safety regulations should be in written form and posted. If an injury occurs and coaches can demonstrate with hard evidence that they continually reminded players of potential dangers, had them written into their playbooks, and posted on the practice plans, it will greatly assist their lawyer if a suit is brought against a staff and a school.

In order to properly instruct, coaches must know the rules. If a neck injury occurred and films show that a player lowered his head and blocked in such a way that his helmet made initial contact, the coach had better have instructed the player repeatedly that this was not a correct blocking technique. If a coach has encouraged the athlete to use his head as a battering ram through using such statements as "lower the boom," "tear his head off," "head to gut," or "helmet in the numbers," a guilty verdict is virtually assured.

Attorney Gene O'Connor, who is a member of the American Football Coaches Association, made the following points that were published in the *Proceedings* of the 55th annual meeting of the AFCA.

1. All the dangers of techniques taught must be explained fully to the players.
2. Be sure you know proper first-aid procedures before working on injured players. Do not invade the field of the physician.
3. Do not overmatch players in practice.
4. All precautions should be taken to avoid injuries in practice and games.
5. No player assumes the risk of a coach's negligence.
6. Players sued for wrongful acts may claim the coach is at fault for permitting them.
7. Players must be taught safety rules. Discipline violators.
8. Spirit and intent of rules must be adhered to.
9. Review and know the AFCA Code of Ethics and the Official Playing Rules.
10. Take words of violence out of your teaching language.

Centralia High School in Washington state has devised the following statement concerning potential injuries in football. It states the coaching staff's position on teaching the basic hitting position and lists the school's obligation concerning equipment.[1]

Football is a contact sport and injuries will occur. The coaches working in our program are well-qualified, professional people. Fundamentals related to playing football will continually and repeatedly be emphasized on and off the field. The information contained within this list of rules and procedures is to inform the young men in our football program of the proper techniques to practice for maximum safety in the contact phase of the game.

Tackling, Blocking, and Running the Ball

By rule, the helmet is not to be used as a 'ram.' Initial contact is not to be made with the helmet. It is not possible to play the game safely or correctly without making contact with the helmet when properly blocking and tackling an opponent. Therefore, technique is most important to prevention of injuries.

Tackling and blocking techniques are basically the same. Contact is to be made above the waist but not initially with the helmet. The player should always be in a position of balance, knees bent, back straight, body *slightly* bent forward, *head up,* target area as near to the body as possible with the main contact being made with the shoulder.

Blocking and tackling by not putting the helmet as close to the body as possible could result in shoulder injury such as a separation or a pinched nerve in the neck area. The dangers of not following the proper techniques can be from minor to disabling to even death. The reason for following the safety rules in making contact with the upper body and helmet is that improper body alignment can put the spinal column in a vulnerable position for injury.

If the head is bent downward, the cervical (neck) vertebrae are in a bind and contact on the TOP OF THE HELMET could result in a dislocation, nerve damage, paralysis or even death. If the back is not straight, the thoracic (mid-back) and lumbar vertebra are also vulnerable to injury with similar results if contact again is made to the TOP OF THE HELMET. Centralia's daily workout includes isometric type exercises; the development of strength in the neck muscles is one of the best methods of preventing head injury and enabling an individual to hold his head up even after getting tired during a workout or contest.

Basic Hitting (Contact) Position and Fundamental Technique

If the knees are not bent, the chance of knee injury is greatly increased. Fundamentally, a player should be in the proper hitting position at all times during live ball play and this point will be repeated continually during practice. The danger is any-

[1]Samuel H. Adams, "Court Decision Hits Hard with New Liability Twists," *Athletic Purchasing and Facilities,* May 1982: 14.

thing from strained muscles, to ankle injuries to serious knee injuries requiring surgery. The rules have made blocking below the waist (outside a two-yard by four-yard area next to the football) illegal. Cleats have been restricted to no more than ½ inch to further help in preventing knee injuries. A runner with the ball, however, may be tackled around the legs.

In tackling, the rules prohibit initial contact with the helmet or grabbing the face mask or edge of the helmet. These restrictions were placed in the rules because of serious injuries resulting from non-compliance to these safety precautions. Initial helmet contact could result in a bruise, dislocation, broken bone, head injury, internal injury such as kidneys, spleen, bladder, etc. Grabbing the face mask or helmet edge could result in a neck injury which could be anything from a muscle strain to a dislocation, nerve injury, or spinal column damage causing paralysis or death.

The illegal play by participating athletes will not be tolerated and all players are repeatedly reminded of the dangers of unsportsmanlike acts.

Fitting and Use of Equipment

Shoulder pads, helmets, hip pads, pants including thigh pads and knee pads must have proper fitting and use.

Shoulder pads which are too small will leave the shoulder point vulnerable to bruises or separations; it could also be too tight in the neck area resulting in a possible pinched nerve. Shoulder pads which are too large will leave the neck area poorly protected and will slide on the shoulders making them vulnerable to bruises or separations.

Helmets must fit snugly at the contact points: front, back, and top of head. The helmet must be safety "NOCSAE" branded; the chin straps must be fastened and the cheek pads must be of the proper thickness. On contact, too tight a helmet could result in a headache. Too loose a fit could result in headaches, a concussion, a face injury such as a broken nose or cheek bone, a blow to the back of the neck causing a neck injury, possibly quite serious such as paralysis or even death.

This report does not cover all potential injury possibilities in playing football, but it is an attempt to make the players aware that fundamentals, coaching, and proper fitting equipment are important to their safety and enjoyment in playing football at Centralia High School.

The above information has been explained to me and I understand the list of rules and procedures. I also understand the necessity of using the proper techniques while participating in the football program.

Athlete's Signature ______________________________

Date of Signature ______________________________

Witness ______________________________

For the high school level and below, it might be a good idea to have the athlete's parent or guardian also sign this statement. A medical examination and filling out a medical history form must be completed prior to each season. An immunization record should also be available on every football player. Players should be protected against poliomyelitis, tetanus, diphtheria, and German measles and mumps if they haven't already acquired immunity.

It is the responsibility of the coach to see that the following safety requirements are met.[2]

1. The field must be free of rocks, obstructions, holes, and glass.
2. Goal posts must be padded.
3. Curbs, benches, fences, and spectators must be a safe distance from the sidelines.
4. There must be no high voltage wires or open electrical boxes close to the field or practice area.
5. Sprinkler heads, if uneven with ground surface or protruding, must be marked.
6. Dust should be kept to a minimum through light sprinkling prior to practice.
7. All dummies, sleds, and equipment should be checked for safety.
8. Horseplay must not be allowed in the locker room.
9. Locker rooms must be well-organized and clean.

The trainer or his assistant should be at the practice field when full-scale scrimmaging is in progress. When the trainer is not present, the coaches should know where he is and have a means of quickly contacting him. Two-way radios might be a useful device.

A training room should be equipped with the following items, which the American Medical Association recommends should be in supply at all times.[3]

Applicators (swabs)
Artificial airway
Blankets
Bulletin board and blackboard
Cleat wrenches
Clippers or razors
Clock
Crutches (adjustable)
Drinking cups (disposable)
Eye patches
Felt (wool, regular, and adhesive)
Fire extinguisher (dry powder or carbon dioxide types)
Gauze pads (sterile—4″ × 4″)
Gauze rolls (2″) for ankles and dressings
Heel cups for bruised heels
Ice (for cold applications)
Mouthwash
Nail cutters (toenail and fingernail)
Ointment (analgesic)
Ointment (antiglare)
Ointment (lubricating)
Powder for minor chafing
Protective pads (miscellaneous sizes)

[2]Bill Murray and Dick Herbert, eds., "A Coach's Guide to Safe Football," *Football Coaching* (New York: Charles Scribner's Sons, 1981), 266–67.

[3]Reprinted with permission of the American Medical Association, *Comments on Sports Medicine.* Copyright © 1973, American Medical Association.

Resin
Rubbing oil (massage)
Safety pins
Salt tablets (enteric coated) and dispenser
Scales
Scalpel
Scissors (for bandage and dressing purposes)
Sink with hot and cold water
Skin adherent for taping
Slings (triangular bandages)
Soap
Spine board (short and long)
Splints (regular and inflatable)
Stockinettes
Suction cup for removing corneal contact lenses
Tables (taping 24″W × 72″L × 32–34″H)
Tape (adhesive, various widths and grades, including 2″)
Tape cutters
Tape removers
Thermometer (oral)
Tongue depressors
Tongue forceps
Towels (paper and cotton)
Tracheotomy tube
Water dispenser
Weight charts
Wraps (elastic and non-elastic)

Football practices generally begin in August. This is one of the hottest months of the year and coaches must be extremely careful, especially during two-a-day practices.

The AMA offers the following suggestions to help coaches prevent heat exhaustion and heat stroke during hot weather activity.[4]

At the start of fall practice, gradual acclimation to hot weather activity is essential. Equally important is the need to adjust salt and water intake to weather conditions. This acclimation can take place over a period of a week.

As an athlete becomes accustomed to hot weather activity, he perspires more freely (thus dissipating body heat) and excretes less salt (thus conserving sodium).

The old idea of withholding water is dangerous. During exercise in heat, it is essential to replace water lost by perspiration. This could be as often as every twenty minutes in extreme cases.

Salt must be replaced daily, especially during the acclimation period. Extra salting of food will acomplish this purpose.

It is advisable to alternate periods of strenuous exercise with periods of rest.

Symptoms of water and salt depletion may include sluggishness, headache, nausea, hallucinations, and weak and rapid pulse. The coach should watch for signs of lethargy, inattention, stupor, awkwardness, or unusual fatigue.

If illness is suspected, prompt attention to recommended emergency procedures is vital.

[4]Reprinted with permission of the American Medical Association, *Comments on Sports Medicine.* Copyright © 1973, American Medical Association.

Additional recommendations were to:

1. Schedule workouts during cooler morning and early evening hours.
2. Acclimate athletes with carefully graduated practice schedules.
3. Provide rest periods of ten to twenty minutes during workouts of an hour or more.
4. Supply clothing that is white to reflect heat, comfortable to permit heat escape, and permeable to moisture to allow heat loss via sweat evaporation.
5. Provide water or electrolyte solution for players to use ad lib or on demand every twenty minutes. Ice can also be used freely. If adequate water is furnished on demand, you will probably not have to contend with the problems of heat exhaustion or sunstroke to athletes.
6. Watch athletes carefully for signs of trouble, particularly those who lose much weight, heavy athletes, and determined athletes who may not report their discomfort.
7. Remember that temperature and humidity are the crucial factors. Measuring the relative humidity, by the use of a sling psychrometer on the field, is recommended. Heat exhaustion and heat stroke can occur in the shade.
8. Alert the hospital emergency room medical and nursing staff of the possibility of heat illness before an emergency occurs so that they are prepared to take care of a stricken athlete.
9. Know what to do in such an emergency. Be familiar with immediate first aid practices and prearranged procedures for obtaining immediate medical care, including ambulance service.
10. Outlaw the hazardous warm weather use of rubberized apparel or other dehydration devices by players.

TRAINING RULES AND ROOM

Drug use and abuse keeps rearing its ugly head in sports as it does in other segments of society. Drugs are chemicals that produce changes in the body. It is hoped that those changes will produce favorable physical responses but often the side effects are undesirable and potentially dangerous.

Drugs can be classified into three major classes according to their effect on the user: stimulants, depressants, and hallucinogens.

The danger inherent in stimulants is that they can produce a false feeling of energy and vitality, when in actuality the subject is exhausted. The athlete is subject to a sudden and complete collapse.

Depressants can cause slurred speech, drowsiness, and a slowed heart rate. Overdoses can cause a loss of control of body functions, restlessness, and open hostility.

Hallucinogens such as LSD and marijuana obviously can't enhance physical or mental performance and must be avoided.

The use of amphetamines and androgenic-anabolic steroids (synthetic male sex hormones) have no place in a sports program at any level. It has not been proven that occasional use of either causes any permanent damage but neither has it been shown to significantly improve performances. Potential dangers are certainly present. The Committee on Medical Aspects of Sports of the AMA strongly condemns the use of both.

Alcohol use and abuse causes more serious social problems than all other forms of drug abuse combined.

1. Alcohol-precipitated cirrhosis is the sixth leading cause of death in the United States.
2. Alcohol abusers shorten their life spans by 10 to 12 years.
3. One-half of all traffic fatalities are associated with alcohol use.
4. One-third of all homicides are associated with alcohol use.
5. One-third to one-half of all fatal accidents (other than traffic) are associated with alcohol use.
6. One-third to one-half of all crimes committed are associated with alcohol use.
7. One-third of all arrests are for public intoxication.
8. Alcohol abuse and alcoholism drain the economy of an estimated $15 billion per year. Of this total: $10 billion is attributable to lost work time; $2 billion is spent for health and welfare services provided to alcoholics and their families; and property damage, medical expenses, and other overhead costs account for another $3 billion.
9. One in every five persons is closely related to someone who suffers from alcohol abuse.[5]

Alcohol is a depressant of the central nervous system. Taken in small doses, alcohol can have a relaxing effect and cause a person to experience a happy feeling. It can serve to stimulate conversation and friendliness. But normal critical thinking is not possible when influenced by alcohol, since cortical function is disrupted and anxieties can be temporarily reduced.

Even moderate consumption of alcohol interferes with coordination, intellectual function, and verbal performance. High doses can cause serious behavior changes. These changes differ with individuals but include hostility, belligerency, and depression.

[5]Paul M. Insel and Walton T. Roth, *Core Concepts in Health,* 3rd ed., (Palo Alto, CA: Mayfield Publishing Company, 1982), 237.

Excessive consumption of alcohol creates a dependency and leads to a tolerance that requires more alcohol to be drunk to get the same effect. Any athlete who wants to perform at peak efficiency will refrain from drinking.

The dangers of tobacco are even more obvious and immediately detrimental than alcohol. Nicotine, the predominant drug in tobacco, enters through the mucus of the lungs into the blood stream. From there it travels, by way of the heart, directly to the brain. The nicotine reaches the brain about seven seconds after the smoke enters the lungs. Nicotine appears to be the substance in the cigarette that causes addiction. It is also the major cause of cardiovascular disease.[6]

Smoking also produces carbon monoxide, which displaces the oxygen normally carried by the hemoglobin in the blood. For this reason smokers become short of breath much more easily. The hazardous effects of smoking have been so well documented that they need not be elaborated on here. No serious athlete can continue this deadly habit.

Getting adequate sleep is important. Top performance demands sufficient rest. College athletes especially are guilty of staying up too late and causing their bodies to become run down. During the football season the athlete must budget time wisely to insure adequate amounts for study, sleep, and practice.

What constitutes appropriate dress has always been a topic of discussion in sport. Coaches who have been around for a number of years have seen the pendulum of dressing styles run full circle. Most coaches require a neat appearance and meet with the captains to determine specifics for a given season.

Hair length and facial hair are additional points of contention. Coaches must be sensitive to the varying mores of different cultures. A black athlete's desire to have a beard need not necessarily be a reflection of an antagonistic attitude any more than certain white athletes' desire for long hair indicates rebellion. Coaches must use a democratic process in arriving at their rules if they want the backing of the team in enforcing them.

When athletes are on trips they must realize that their conduct reflects on themselves, the coach, the team, and the school. The public is very quick to praise and criticize the conduct of athletes both on and off the field.

If a school is fortunate enough to have a training room and trainer, his input must be valued, respected, and followed. Nothing erodes the confidence of a trainer on the coaching staff and the credibility of the trainer in the eyes of the players more than to have his medical decisions overruled. The day after a game is an important time to have the training room open with the trainer present. Players that are injured or have some aches and pains must see him.

[6]Insel, *Core Concepts in Health,* 204.

The trainer should give a status report to the head coach on the health of the team each day, but this is especially important on Monday morning. This can't occur if the players aren't reporting to him. Coaches should come down hard on players who call in sick or injured and haven't checked with the trainer.

The trainer must know that he has the respect of the coaching staff and that his recommendations will be followed. If coaches play individuals in a game against the recommendation of the trainer, rapport is quickly broken and the trainer's effectiveness negated.

DIET

Proper nutrition is essential for maximum physical performance. There are three categories of foods: proteins, carbohydrates, and fats.

During the past few years foods high in protein have been glamorized. Health food stores have featured them. Diets high in protein have become popular. At the same time fats and carbohydrates that tend to be higher in calories have undergone criticism. The best sources of protein are meat, fish, fowl, milk, eggs, nuts, cheese, and whole grains.

Carbohydrates are the main source of all food energy and are the most efficient fuel food for athletes. They can be mobilized more quickly as an energy fuel than either proteins or fats. Fruits, vegetables, cereals, and grains contain significant portions of carbohydrates. The training meal of spaghetti or pancakes is higher in carbohydrates and lower in fats than the traditional steak or hamburger.

The word *fat* conjures up negative images for most people. Fats, however, have positive aspects. The body can store fat efficiently as a reserve fuel supply, and fats contain over twice as much caloric energy per gram than the other two categories of food. Sources of fats include butter, lard, margarine, pork sausage, and bacon. Fats also appear in significant amounts in nuts, cream, milk, grains, and egg yolk.

Growing young men need to include food in their diets from each of the four basic food groups.

Group I: Milk. Teenagers need four or more eight-ounce glasses daily. Substitute foods are cheese and ice cream. Milk complements cereal or bread to make a complete protein.

Group II: Meat. Americans in general eat much more meat than is either necessary or good for them. The basic problem is usually the size of the portion. Four to six ounces of meat is all that is necessary per day. Poultry or fish are recommended substitutes.

Group III: Vegetables and Fruits. Most people, football players included, don't eat enough of these. Four servings a day should be a minimum. They are good sources of vitamins A and C and also provide roughage. Roughage is coarse food (bran, celery, vegetable peels) that contain a relatively high proportion of cellulose. It aids in excretion and can cause a person to feel "full" without excessive caloric consumption.

Group IV: Breads and Cereals. One should have four servings a day. One slice of bread or one ounce of ready-to-eat cereal is considered a serving.

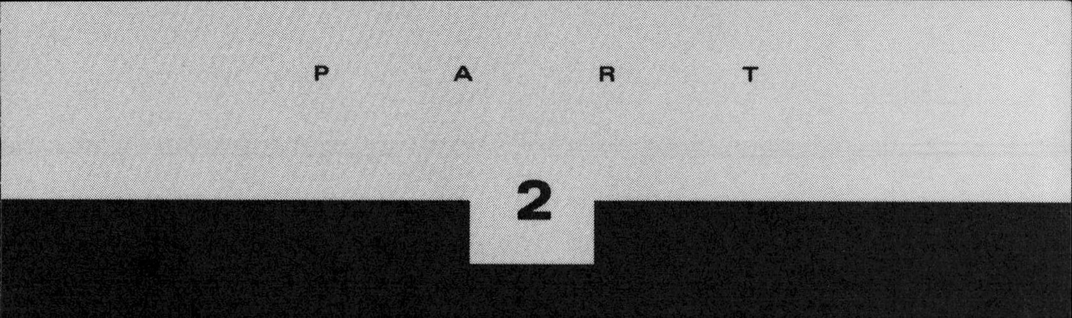

PART 2

3

Off-Season Planning

A thorough knowledge of all the Xs and Os of offensive and defensive football and the ability to devise the best game plan will be wasted if the coach cannot organize and plan in a systematic, coherent manner.

Time spent planning practices should equal or exceed actual practice time. In addition, every successful coach spends a lot of time organizing and planning for the involvement of coaches and athletes during the off-season.

Organization and planning are broken down into two areas. This chapter covers what coaches and athletes should be doing during the off-season. Chapter 4 covers in-season planning.

CONDITIONING PROGRAMS

General Principles

1. Allow enough flexibility in the program so that the athletes can concentrate on overcoming weaknesses (strength, speed, agility, endurance, flexibility, etc.).
2. Make the program fun. Encourage camaraderie, especially between the younger and more veteran ball players.
3. A warm-up time is important prior to engaging in vigorous stretching or calisthenics. Many athletes don't take time to warm-up adequately. Warm-up elevates core body temperature, increases the contractile force and speed of muscles, and reduces the chances of injury.
4. Stretch muscles slowly and progressively. Don't bounce. When a jerky stretching action is employed, as is the case with the traditional four-count toe toucher, body mechanisms are triggered to prevent overstretching. When

the stretch is performed slowly and held for ten seconds, the muscle is allowed to relax and effective stretching is made possible. Stretching improves flexibility and circulation and relieves stiffness in joints and soreness in muscles.

5. When engaging in rotating action at various areas in the body, go through a full range of motion. Pay particular attention to the neck, waist, and shoulders.
6. Cooling down gradually is as important as warming up. Don't stop activity abruptly. Blood can pool in muscles that suddenly aren't being used and cause soreness. The muscles of the body act as pumps in assisting the flow of blood in the veins back to the heart. If they aren't being used, a greater demand is placed on the heart in performing this function.
7. Calisthenics can be beneficial. They can: a) be used in the warm-up and cool-down portions of a workout; b) assist in developing flexibility and agility; and c) serve as conditioners both for strength and endurance. Calisthenics do not require specialized equipment. All the muscle groups of the body can be exercised and a cardiorespiratory benefit can result if the person has the necessary motivation. Some calisthenics are included in a recommended workout later in this section.
8. In order for a muscle to develop, it must be made to overcome progressively increased resistance. This is called the overload principle. There are no short-cuts to physical fitness.
9. If an athlete wants to gain strength, he must work with a resistance (weight) that does not allow him to exceed twelve repetitions. If he wants to increase endurance, he must work with less weight but repeat his movements many more than twelve times. Cardiovascular efficiency is improved through exercises that place a steady but submaximal stress on the heart, lungs, and circulatory system.

Principles of Strength Training

Since the development of strength is such a crucial aspect of a football player's off-season conditioning program, several principles will be noted.

1. Do eight to twelve repetitions of an exercise. If an athlete can exceed twelve repetitions, he should increase the weight.
2. Perform each exercise to the point of absolute muscular fatigue. In the early repetitions the weight will be too light to maximize strength gains. Forcing yourself through the final two repetitions will produce more strength gains than doing many sets but always quitting prior to muscular failure.

3. Perform one set of each exercise per workout session. The key factor is not the number of sets. Do one set, but to the point of muscular failure.
4. A workout session does not need to exceed thirty minutes. It's the intensity of the work, not the duration, that increases strength.
5. The negative work (lengthening contraction) is just as important as the positive work (shortening contraction). Most experts recommend that the first half of the exercise (extension on a bench press, flexion on an arm curl, extension on a leg press) take two seconds and the final movement or return to the original position take four seconds. Beginning weight lifters fail to realize the importance of the second half of the movement.
6. If possible, workouts should be supervised. Most individuals are not capable of pushing themselves to the point of muscular failure without supervision.
7. Have the football players work in pairs. The partner can help lift the weight on the first half of the exercises when the performer can't lift it any more, and in this way let the performer continue lowering the weight (negative work) for several more repetitions. He can also help by being a motivator and recorder.
8. Record every workout.
9. Exercises should be done at a slow, steady pace.

This final principle needs some explanation: It might seem logical that speed of movement on the football field can best be achieved if weight work is done explosively. This is not true. What happens when weight work is done explosively? First, the athlete is not using enough weight to maximize strength gains. If he was, explosive or fast movement of the weight would be impossible. Second, momentum becomes a factor and after the initial muscular contraction, the weight just "rides" through the rest of the range of motion. Third, the brain only recruits enough muscle fibers to lift the required weight, and less weight obviously implies the utilization of less muscle fibers. Fourth, injury most frequently occurs at the initial explosion. At this point a large amount of force is directed on the muscles and joints, which is dangerous as well as counterproductive. In order to improve the performance of any skill, build the strength component in the weight room and the skill component on the football field.

Weight Program

The creative coach can build a good program with very little equipment. A squat (leg press) can be done with a partner on the back of the exerciser. A dip can be done on parallel bars or between two chairs. Chin-ups can be done almost anywhere. Cement blocks can be hung on the performer to increase resistance. Neck exercises can be done very effectively with a partner providing the resistance. Sit-ups can be done with a partner sitting on the legs of the exerciser and offering resistance with his arms.

Free weights, nautilus, universal gym, or most of the other equipment on the market will enhance a program, but they are not necessary.

In the following exercises the precise names of the muscles are generally used. Sometimes only the area of the body is mentioned.

Warm-Up

As was stated earlier, warm-up is important. It would not be wise to engage in a strength building program without it. Easy jogging or cycling for four to five minutes will elevate core body temperature slightly and make subsequent stretching more beneficial.

Static Stretching Exercises

The primary focus of calisthenics should be stretching and the guidelines noted earlier should be followed. The following stretching exercises are recommended.[1]

Upper Trunk Stretcher

1. Prone (face-down) position, hands under shoulders
2. Keep pelvis on floor
3. Extend arms

Lower Trunk Stretcher

1. Prone position
2. Grasp ankles from behind and pull
3. Hold head up

Lower-Back Stretcher

1. Sitting-up position, knees locked
2. Legs extended, toes pointed
3. Grasp outer borders of feet and pull head downward

[1]Mike Bobo, *Principles of Coaching Football* (Dubuque, IA: Wm. C. Brown Publishers, 1987), 16, 17.

Upper-Back Stretcher

1. From supine (face-up) position, bring knees to chest and raise legs up and over head
2. Rest extended toes on floor above head
3. Leave hands and arms flat on floor
4. Return to starting position

Toe Pointer

1. Sit on feet, toes and ankles stretched backward (passive plantar flexion)
2. Raise knees from floor slightly
3. Balance weight with both hands on floor just behind hips

Shoulder Stretcher

1. From standing position, bring right hand to upper back from above
2. Bring left hand to upper back from below and hook fingers of the two hands
3. Repeat to other side

Trunk Lifter (Abdominal Curl)

1. Supine position, have partner hold feet
2. Hands behind neck, lower legs flexed at knee, feet flat on floor
3. Raise head and chest vigorously, hold

Leg Lifter

1. Arms down at side, prone position
2. Raise both legs off floor about six inches, return rapidly
3. Partner hold shoulders down

Trunk Bender

1. Sitting up, legs apart and straight (extended)
2. Hands behind neck
3. Bend trunk forward and downward, attempt to place elbows on floor, hold
4. Keep back straight

Trunk Rotator

1. Arms extended laterally
2. Twist trunk to left and then to right

Gastrocnemius Stretcher (Wall Push-up)

1. Feet 2½ to 3½ feet from wall
2. Keep body straight, place hands on wall
3. Keep feet parallel and *heels on floor* (very important)
4. Lean forward
5. Repeat with one foot in front of the other (leave back foot heel down)

Exercises

The following strength building exercises are recommended.

1. Squat or leg press—quadriceps (thighs) and gluteals (buttocks)
2. Lower leg extension—quadriceps
3. Lower leg flexion (curl)—hamstrings
4. Bench press—pectorals (chest) and triceps
5. Chin ups—latissimus dorsi (lats) and biceps
6. Shoulder press—deltoids (shoulder) and triceps
7. Upright rowing—deltoids, trapezius, and biceps
8. Dips—triceps and chest
9. Pulldowns—latissimus dorsi, biceps, and shoulder girdle
10. Curls—biceps and wrist flexors
11. Neck—neck flexors and extensors
12. Shoulder shrugs—trapezius and shoulder girdle

STAFF PREPARATION

A head coach may not have much choice in selecting his staff. If he does, it is crucial that he select people who complement him. If he is quiet and reserved, it would be wise for him to select an assistant with a more outgoing personality. Oftentimes scholarship and motivational ability are not present in the same person. Both qualities are essential and should be present on the staff. Attention to detail versus conceptualizing the overall design or game plan are two additional elements that are crucial, but often not present in the same person. The ideal staff has coaches with varying abilities and talents but with a genuine respect for the contributions that each makes to the program.

If a new head coach inherits an existing staff, they should meet as soon as possible. The new coach must be extremely sensitive to the concerns of the other coaches and listen carefully to their opinions. This is no time to autocratically lay down rules unless the new coach feels that he can do the job alone! The former head coach may be on the staff, and one of the assistants may have wanted the head job, so democracy in decision making is essential. Only through carefully listening and asking the right questions can a new coach begin to identify strengths and weaknesses on the staff and delegate responsibilities wisely.

A head coach must not surround himself with a bunch of "yes" men. Loyalty to each other is essential and a united front must be presented to the players, but staff meetings should be alive with disagreement and alternate opinions.

Assistants must be given responsibilities that have been carefully delineated and written out. The day of the one-man operation is over. Along with responsibility, the coach must be given enough freedom to function effectively. There is a fine line between constantly looking over an assistant's shoulder and offering meaningful, supportive assistance. In this way the new head coach can discover which assistants want and can effectively assume responsibility and which will need help.

It goes without saying that the head coach must be a model of correct behavior. If he is sloppy in his preparation, tardy to meetings, and unorganized, it will eventually rub off on the total staff. He must earn the respect of his assistants.

Personal relationships outside of football will affect each coach's performance. A coach who has the full support of his family will be much more productive. Before the season gets underway a family outing or picnic could pay greater long-run dividends than a full day of looking at films.

Many schools depend on volunteer help, but it should not automatically be accepted. Many times volunteers are recent graduates who can help in bridging the generation gap, but they must understand and agree with the goals and objectives of the program. It is difficult to meet regularly with volunteer help, but without it their effectiveness and sense of contribution is limited.

The first formal staff meeting the head coach calls is crucial. The atmosphere should be one of warmth but with definite direction and purpose. He must have job responsibilities carefully thought out and typed up for distribution. Each coach should look over his job description and react to it. If he feels that he has been given too little or too much responsibility, he should speak up immediately and not wait or complain through another channel.

A football staff must be careful that they don't become so wrapped up in football that they cease to make time for relationships with the rest of the academic community. Support from the community is essential to the ongoing success of the program. Time should be made to meet and talk with faculty colleagues. Many coaches set up a time when faculty can meet with them, view game films, and ask questions. A coffee break with the faculty occasionally is a good idea.

Clinics provide an ideal setting for learning and camaraderie, and they don't have to be on the scale of the National Football Coaches Association Convention to be valuable. Many times a small clinic with two or three qualified coaches as presenters has more potential value.

A coaching staff can put on their own clinic for coaches in the area. Coaches love to get together and share ideas, and oftentimes it just takes one school to get things started.

Visiting practices at a local college or university can be a valuable learning tool. By watching how they administer their practices, new ideas can be infused into a program.

Coaches can be assigned specialty areas in which they stay abreast of all current research and information. A report could be made by each coach at a summer meeting, summarizing the latest findings.

INCENTIVES AND AWARDS

Any coach who gets so caught up in incentives and awards that he forgets the less skilled players, or who follows a philosophy that suggests that one should not spend time with athletes who can't help immediately, will eventually experience difficulty. An enthusiastic red shirt team that each week learns the opponent's offense and gives the varsity a good picture is essential to the success of a program. If having a team goal to hold the other team scoreless prevents a coach from playing his substitutes, that team incentive should be discarded. Individual and team incentives and awards must not be at the expense of morale and esprit de corps.

Each year the coaching staff should evaluate the incentives and awards that are used in the program. The captain(s)-elect of next year's team can assist the coaching staff in determining what to keep, discard, or add.

The selection process for the captain(s) of next year's team must be carefully thought through and fairly administered, since this is one of the most valued awards. The players on the current team should select the captain(s) for the following year. A team meeting should be called immediately after the season is over. The head coach should speak to those qualities that a captain exhibits, and the ballots should be distributed. The process should be completely confidential. Other awards can be: 1) most improved player, 2) best lineman, and 3) most valuable player.

An award that can be very meaningful to the athletes is an award, given by the coaches, often in the memory of a former player, to the athlete that exhibits certain qualities other than natural athletic ability or physical skill. Some of these qualities that can be included on a citation are: stick-to-itiveness, willingness to go the "extra mile," loyalty, maximizing potential, and the like. Coaches who haven't given an award decided on and presented by the coaching staff, are often surprised at how valued a recognition it is.

Helmet decals are used by many coaches. The criteria for earning helmet decals should be spelled out to the team, and the coaching staff must be impartial in distributing them. Many coaches have negative feelings about their use. They feel that the regulars get enough recognition and giving them more will affect team morale. The success of a program over the years will depend on the support of all squad members. If helmet decals discourage younger, talented players, a coaching staff must look carefully at their use.

A time should be set aside for the entire team to look at game films. This should be an instructional time but not so tense an environment that the players can't enjoy themselves. It should be early in the week so that feedback is as immediate as possible and corrections can be made. The options available to the staff for giving feedback to the athletes, after films have been viewed and broken down, are presented in Chapter 4 under the heading of Individual Player Evaluation.

Some coaches keep careful records of individual and team progress each week in a variety of areas. Sometimes these are posted on a board for the entire team to see. Some potential areas are: 1) individual and team tackles and assists, 2) tackles producing fumbles, 3) interceptions, 4) quarterback sacks, 5) punt blocks and returns, 6) third-down conversion rate (offensively and defensively), 7) fumble recovery, 8) "hit of the week," 9) turnovers, 10) number of first downs, and 11) yards rushing and passing (offensively and defensively). Goals can be set in each of these areas.

Recognition on all-conference, all-city, all-state, and all-American teams are certainly cherished awards that will motivate the gifted athletes. Many conferences pick a "player of the week" and his name is distributed to the media.

Many coaches give physical and mental tests at the start of the season. If playbooks are distributed before the summer months, a knowledge test early in the fall might motivate summer study. Physical tests on the first practice day serve more as a motivational technique for summer workouts than as a reliable assessment of ability. Some of the tests most frequently administered are: 1) 40-yard dash, 2) bench press, 3) leg press, 4) standing long jump or vertical jump, 5) shoulder press, 6) mile or half mile run, and 7) an agility test. Many coaches are getting away from pure strength as demonstrated by maximum force on one repetition and are evaluating weight that the athlete can repeat six, seven, or eight times. In this way the athlete is less prone to injury. The test is also a more realistic use of weight.

GOALS

As was mentioned in Chapter 1, successful coaches are goal oriented. Each member of the team must also be goal oriented. Players should write out for themselves what their goals are for the off-season and how they plan to achieve these goals. Mike Bobo, in his book titled *Principles of Coaching Football,* tells the following story of a technique a coach used in an attempt to generate self-motivation within the players.[2]

> As the players came in I told each group that I wanted to induct them into a secret society. They all looked at me strangely as if to say "What do you mean?" So I took out the gold dots, pulled off the backs and put one on each player's watch. I told them that the gold dot meant that as a football team and as individuals we had set goals. In order to attain those goals we had to diligently, day-by-day, work toward attaining them. "If you guys leave here after all we have done throughout the spring without the incentive to continue to believe and work, then we have wasted our time. This dot will remind you of that every time you look at your watch. That gold dot is going to slap you in the face and you're going to be reminded. You look at your watch approximately forty times a day, and that gold dot will remind you forty times a day of your individual goals and team goals." I did that with each of the groups and explained that the reminder would be this: Gold, G-O-L-D. *G* stands for the goals you set individually, and team goals. *O* stands for the oneness it takes as a team. The *L* stands for the loyalty it takes as a team, and individually to your teammates, coaching staff, and school. Loyalty is a vital part of success. The *D* stands for determination to get the job done. The reason for the Secret Society of the Gold Dot was to stimulate within the players the tough line, the positiveness toward the goals that they have to accomplish.

LETTERS AND INTERVIEWS

Coaches must express genuine interest and concern in each athlete during the off-season. A personal interview provides an excellent opportunity for the coach to share his observations, concerns, and wishes. At the same time he can listen to the suggestions, complaints, and aspirations of each player. They should mutually agree on areas of effort. Some of these might include academics, strength, agility, speed, endurance, and football knowledge. Coaches must be honest with the players. If an athlete isn't going to fit into the program, tell him. If a coach is thinking of changing an athlete's position, this would be an excellent time to discuss the move.

The initial interview with a player should be followed with periodic mailings. These can be overdone, but two or three mailings during the summer serve as

[2]Mike Bobo, *Principles of Coaching Football* (Dubuque, IA: Wm. C. Brown Publishers, 1987), 224.

reminders that football is coming. Letters should include the expectations of the coaching staff (body weight, expected times for running events by position, expected strength gains, etc.), workout directions, capsule summary of upcoming season, program philosophy, and possible staff additions.

Periodically, the coaching staff should include a postcard for players' responses. Specific questions can be asked on the preceding information and space should be left for their comments. Invariably, certain problems will arise and a card will encourage the athletes to share them.

EVALUATION OF PAST SEASON

Film Breakdown

Approaches to film breakdown are discussed in Chapter 4 under the heading, Scouting. The off-season can provide an excellent time for the coaching staff to analyze their offense, defense, and kicking game in a more objective manner. A total season summary of your own team's tendencies in the following areas could be very revealing: 1) number of times team passed and ran from various formations; 2) number of times each play was run; 3) average yardage for each play; 4) number of times each player ran with the ball; 5) what plays were run on first and ten, second and long, etc.; 6) plays run inside the 20-yard line; and 7) defenses that you select on first and ten, second and long, etc.

Any data that is considered worth gathering on an opponent should be gathered on oneself so that team tendencies can be uncovered and corrected. This breakdown doesn't have to be done by the coaching staff. Any competent individual, given the proper instructions and the game films, can produce this information.

Player Evaluation

Following the season the coaches will get together, remove the names of graduating seniors from the offensive and defensive depth charts or boards, and move up reserve players. Gaps at various positions become evident and the shifting of certain players must be discussed.

Some coaches fill out a very detailed evaluation of every returning player that includes such things as weight, attitude, speed, strength, agility, and factors specific to each position such as pulling ability, pass blocking, or drive blocking. While memories are still fresh, it may be a good idea for each coach to write an analysis of each returning player.

Evaluation of Coaches

The coaching staff must honestly evaluate their own performance. If knowledge is lacking in a given area, attendance at a clinic or the study of an appropriate book might remedy the problem. Poor performance on the field might be the result of ineffective teaching strategies. Maybe a new approach should be taken.

The dynamics of staff relationships must be evaluated. Friction between staff members will lessen team productivity. Some things that can create problems are: preferential treatment, unfair publicity, unclear lines of responsibility, inappropriate job assignments, unfair workloads, nonconformity to established policies and procedures, and an unfair pay scale. Sometimes these can't be resolved. If this happens, it is better to replace one person or even function with a reduced staff for a year.

Program Evaluation

Each year the training rules should be reevaluated. Times change, young people's attitudes change, and effective forms of discipline change. It is impossible to simply turn the clock back and impose the disciplinary philosophy of a previous generation. The captains can assist the staff in this evaluation.

Practices should be critiqued. Areas that might be considered are: innovativeness, punctuality of coaches and players, hustle (on the practice field and to and from practice), attentiveness, appearance (coaches and players), conditioning, progression of teaching, and teaching techniques.

The coaching staff must evaluate strategies in light of anticipated returning personnel. A wide open passing attack necessitates a good passer, speedy receivers with good hands, and an offensive line capable of protecting the passer. An I-formation offense requires a hard-nosed blocking fullback, a rugged multitalented tailback, and an offensive line with strength and technique at least equal to the defense. If a quarterback lacks experience in running a triple option attack, it would be foolhardy to expect offensive success, especially in the early games.

The same is true defensively. A 5–2 angle defense is built around a strong, quick middle guard. If a team is light on returning linebackers, a 4–4 would probably not be the best defense to run. It might be wise to shift from a four-deep secondary to three deep if all the personnel in that area graduated. If quickness in the defensive front is not returning, a read defense may be better than an angle or stunted defense.

PLAYBOOK

After a complete evaluation of the past season has been done and returning personnel have been thoroughly evaluated, the playbook should be revised. It is important that the playbooks be collected at the end of the season. This can be done at a team meeting following the last game.

Some of the sections most frequently included in playbooks are: 1) a letter from the head coach; 2) terminology section; 3) information on huddle, cadence, sequence at the line of scrimmage; 4) offensive plays; 5) defensive information (lineman, linebackers, secondary); 6) short yardage and goal-line defense; 7) kick-off returns; 8) punt coverage; 9) kick-off coverage; and 10) field goal and P.A.T. protection.

A key element of a playbook is the presentation of the offensive plays and blocking assignments. The manner in which this is done must be carefully determined by the coaching staff. The most common system is to diagram every offensive play against every defense a team anticipates facing. This makes for a thick playbook! The technique system presented in Chapter 8 allows the entire offense to be presented on two pages.

Chapter 9 develops how the offense can be presented to include play calling, huddle and break, and a recommended sequence at the line of scrimmage. Chapters 8 and 9 should be read carefully before any final decisions are made on the content of the playbook.

EQUIPMENT INVENTORY

The personal and practice equipment that a coach must consider for his program was outlined in Chapter 2. After each season the head coach or his designated representative must inventory all equipment. Equipment changes as the rules change and better items come on the market. The head coach and equipment manager should meet with representatives of various sporting goods companies and have them present their equipment.

The head coach must insure that the equipment is being stored, repaired, and maintained properly. An accurate record must be kept on all equipment to include condition, size, and age.

Items such as game balls and yard markers should be reordered, if necessary. Practice equipment must be checked for damage and wear. Dummies should be replaced each year. Sleds must be checked for breakage and cracks and the pads replaced at regular intervals.

REPORTING DAY PROCEDURES

First impressions are important and the coaching staff must spend extra time insuring that the administrative details of reporting day are in order.

Equipment distribution must be planned so that there is a minimum of confusion. The lockers should be assigned well in advance and all items except the helmet, shoulder pads, and shoes placed inside.

Fitness and knowledge testing can be done on the first day. Possible test items were suggested earlier in the section on incentives. Each coach should take a station to supervise and record scores.

A formal team meeting should precede the first practice. A meal followed by a time for introductions, announcements, and talks is ideal but not necessary. At this team meeting the head coach should introduce his staff and other key personnel in the program. The players can introduce themselves, and the head coach can share a little bit about his philosophy of sport and expectations for the coming season.

4

In-Season Planning

NO PAD DAYS

Many schools have several "no pad" days. During these days, skill development should begin and the conditioning and stretching begun during the summer months should continue.

The physical condition of the athletes upon arrival will dictate the percent of emphasis placed on stretching and conditioning. It is a common error for coaches to do too much of this in the first practices. Remember that the objective is to get ready for the first game and not to exhaust the players the first day!

Recommended stretching exercises, along with guidelines for their execution, were included in Chapter 3. Each exercise should be carefully demonstrated and explained prior to being incorporated into practice. Slow, sustained stretching is very important for any athlete and too many football players and coaches don't place the necessary emphasis on this portion of the practice.

More and more athletes are working hard at off-season strength programs. Unfortunately, if this emphasis is not continued during the season, much of the strength gains are lost. The ideal situation is a carefully designed in-season strength program that is required two days a week outside of practice time. Few head coaches make this commitment and, consequently, a segment of several practices per week must include a strength emphasis.

There is not universal agreement on the value of overdistance running as a cardiovascular conditioner for the football player. It primarily involves the large muscle groups of the lower body, is submaximal in intensity, and is a limited, midrange motion. For these reasons, if it is done in excess without a strength and stretching routine, strength and flexibility can actually be reduced.

If a team has a carefully designed in-season strength program that moves at such a pace that the pulse rate hits 180 beats per minute and does not drop below 150 for the duration of the workout, a modest cardiovascular training effect can take place at the same time that strength is developed. If equipment like Nautilus is available that forces the muscles through a full range of motion, stretching also occurs and flexibility can be increased.

Since very few schools have a strength program that meets these criteria, running in excess of one mile and stretching around all major joints of the body should be included in these early no pad practice days.

A mechanically correct stance and start (Double S) must be introduced at the very first practice and drilled at every practice thereafter (correct techniques are covered in Chapter 6). Make time to give individual attention and instruction. Everything in football begins from a correct stance, and if the stance is learned incorrectly, it can be difficult to change.

Once this basic skill has been practiced, other skills can be introduced by the position coaches. These are covered on the sample practice schedules.

Agility (grass) drills deserve special emphasis in these early practices. Many coaches make the mistake of turning agility drills into conditioning drills. By definition, agility is the ability to rapidly and accurately move the body or parts of the body through space. Allow the athletes enough rest between drills so that they can do each one explosively. Several drills of a general nature will be mentioned here. Specific drills to improve offensive and defensive skills and an elaboration on the following drills is included in the coach's manual.

1. Up-downs
2. Quarter eagles
3. Carioca
4. Crab walk
5. Monkey rolls
6. Kangaroo hops
7. Stance & starts
8. Wave drills
9. Whistle turns
10. Hand balance
11. Back-up run
12. Jingle-jangles
13. Pulling
14. 4-point spinout
15. 2-point spinout

Instruction in a blocking progression should begin immediately. If the forearm lift (palm punch) technique covered in Chapter 6 is being used, the first two or three days do not require pads. The basic principles for correct blocking and tackling are virtually identical and practice on one constitutes practice in both. If the shoulder block is taught, the techniques cannot be broken down and executed at full speed until pads are worn.

These early practices are excellent times to begin learning assignments, both offensively and defensively. Chalk talks in a classroom should be used to introduce assignments, followed by actual physical practice on the field. Position coaches should cover assignments first, and then the team should be brought together for team execution. In these early practices it is best to have returning football players go through a play first, followed immediately by new players executing the same play. Once the new players understand the system, they can run different plays. If the squad is large, the running of plays can be done in two groups. Whenever the numbers on the field warrant a portion of practice being done in two groups, it should be done.

Creative ways of finishing practice should be explored. Wind sprints or a short, fast circuit are two ideas that are effective. Psychologically, as well as physically, it is a good idea to make the final period of the practice physically intense and an entire team effort.

If these early practices are before school starts and the squad is large, the coaching staff might consider dividing the team into two groups and holding separate practices. Personal attention can be doubled and the athletes will know that the coaches are getting a closer and more reliable look at them.

Schematically, one format that the first two practices could take follows.

Practice One

2:40–3:00	Specialty or mile run (centers and QBs, deep snappers, kickers and holders, receivers)
3:00–3:15	Calisthenics
3:15–3:30	Agility drills
3:30–3:45	Blocking progression (groups)
3:45–4:00	Play review (groups). If dummies and sleds are limited, the team can be divided in half for the previous two periods.
4:00–4:05	Sprints (8 × 25 yards). Blocking progression practice and play review are not physically intense periods and sprints prior to a mid-practice break can help pick up the tempo.
4:05–4:15	Break. Liquid replacement is essential, especially on hot days.
4:15–4:25	Huddle and breaking from the huddle (team)
4:25–4:55	Team play review. Everybody should have the opportunity to run the plays, so break up into several groups if necessary.
4:55–5:05	Short circuit or sprints

Practice Two

2:40–3:00	Specialty or mile run
3:00–3:10	Calisthenics
3:10–3:25	Agility drills
3:25–3:40	Blocking progression or play review
3:40–3:55	Play review or blocking progression

3:55–4:05	Introduction to punting. All individuals not on a punting team line up outside the ends on the line of scrimmage and sprint past the punt receiver.
4:05–4:15	Break
4:15–4:30	Team play review (passing)
4:30–4:55	Team play review (running)
4:55–5:00	Circuit!

These two sample practice plans include several elements. The coaching staff must identify specialists early. Deep snappers, punters, field goal kickers, kick-off specialists, and holders must be observed immediately.

The C-QB exchange must become automatic as soon as possible. It's a good idea to have several sets of centers and quarterbacks exchanging on a single cadence. In this way the coach can watch the reactions and movements of one group in relation to another.

Extra time must be allocated for calisthenics and agility drills in the first few practices since every exercise and drill must be explained. Take time to insure that every athlete understands exactly how each activity is done and the reasons for its inclusion in practice.

Some form of blocking review should be included in every practice. The part-to-whole method outlined in Chapter 6 allows meaningful practice to begin immediately, regardless of whether pads are worn.

The initial play review should be done by position and with the position coach. It is a serious error to have the head coach do this for the entire team. All coaches, even if they are primarily working with the defense, should be assigned as offensive area of responsibility for these early practices. This is obviously not necessary if a team divides itself totally and exclusively into offensive and defensive units.

Early practices require additional verbal explanations by the coaching staff and periods of less intense physical effort while the athletes learn technique assignments. For this reason it is a good idea to inject a sprint period or a brief intense circuit into these segments of practice.

The order in which plays will be introduced is important. Consideration should be given to the following points: 1) varying the ball carrier, 2) balancing passing and running, 3) keeping series integrity, 4) varying blocking patterns, and 5) simplicity.

The new players can't possibly run the offense smoothly on the first day. It is best to let them repeat the play of the unit in front of them during team play review. Some type of defensive alignment should be present (people, hand dummies, standing dummies) so that blocking assignments can be checked.

BY THE FIRST GAME

The coaching staff must itemize everything that needs to be accomplished by the first game and when each element should be introduced into the practice schedule. Following is a list of some key considerations.

1. How much offense to put in and in what order. Most young coaches err on the side of putting in too much, too early.
2. When to introduce various aspects of the kicking game and how specialized to make these units.
3. How quickly to introduce live hitting and full scrimmages.
4. What percent of practice time to allocate to defense, offense, and the kicking game (if teams are not divided).
5. How much live hitting to do.
6. Goal line (short yardage) offense and defense.
7. Special offensive formation or plays in case primary attack gets stalled.
8. Special defenses for specific situations.
9. Substitution plan (to allow key individuals to work with first unit if they might in a ball game).

PRACTICE WEEK AT A GLANCE

The following suggestions will assume that games are played on Saturday afternoon. If games are on Friday evening, the recommendations will have to be compacted.

Sunday

Sunday activity will vary depending on the amount of playing time each athlete had. Treatments for injuries cannot wait until Monday. The training room should be open on Sunday afternoon, even if only for a short time, to allow injured athletes to receive attention. This can also be an ideal time for the players to talk over the game with its high and low points and then put it behind them. Stretching and jogging should be done by all members of the team.

If the coaching staff has had time to thoroughly review the game films, Sunday evening is a good time to show them to the squad. If they haven't, it is better to wait until Monday afternoon or evening.

Monday

The coaching staff should have the game plan fairly solidified by Monday's practice. It takes some athletes a lot longer than others to assimilate adjustments in blocking techniques and assignments or changes in defensive keys. It is a mistake to change basic strategies throughout the week after closer examination of films of upcoming opponents. The athletes must clearly understand what it is that they are doing and must be given ample time to physically practice, or the adjustments won't be automatic on game day. The coach or person who scouted the upcoming opponent should take a few minutes to highlight his scouting report. This is a crucial report since it can set the tenor of a team's attitude for the entire week. The scout must be honest in what he says if he hopes to maintain his credibility throughout the entire season. Don't attempt to peak a team needlessly for an obviously weak opponent. Young scouts can also be misled in the opposite direction. Any team can have a bad day and it is an error to report back that a team will be a pushover.

Most schools have a group of players that run the upcoming opponent's offense. Monday is the day to get that team together. The plays that you intend to have them learn should be drawn on large cards and practiced prior to running them for the defense.

Athletes that played a lot in Saturday's game need a different type of practice than those who did not. If a significant number of players did not play in any game over the weekend and don't have a game coming up until the next weekend, a lively scrimmage can be an excellent part of the practice. Scrimmages provide an excellent opportunity for the coaching staff to observe and evaluate the talent of the future.

Athletes that did play a lot should do a lot of stretching and running. A coach should be assigned to supervise this activity. If the staff is committed to the importance of an in-season strength program, Monday could be one of the two days that this is done. Adjustments in offensive and defensive techniques and assignments should be introduced. Since Monday practices are generally less intense, this can be done in an informal atmosphere with input and reactions from the players being encouraged before the final game plan is committed to writing.

If this is the first meeting of the full squad since the game, practice should begin with a talk. The head coach should make a few comments about the past game and challenge the team in their preparation for the upcoming contest.

Tuesday and Wednesday

The hard physical elements of the week's preparation should be done during these two days. The amount of scrimmaging done will depend on the age-level of the athletes, depth of the squad, and the quality of the week's opponent. High school players need more complete scrimmages than college athletes. Also, the heavy hitting should occur prior to the easier ball games. This will minimize the chances of a key injury before a big game and will help maintain a sense of discipline and effort before the easier games.

If a team is not divided into offensive and defensive units, it is a good idea to have one of these work days emphasize defense and the other offense. Obviously, both must be practiced both days, but the practice might end with a defensive scrimmage or emphasis one day and an offensive emphasis the other.

If the squad is not large enough to warrant complete division into offense and defense, but large enough so that many players are standing around much of the time, have a defensive emphasis at one end of the field and an offensive emphasis at the other. The first team offense can work against the second or third team defense at one end while the first team defense works against the second or third team offense at the other. After a certain period of time the second offense might work against the first defense and vice versa. This may require juggling the team so certain individuals play with the offensive or defensive units, but it will minimize the time that players are standing around.

Time spent scrimmaging will vary from school to school and from week to week, but conditioning must always be stressed. It is unfortunate that for most players their skill level increases during the season but their conditioning level deteriorates. Push the players physically. Agility drills must be done with intensity. If excessive repetition is creating boredom and a loss of effort, vary them. There should be no cheating on wind sprints. Don't let anybody consistently jump the start count and coast. Require them to run through the full distance.

The specific blocking techniques to be used in the game must be practiced, and a portion of this practice should be full tilt. A reserve QB and ball carrier can enhance the intensity of this group period. Defensive adjustments to offensive formations and movements must be practiced during these two days. Repetition is the key to learning. Allow each player that will see action in the ball game many opportunities to physically practice correct responses to offensive and defensive movements.

Offensive backs should spend time with the offensive line in group work sessions. Running backs need to know where the key blocks are coming from and linemen need to know how each play develops in the backfield. This can be an ideal time for the offensive line coach to take over while the backfield coach assists in another segment of practice. The backfield coach could be running a skeleton offensive passing attack against the defensive secondary.

Goal line offense and defense must be stressed on these days. A team must maximize its scoring percentages when it penetrates inside the opponent's 10-yard line and must minimize the opponent's scoring percentages when it does. This only happens if quality practice time is devoted to it. The players must believe in their goal line offense and defense. The opponent's goal line defense must be carefully scouted and blocking assignments drawn up and practiced specifically for it.

Most coaches feel that kicking should be included in every practice. Some feel that the repetitious nature of kicking causes athletes to perform at less than 100 percent intensity and, therefore, the practice does more harm than good. The periods for punting and field goal practice need not be long and live, but they should be executed with full intensity so that a realistic picture of the protection and coverage is provided.

A sample midweek practice may look like:

3:45	Specialty period
4:00	Calisthenics
4:10	Agility period (grass drills)
4:25	Individual drills (blocking progression, form tackling, one-on-one)
4:35	Group drills (defensive backs, offensive line, etc.)
4:50	Goal line offense and defense
5:05	Kicking game
5:20	Team offense and team defense
5:50	Circuit

Thursday

Many coaches make Thursday a day for extra kicking emphasis. The kicking corps takes center stage! This is an area of disagreement with many coaches. Is it a valuable expenditure of time to have the kick-off unit run down the field ten times? Does the punt block team benefit from going through a blocking scheme, or would this time be better spent on polishing the pass defense and goal line offense? These are decisions that each coach must make.

The kicking corps certainly appreciates the attention they receive from the entire squad and coaching staff when a significant portion of practice is devoted to this aspect of the game.

Most teams will not do any live work on Thursday. This can be a good day to polish the passing game, with the linemen working on their agility and positioning against a rushing defense. The defense can review their game plan with the secondary coach, especially observing the correctness of the coverages.

If a team has made the commitment to an in-season strength program, Thursday along with Monday would be possible days to incorporate it.

If significant changes in emphasis have been made offensively or defensively, they should be written up and distributed to the players. By Thursday all experimentation and changes should be concluded so that what is distributed will be correct at game time.

An excellent format for summarizing information the defensive secondary needs to know is outlined in Figure 4.1.

Friday

The day prior to ball games becomes quite ritualistic for most teams. Game uniforms are often worn and an almost pregame type warm-up is conducted. Offensive units will put the final polish on their running and passing plays, while the defensive units check alignments and adjustments to the opponent's formations and movements. Special punt blocks can be practiced and portions of the kicking game reviewed. Every player should know what teams he is on and these assignments should be typed and distributed. The head coach should finish this practice with a brief, stimulating talk.

Saturday or Game Day

For many teams game day, in a sense, begins the night before. The team might have dinner together, followed by a brief meeting and a movie. This certainly depends on the level of competition.

The pregame meal should be three to four hours prior to the game to allow time for digestion. The primary ingredient of a training meal should be carbohydrates, since they can be mobilized most quickly as an energy source. For this reason, pancakes or spaghetti have become popular training meal staples. More was said about diet in Chapter 2.

After the training meal, many teams will meet as a group and the head coach will give a brief talk. A final look at the opponent on film can be a part of this presentation. Then the team will break into offensive and defensive units for a final review of assignments and strategy. Sufficient time must be left for taping.

When to take the field will depend somewhat on the temperature and weather conditions. Linemen do not need as much time for warm-up as specialists, receivers, and quarterbacks. Under normal circumstances, specialists should take the field 45–50 minutes prior to kickoff. The remainder of the team can come out approximately 15 minutes later. If the weather is cool, more time will be needed. If it is extremely cold, some of the warm-ups can be done inside, thus limiting unnecessary exposure.

1. KEYS FOR SECONDARY ALIGNMENTS:
   SS: side of two receivers
   SHB or CB: side of tight end
   WS: opposite two receivers
   WHB: opposite tight end
2. OPPONENT FORMATIONS AND YOUR MATCH-UPS:

I-PRO 52 SS B B SHB WS WHB	BREAK WEAK PRO SLIDE SS E T M TE B B SHB WS WHB	POWER I 52 B B SS SHB WS WHR
I-SLOT 52 B B E SS SHB WS WHS	DIVIDE PRO CLOSE B E T M TE B WHB WS SHB	BREAK STRONG SLOT 52 B B SS SHB WS WHB

3. KEY FOR FLOW: No key for flow this week; all pre-rotate. Must be a corner call each play by safeties.
4. REACTION TO MOTION: SS will follow motion man in all long motion situations
5. SHORT YARDAGE FORMATIONS AND COVERAGE:

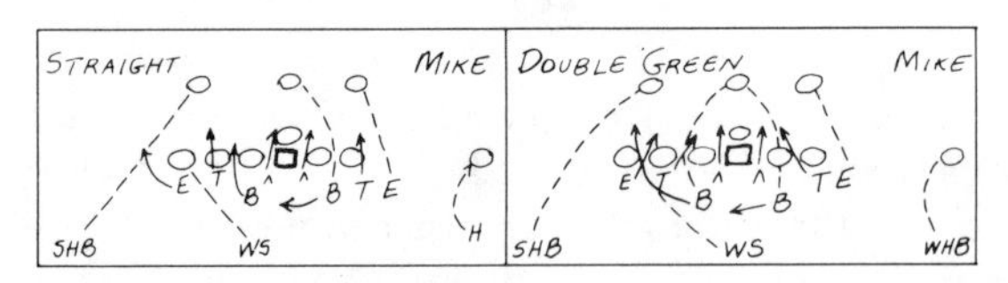

6. PREVENT COVERAGE

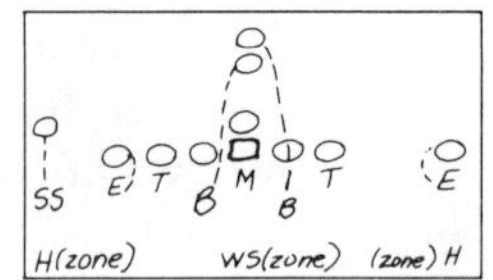

7. FAVORITE OPPONENT PASS PATTERNS:

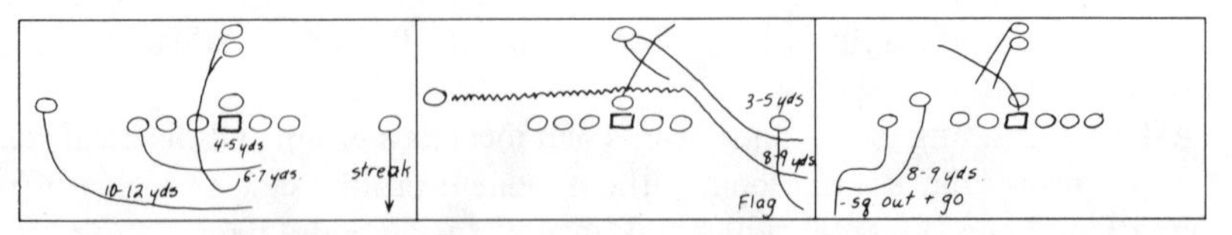

8. OTHER COMMENTS, RULES, OR SPECIAL COVERAGES: "40 slide pass" (regardless of formation)

This will be a real test for us. They like to pass and they do it well. The designed defenses allow the secondary to Concentrate especially on the pass. Stay behind receivers in your zone, make sure tackles, and do not allow an easy score.

SS B B
SHB WB WHB

▶ **Figure 4.1** Defensive Secondary Game Plan

Specialists should spend the first fifteen minutes loosening up gradually. Kickers should progressively increase the length of their kicks and quarterbacks should loosen up their arms. Receivers for punts, kicks, and passes can check the turf and wind conditions as they receive footballs.

Team calisthenics follow when the entire team joins the specialists about 30–35 minutes prior to kickoff. Stretching exercises noted earlier should be done following the guidelines noted. Some exercises can be done to a cadence for esprit de corps.

After seven to ten minutes of exercises, the players should separate with their position coaches for the final tune-up on specific techniques. Some agility drills are often done by linemen, followed by increased contact on blocking technique or defensive maneuvers. Quarterbacks and receivers review pass routes.

At this point some schools will send the linemen into the pregame meeting room prior to the rest of the team. Other coaches prefer to have the first offense as an entire unit run some plays against the second defense. The second offense can run some plays against the first defense. This can serve as a final team tune-up.

During the game, bench control is crucial. One coach should be assigned to monitor this. The players should be assigned a location by position so that a coach can readily contact a player.

Every head coach must decide the degree of responsibility he wishes to maintain during a ball game and how much he is willing to delegate to his assistants. Items he must consider are: play calling, substitutions, kicking decisions, scoring combinations, adjustments to the game plan, and contact with coaches in the press box. Once he has made his decision, the staff should be informed, so that there is no confusion on responsibilities.

Organization at halftime is crucial. It can logically be divided into three sections. During the first period the players should check with the trainer, sip soft drinks, or eat orange slices. It is a time to unwind and relax. While the athletes are doing this, the coaches can meet in a separate area to assess the first half. In the second period the coaches should ask key questions of certain players. The players can ask the sideline coaches, and especially those coaches stationed in the press box, any questions that they have. Following this period, the athletes should sit quietly but attentively while the coaches review the game plan and make adjustments for the second half, if necessary.

Comments immediately following the game need not be long. Regardless of the outcome, they should be positive. This is not the time for a negative tirade!

SCOUTING

At most levels of competition the league determines the number of times teams are allowed to scout an opponent. If this hasn't been determined, the coaches should establish a policy.

Football is an extremely complex game. Every coach wants as much valid and reliable information as possible about each opponent. Effective scouting is the vehicle by which this can be accomplished.

The intensity and amount of scouting will vary with the level of competition. Assistant coaches can be on the road so much of the time that they seldom see the athletes they coach in a game situation.

One solution to this dilemma is greater use of video exchange. Some leagues do no on-site scouting. Instead, the previous week's game of each team is exchanged on Sunday or Monday evening. This is accomplished by having two people meet at an agreeable predetermined site. An exchange system does delay final game plan decisions until the video can be broken down, but it allows all coaches to be at contests and, in essence, to also scout every opponent.

On-site scouting can be done most effectively by coaches on the staff. They can be assigned to teach the scout teams the opponent's offense and defense. They are present at staff meetings to clarify any confusing points on the scouting report and to give added input.

Every school has a slightly different scouting system, but there are basic ingredients that are common to any successful program.

What Information to Gather

Information of a general nature that a scout should gather can be categorized into three areas. They are: 1) offensive information, 2) defensive information, and 3) the kicking game.

Questions of an offensive nature that need answers are: 1) What is the stance of the linemen and backs? 2) Do they set immediately or on command? 3) Do they shift? 4) Do they use automatics? 5) Do they run plays in a sequence? 6) What type of cadence do they use? 7) Do they repeat successful plays? 8) Do they use motion? 9) Do they go on a long or short count? 10) Are they primarily a trap, lane, or power blocking team? 11) Do they have keys to their passing game? 12) What type of pass protection do they use? 13) Are they primarily a drop-back, sprint-out, or roll-out passing team? 14) What percent of their passes are short versus long? 15) What are the names and numbers of their favorite receivers and passers? 16) Are their passers good scramblers? 17) On what downs and where on the field do they begin to pass?

Some defensive concerns are: 1) Who are their defensive personnel? (The scout should bring home a program.) 2) What defenses do they use? (These should be diagrammed and should include goal line and/or short yardage as well as prevent defenses.) 3) What adjustments do they make to split ends, flankers, motion, pro-set, etc.? 4) Do they use a three-deep alignment, four-deep alignment, or both? 5) How do they rotate? 6) Is their pass defense zone, man-to-man, or both? 7) Do they stunt line backers? How often? 8) Where and whom can we pass and run against? 9) How do they adjust to motion? 10) Do their ends play a role in pass defense? 11) Do they shift from one defensive alignment to another at the snap of the ball? 12) What plays went well against them? 13) Do they pursue and gang tackle well?

The scout should observe an opponent's kicking game carefully. Their punt formation should be diagrammed with the protection and coverage noted. The scout should note any vulnerable areas in their protection. Their punt return and block should be diagrammed. Their punters and kickers should be listed with speed, delivery, and distance noted. The effectiveness of the snap should be checked. Their kick-off and kick-off return teams should be listed along with the strategy. The field goal and P.A.T. formation should be diagrammed.

After the game has been scouted, a summary of the following information should be compiled: 1) a list of every play run from every formation; 2) a list of every play run and the average gain per play by every ball carrier; 3) a list of every play run on first and ten, second and long, second and short, third and long, third and short, and fourth and short; 4) a summary of the average gain for every play; 5) a sequence of plays run inside the twenty-yard line; 6) a list of plays run into and away from the strength; 7) a list of plays run from the right hash, left hash, and center of the field; 8) a list of every pass play attempted with completion ratio and average gain noted.

How to Gather the Information

Booklet. Many schools have a football scouting report booklet that the scout fills in while he is watching the game and completes afterwards. In addition to leaving areas for answering the questions already noted, many booklets include a number of worksheets for recording offensive information. Figure 4.2 shows the format a typical worksheet might take.[1] As the scout watches the game, he fills in the information.

Tape Recorder. Other scouts lean heavily on recording information into a tape recorder. It enables the scout to keep his eyes on the playing field all the time and to gather more information, since he can talk much faster than he can write. The disadvantage of using recorders is that the information must be transferred from tape to writing before it can be processed and summarized.

[1]John Ralston and Mike White, *Coaching Today's Athlete* (Palo Alto, CA: Mayfield Publishing Company, 1971), 425.

OFFENSIVE WORKSHEET

Down Yards	Position	Formation	Play No.	Runner Passer	Receiver	Gain Loss
1/10	-36L		59 FB cpt.			0

15 Defense

10

5

LOS

Down Yards	Position	Formation	Play No.	Runner Passer	Receiver	Gain Loss
2/10	-36	R	42			+2

15 Defense

10

5

LOS

Down Yards	Position	Formation	Play No.	Runner Passer	Receiver	Gain Loss
3/8	-38	M	59 RO		INC.	

15 Defense

10

5

LOS

Down Yards	Position	Formation	Play No.	Runner Passer	Receiver	Gain Loss
1/10	-14	L	59 ROLL		Inc.	

15 Defense

10

5

LOS

▶ **Figure 4.2** Offensive Worksheet

Play #	Down	Yards to Go	Hash	Field Position	Time	Formation	Type	Play	Player	Direction	Strength	Gain	Play Action	Result	Comments
1	1	10	R	−20	14:20	1272	R	24DV	24	R	I	0			Fumble
2	2	10	R	−19	14:10	2441	P	18PS	81	R	A	+12	Y	3	Pass Intercepted
3	1	10	M	−45	12:01	1272	R	26PR	34	R	I	+ 6			
4	2	4	R	+49	11:38	1272	R	24DO	24	L	A	+ 5			
5	1	10	L	+44	11:16	2441	P	26PP	83	L	I	0	Y	1	
6	2	10	L	+44	11:10	2441	P	91PP	81	M	I	+ 9	Y	2	
7															
8															

▶ **Figure 4.3** Scouting Summary Sheet

Summary Sheet. A third system that can be used alone or in conjunction with computer input is illustrated in Figure 4.3. Each play is one line in the diagram. Most of the information is the same as that recorded on the worksheets in the first system. The only sections that need further explanation are formation, play, direction of play, strength, play action, and result.

Rather than diagramming the formation, the scout uses a sequence of numbers to indicate the formation. In Figure 4.3, the four numbers on the first line under "Formation" could identify the location of the following personnel: left end, odd back, set backs, and the right end. The "1272" could designate a tight left end, a flanker left for the odd back, a divide backfield for the set backs and a split right end. Any convenient system for identifying the formation can be used, but to serve as input data for a computer the information must be coded in a consistent manner.

Under "Play" the scout can use any four letters or numbers that identify the play. In this scouting format, the direction is indicated by an "L" for left, an "M" for middle, and an "R" for right. "Strength" is indicated by an I, A, or M designating whether the play went into, away, or up the middle in relation to the strength of their formation.

The play action column indicates with a Y(yes) or N(no) whether a pass was play action or not. The result column identifies with numbers the result of the pass. For example, a "3" in the result column might mean the pass was intercepted.

The scout uses this sheet to provide the summary information noted in the previous section.

Key Sort Cards. A fourth process involves using key sort cards as illustrated in Figures 4.4 and 4.5. A key sort card has the same basic formation on it as the offensive worksheets and summary sheets, but the information is arranged around the edge of a card.[2] Rather than writing information, the scout pencils over the appropriate down, distance, yard line, and so forth. After the game the scout then punches each pencil mark with a regular paper punch. The time saved in this system is in sorting out information. If the scout wants only first down plays he inserts an ice pick into the first down hole and shakes out those plays. If he wants plays run by a certain ball carrier, he inserts the ice pick into these holes and sorts out the appropriate cards. Once the cards containing a specific piece of information have been sorted into a separate pile, they still have to be summarized into an easily readable package. The system does not save that much time.

[2]Mike Bobo, *Principles of Coaching Football* (Dubuque, IA: Wm C. Brown Publishers, 1987), 205–206.

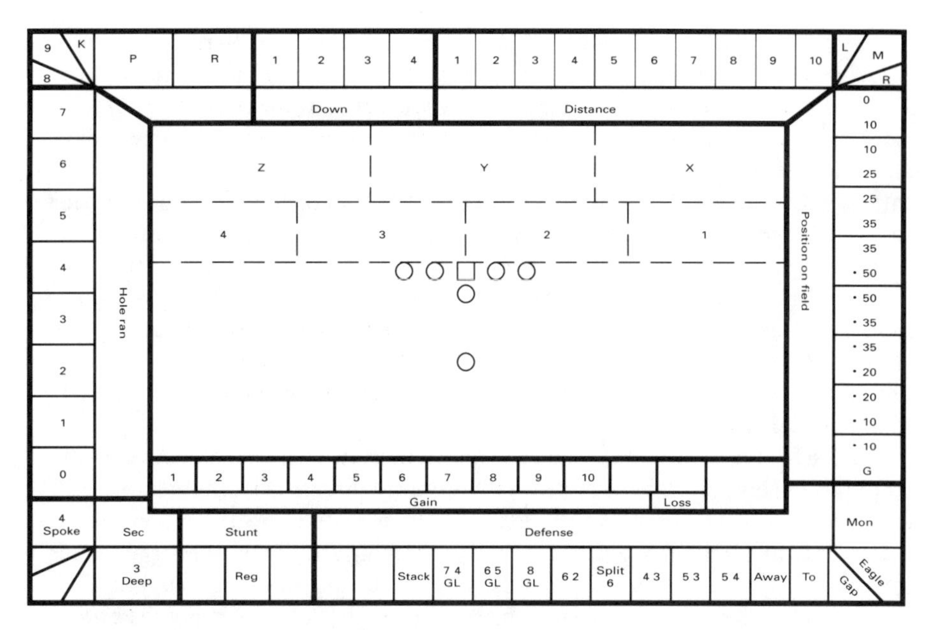

▶ **Figure 4.4** Defensive Key Sort Card

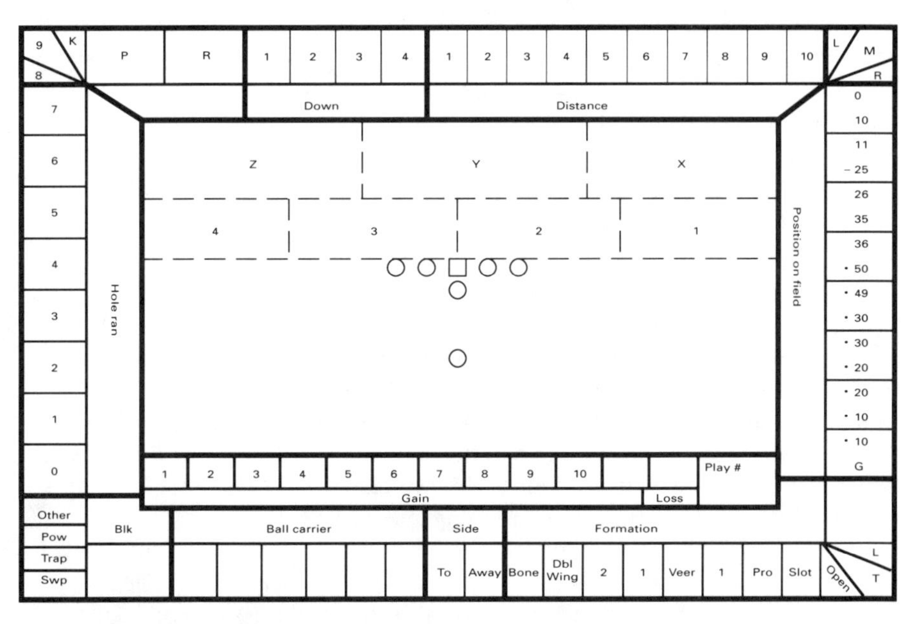

▶ **Figure 4.5** Offensive Key Sort Card

Computer. The greatest advantage to using a computer is that it saves time. It can process information in an instant that takes hours of human calculation. A few examples will make this obvious. If a scout uses the summary sheet technique explained earlier, he can complete the sheet by the time the game is over. After he returns to his campus or school, the coach gives that sheet to a data entry person who enters the data into a terminal. Once this information has been entered, a computer has the capacity to generate much meaningful data. It can scan the "Down" column, pull out every first down play, and print out the plays that were run. It can scan the "Formation" columns and print out every play run from every formation. It can print out every play run by every ball carrier. The information breakdown available is limited only by the ingenuity of the coaching staff. The eight summary areas listed at the conclusion of the previous section would be logical breakdowns to obtain.

If a school has a computer and the coaching staff wants an objective breakdown of information, computerized scouting is by far the best method to use. If the scout enjoys spending his time on Saturday or Sunday breaking down information into meaningful segments, or if the coaching staff only wants the scout's opinion of a team's tendencies, then it is not necessary to use a computer. The laborious task of breaking down information manually, however, serves no professional purpose. Let the computer do that task so the coaching staff can spend more time analyzing and interpreting the data.

Many people feel uneasy when they receive a computer printout. There is no need for this. The printout can provide the information the coaching staff wants in almost any format they wish. For example, if a team runs and passes from multiple formations, the coaches will certainly want a listing of all plays run from every formation. This could be presented as in Figure 4.6.

How to Report the Information

Information should be reported in a consistent, readable format. A team's personnel should be listed at the beginning. A program of the game can be included. Regular substitutes should be noted.

Offensive information should include answers to all the questions asked in the section, What Information to Gather. After the questions have been answered, the summary breakdowns should be written out. If the scout believes that the offensive tendencies displayed by a team in the game he scouted are not indicative of what they will do against his own team, he should explain and list what he feels will be their favorite running and passing plays.

Defensive information might logically come third. Most teams do not do much data analysis of defensive tendencies. Instead, the scout diagrams the opponent's alignments, secondary rotations, stunts, goal line, and short yardage defenses.

FORMATION: WIDE --FLANKER RIGHT --BREAK STRONG--TIGHT			
		TOTAL YARDS	AVERAGE
PLAY	TIMER RUN	YARDS GAINED	YARDS GAINED
42TP	1	0	.0
28TS	2	8	4.0
34WH	7	31	4.4

FORMATION: WIDE --FLANKER RIGHT --I --TIGHT			
		TOTAL YARDS	AVERAGE
PLAY	TIMES RUN	YARDS GAINED	YARDS GAINED
28PS	1	4	4.0
28TS	1	10	10.0
42TP	1	1	1.0
QBSN	1	2	2.0

FORMATION: WIDE --FLANKER RIGHT --DIVDE --TIGHT			
		TOTAL YARDS	AVERAGE
PLAY	TIMES RUN	YARDS GAINED	YARDS GAINED
17PX	14	46	3.3
92PP	1	0	.0
P8PR	6	74	12.3
P8PL	1	0	.0

▶ **Figure 4.6** Computer Printout Listing All Plays From Every Formation

If a team does run multiple defenses, it is valuable to record the situations in which the various defenses are run. If the offensive coaches can know when a team will go into short yardage, goal line, a pass defense, or use a particular stunt, this will certainly help in play selection.

The kicking game might be presented last. Items noted in the section, What Information to Gather, should be clearly diagrammed along with appropriate comments.

Tips for Effective Scouting

The following tips should be followed, especially by the inexperienced scout.

1. Learn something about the team before the scouting assignment. School and community newspapers can provide valuable information.
2. Arrive at the stadium at least thirty minutes prior to game time. During warm-ups a scout can watch the kickers, passers, and pass receivers. He can buy a program and review the probable line-up.
3. Don't try to get too much. This is especially true for the inexperienced scout. It is better to come back certain of what information you do have, than to have double the information but be uncertain as to its correctness.

4. Bring along a second person even if that person knows nothing about football. Between offensive plays there is basic recording that must be done. The second person can write down such things as down, distance, yards to go, position of field, gain, etc., while the chief scout does the more sophisticated recording. A girlfriend or wife, if she is interested, can perform this function nicely.
5. Use a tape recorder if you are scouting alone. There is only so much time between offensive plays, and a tape recorder lets you keep your focus on the field all of the time.
6. Break down the information accurately. If the data is being entered into a terminal, be sure that it is entered correctly.

Scouting Your Own Team

Through scouting oneself, a team can discover what information opponents are getting on them. If budget and staff permit, a team could have a scouting report on their game presented to them each week. In this way any tendencies that a team might develop can be detected and corrected.

INDIVIDUAL PLAYER EVALUATION

Player evaluation is similar to scouting in that it can be an unending task. Like scouting, however, it is an essential ingredient of successful football programs. The perceptive coach is always observing individual athletes and making suggestions that will improve their performance. Disagreement arises as to how important it is to objectify this process. Large staffs at major schools will go through an entire film looking at each player individually and provide him with a grade on every play in every game. He is evaluated on the execution of his assignment, effort in that execution, and correctness of the techniques used. He receives a positive or negative point value score for every play. These are totaled to give him a score for the game.

Other coaches feel that reducing a performance to a score or percentage level creates a negative feeling on the part of the athlete. A performance rating is meaningless unless it is followed with feedback. A card can be filled out on each athlete for every game with as many suggestions or comments on it as the coach wants to make. Other coaches will call athletes aside and talk to them before, during, or after practice.

At any level, when films are taken, time should be set aside to allow the athletes to view them. This might be done on Sunday evening, Monday evening, or during a portion of Monday's practice. It should be early in the week but only after the coaches have had time to thoroughly break down the film. Coaches can make this time more efficient and productive if they have the order of offensive plays and defensive calls with them, so the film doesn't have to be run through once before these are established. A coach should call out the play or defense before it appears on the screen. Comments that each coach intends to make should be written down by play number so that they can be made at the appropriate time with the necessary visual reinforcement.

The attitude that the coaches take to these film sessions is crucial. It is best not to let these sessions get negative and morose. Constructive criticism can be made without undue harassment. If individual players need to be singled out for serious mental or physical errors, it should be done in private. Make these group film sessions a time the players look forward to, not dread. The motivation for coming should not be fear. Genuine positive feedback goes farther than negative feedback in producing desired results. Each coach must be willing to evaluate his own personality and be conscious of his own tendencies. At no time is this more important than at the film session after a crucial loss. Certain mistakes are obvious to everyone in the room and do not need to be belabored by any coach.

THE DEPTH CHART

Every coach keeps a depth chart. Before the first practice, players have to be ranked by position if for no other reason than to facilitate the running of plays.

Whether or not to post the depth chart and how soon to post it are points on which coaches disagree. A depth chart serves two valuable purposes. It facilitates practice organization in that every athlete knows what teams he is on before coming to practice. It also serves as an indication to the players of the coaches' evaluation of them each day.

Different players react differently to having their names moved up or down or from one position to another on a depth chart. Some players see that the coaches have moved a good athlete to their position, and they quit, sometimes without even coming in for a talk. Demotion brings out the best in some athletes and the worst in others. Before major changes are made on a posted depth chart, a coach should talk to the athletes involved. A conversation with the athlete involved lets him know that the move wasn't done arbitrarily.

A large board for the offense and defense with hooks on it under each position is a valuable visual aid. Each player has his name on a tag. Each day the coaches evaluate personnel, find out who is injured from the trainer, and position the tags on the board for that day's practice.

DAILY STAFF MEETINGS

Regardless of the level of coaching, the head coach must get together with his assistants before each practice. When this doesn't occur, the head coach often ends up doing most of the on-the-field instruction himself. This is destructive in two ways. It is a very inefficient use of time. If the head coach instructs the whole team at once, he is wasting the time of the players when his instruction doesn't relate directly to them. If he moves from group to group, he is wasting his own time. It also destroys the relationship of the assistant coaches to their players. Each assistant coach must be perceived by the athletes in his area as knowledgeable and competent. Without daily staff meetings this is impossible.

At these meetings coaches can assess personnel, plan the day's practice, evaluate progress, formulate or refine the game plan, assess injuries, recheck video, and adjust the depth chart. The meetings also serve in cementing a bond between staff members. Coaches can share concerns outside of football that may be affecting their ability to function productively.

THE PRESS BOX

The coaches on the sideline have the worst seats in the house! Players both on and off the field can block their vision. Some fields are crowned to such a degree that vision is even blocked by terrain! It didn't take long for coaches to begin looking for some "crow's nest" where they could get a better view of the action. Shortly after World War II, the practice of placing one or more coaches in the press box became popular. Continuous communication between coaches on the field and in the press box soon followed. Television and film crews always sit up as high as possible, usually on top of the press box.

Play development, offensive and defensive alignments, formations, and field position can only be seen from a higher vantage point. If the scout in the box does nothing more than relay the field position and situation to the head coach, he serves a necessary function.

A coach in the press box is not immune to the temptation to "watch the game." If the coach is doing his job right he should be watching the opposing team's alignments, shifts, and movements more than his own. For this reason it is necessary to organize a strategy for effective press box procedures.

Down and Distance Play and Gain Opp. Defense

1st Down	2nd & L (7+)	2nd & M (4–6)	3rd & L (7+)
25DV + 4(5-2∠) 24DO + 1(5-2D) 30MN + 6(5-2)	26PP 0 (4-3) 11DR + 11 (4-3)	91PP 0(5-2R) 26DR + 5(5-2)	17HK + 25 (4-3) 18ST 0 (4-3) 19PP + 6 (4-32)
3rd & M (4-6)	2nd & S (1-3)	3rd & S (1-3)	Goal Line
30MN + 2 (5-2) 31MN + 4 (5-2∠) 24DO + 15(4-3) SCRN + 50(5-2)	17SK 0 (4-3) 24WH + 6 (5-2∠) 25WH 0 (5-2D)	30MN + 1 (G-8) 31MN + 4 (6-5) 91PP 0 (6-5	37SL + 2 (6-5) 37SL + 2 (6-5)

Offensive Chart

▶ **Figure 4.7** Offensive Play Analysis Chart

The sophistication of the procedures will depend on the level of competition and the number of coaches in the press box. At any level it does no good to gather a lot of information if it isn't processed and summarized into a potentially useful format.

Most teams will chart their own offense. All plays run on first down, second and long, second and short, etc. will be listed in one column with the result. This allows the coaching staff to see the success or failure of certain plays throughout the game. On the same chart could be listed the defense that the opponent ran in each situation. One coach can perform both of these duties when his team has the football. Figure 4.7 presents a format this chart could take.

When a team is on defense, a defensive chart showing down-and-distance tendencies and the holes the opponent is attacking can be plotted. The information should be recorded in such a way that it does not require further compilation. It should provide meaningful information as recorded or it shouldn't be kept. For example, information should not be written down in a list format and then transferred to a chart. Record it on the chart directly. Figure 4.8 presents a format this chart could take.

Figure 4.9 is merely a chart with the opponent's formations drawn and the appropriate place marked as the plays are run during the football game.

Down and Distance	Holes 9	7	5	3	2	4	6	8	Passes (Rt., Left, Short, Long) R-S	R-L	L-S	L-L
1st & 10	DO + 16 SW + 4	PR + 6 SL + 2	DV 0	TR-4		DV 0 BL + 6		SW + 4				
2nd & L											FBF1 + 6 RED + 2	LES + 20
2nd & M												
3rd & L	RV + 10 SW 0											
3rd & M					TR-0							
2nd & S									91P + 16			
3rd & S	30 + 2 31 + 3											
Goal Line	SW T.D.				30MO							

Defensive Chart

▶ **Figure 4.8** Defensive Analysis Chart

IN-SEASON STRENGTH PROGRAM

More and more athletes are taking out-of-season strength programs very seriously. These athletes will lose strength during the course of a season unless an in-season strength program is adopted. Some coaches know this but feel that practice time must be spent on skill development and not strength maintenance.

More and more coaches are requiring strength workouts twice a week during the season. Strength can be maintained with two workouts a week of thirty minutes. The workouts must follow the guidelines noted in Chapter 3. Interior linemen could have a portion of Monday's and Thursday's practice devoted to strength maintenance. Coaches should be there to supervise the program. In larger

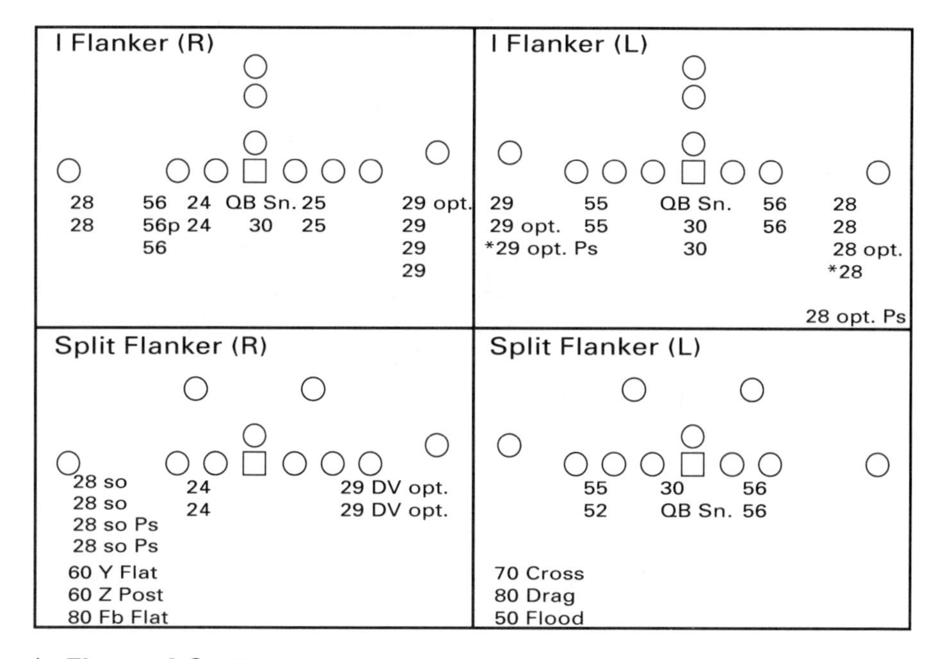

▶ **Figure 4.9** Formations and Plays

programs this could be required in addition to the regular afternoon workout. The key to the success of these strength maintenance sessions is not in the length of the sessions, but in the intensity of the effort. Most athletes lift weights for too long a period of time; few lift with the necessary intensity.

In-season strength programs should maintain the muscular strength and endurance that the athletes have developed during the off-season and continue the emphasis on flexibility and agility. The following definitions of these four key ingredients relate to the football player. Flexibility is the range of motion in the joints of the body. Full range of motion is required for peak performance. Many injuries occur when a joint is forced beyond its normal range of motion and the strength isn't present to resist the unexpected demand.

Agility is the ability of the football player to make quick and accurate changes in direction, an obviously important skill for all football players, but especially those at the skill positions.

Endurance involves both the cardiovascular and muscular systems. The ability to repeatedly perform submaximal muscular contractions over an extended period of time is one definition of muscular endurance and is obviously crucial to success in football. Granted, these muscular contractions are required in short bursts, but when executed many times over the course of an entire football game, the oxygen delivery system of the body is brought into play. The ability of the body to deliver oxygen to the working muscles and remove the waste products (carbon dioxide and lactic acid) from these muscles is a measure of the efficiency of the cardiovascular system.

Strength, the contractile force a muscle can exert, is of the utmost importance to a football player. It not only aids in injury prevention since muscles and connective tissues support the joints, thus strengthening the joint so it can withstand the stresses that are placed upon it; but it is an essential component of power that enables an athlete to move his opponent, break tackles, or bring down a ball carrier. Power is the ability to utilize strength explosively and was explained in Chapter 3.

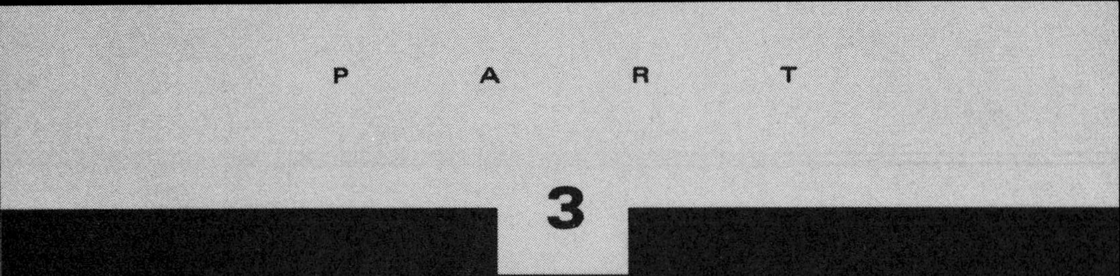
P A R T
3

5

Offensive Terminology

Fortunately, most terminology pertaining to the offensive aspects of football is fairly standardized. Yet, every coach and school have some unique terms that have significance and meaning only to them. As a result, the following list cannot be complete, but it does cover most of the terms that coaches use. The terms are broken down alphabetically under five categories. The abbreviations are initially presented in parentheses, and used frequently thereafter. Terminology is presented now to assist the reader as he studies this part of the book.

POSITION TERMINOLOGY

Center (C)	The offensive lineman who lines up over the football and snaps it to the quarterback (QB).
Flanker (F)	An offensive halfback set over four yards outside a tight end.
Fullback (FB)	A back lined up directly behind the center and quarterback. If two backs are directly behind the C and QB, the FB is the first one.
Guard (G)	Offensive linemen lined up alongside the C.
Strong Guard (SG)	G lined up on tight end side or power side of the formation.
Quick Guard (QG)	G lined up on split end or quick hitting side of the formation.
Halfback (HB)	A back lined up approximately behind the offensive tackle.

Quarterback (QB)	Back who receives the ball from the C in most formations.
Slot Back (SB)	A back who is set between a split end and the next interior lineman.
Split End (SE)	An end who is split more than four yards from his tackle.
Tackle (T)	Offensive lineman lined up next to the G.
Strong Tackle (ST)	T lined up on tight end side or power side of formation.
Quick Tackle (QT)	T lined up on split end side or quick hitting side of formation.
Tailback (TB)	When three backs (QB, FB, and TB) are lined up behind the C, the deepest one is called the TB.
Tight End (TE)	An end who is split less than four yards from his tackle.
Wingback (WB)	An offensive halfback set less than four yards outside the TE.

BLOCKING TERMINOLOGY

Running Plays

Angle	A block away from the hole on a man lined up in the gap.
Area	When the offensive line blocks anyone in the attack area. Freelance blocking.
Inside Fold	When the interior lineman blocks to the outside on a lineman and the lineman next to him "folds" behind and blocks LB.

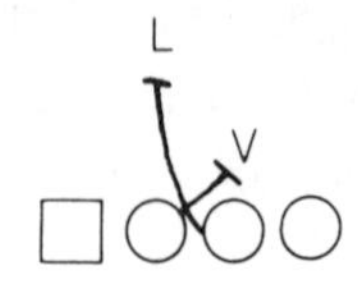

One-on-One	Same as drive blocking.

Outside Fold — When the outside lineman blocks down on a lineman and the lineman next to him "folds" behind and blocks LB.

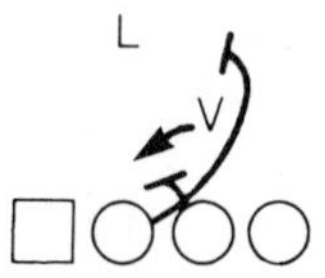

Post-Lead — A double-team block where the man with the defensive man on him executes a drive block and the other blocker executes an angle block.

Pulling — When an offensive lineman runs behind the line of scrimmage and turns upfield.

Reach — When the offensive linemen reach in the direction of the play in an attempt to prevent penetration and seal off the opponent.

Bounce — When a lead blocker has the man he's blocking angling away from him, he "bounces" to a linebacker.

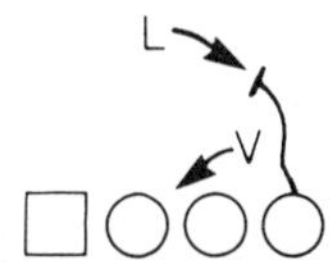

Brush — When a blocker makes contact (usually on an opposing lineman) then slides off (usually to a linebacker), leaving that person to be blocked by someone else.

Cross — When two adjacent offensive linemen block defensive linemen that are facing them.

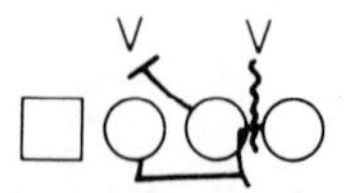

Cross Body — Used in crossfield block when blocker throws his body by and high past the defensive man in an attempt to chop him down.

Crossfield — Blocks made by offside linemen on defensive secondary men.

Down — Same as angle block.

Drive, One-on-One, Base — Blocking a man that is straight up and taking him out of the hole.

Gap — Blocking a man on your inside seam.

Influence — An attempt to decoy the defensive man into thinking that something other than the intended action is going to happen.

Reverse Shoulder — A shoulder block when the head is *not* put on the hole side of the play.

Scramble — When the blocker lunges forward onto his hands, brings up his feet, and assumes a crab-like position.

Trap — When a blocker (usually a guard) pulls behind the line of scrimmage and inside-out blocks a defensive lineman or penetrating LB.

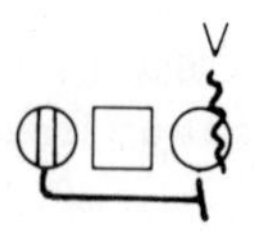

Passing Plays

Cut Down (Chop, Quick) — This block is used on quick passes. Blockers immediately go after defensive linemen to get their hands down.

Draw — When a blocker sets up in drop back protection to influence the defense and then blocks man away from the hole.

Drop Back (Cup) Protection — Protecting a spot five to seven yards behind the center.

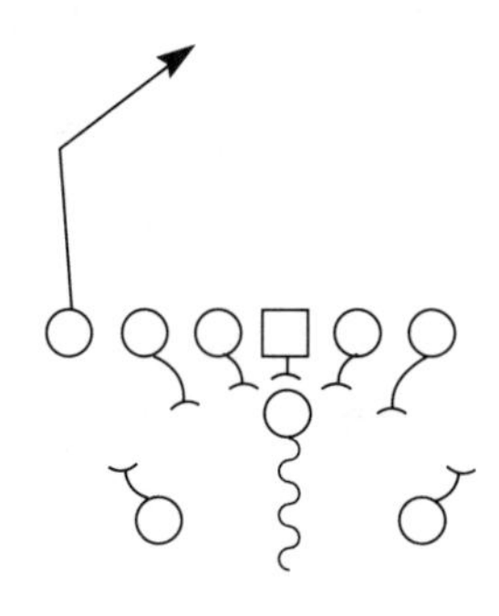

Hinge Block — Technique used by an offensive lineman assigned to protect the QB's backside.

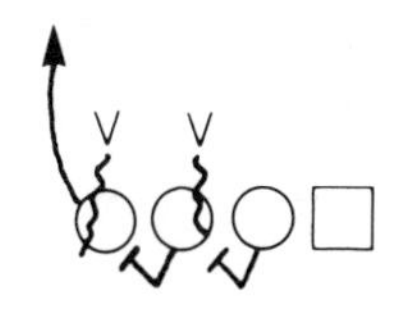

Play Action — A pass play that comes from a running fake. The blockers attempt to block like the running play.

Screen — The blockers set up in drop back protection to influence the defense and then set up a "screen" in front of receiver.

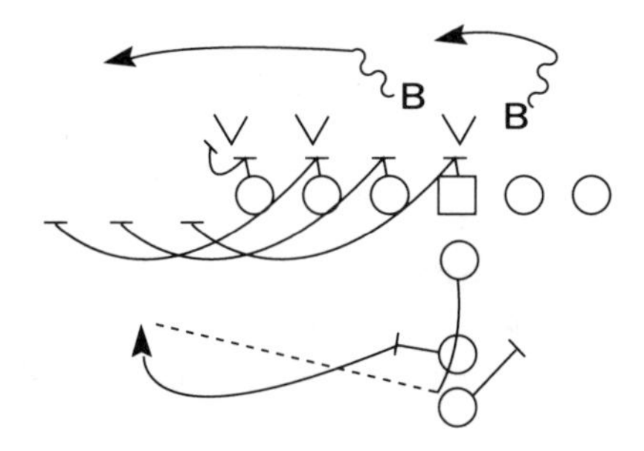

RECEIVER TERMINOLOGY

Check Swing (Safety Valve) — The running back or end check blocks first and then slides laterally to outside.

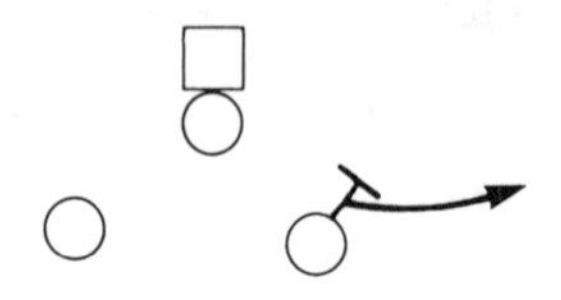

Crack Back — This block is used by wide receivers on sweeps or tosses and is executed as diagrammed.

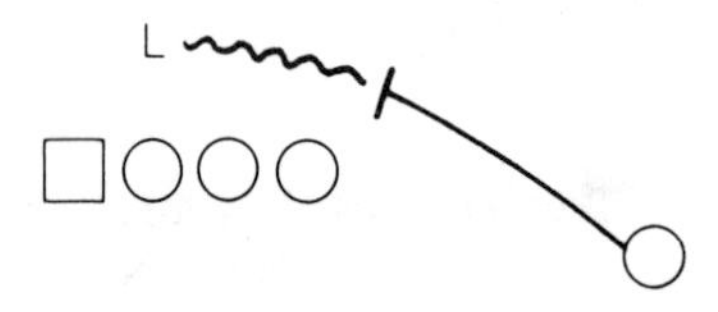

Cross — Pass route normally executed by TE in which he runs across the formation.

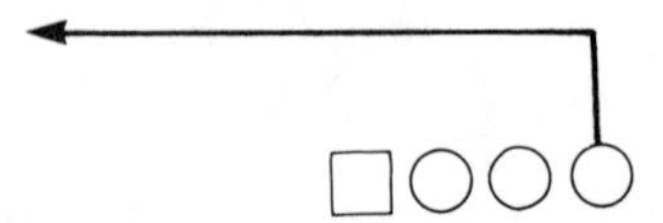

Curl — A pass receiver who goes straight down field for 8–15 yards and loops inside or outside.

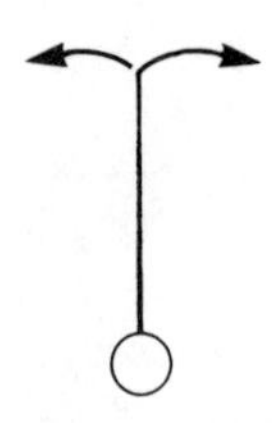

Delay — A pass receiver delays before running his route.

Flag (Corner) — Receiver makes outside break to end zone flag after driving 10–12 yards down field.

Flare — A back or end runs the route shown.

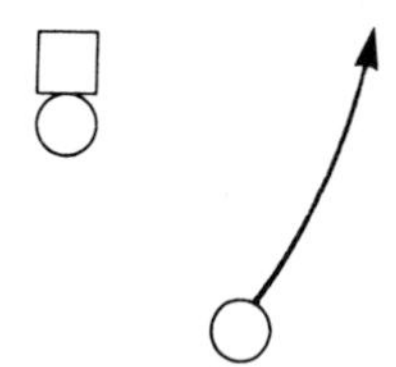

Flat — A back or end runs the route shown.

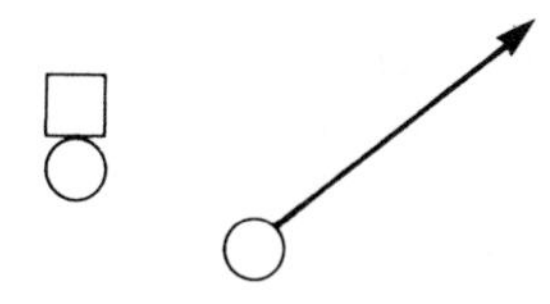

Flex — When a TE assumes a wider split than normal but is less than four yards from T, he is flexed.

Flood — When two or more offensive receivers are sent into one area of the defensive secondary.

Hitch — When a wide receiver drives a few yards off the line of scrimmage and turns sharply to the inside.

Hook — When an end drives off the line of scrimmage for 10–15 yards and turns sharply back to the inside or outside.

Out — When an end drives off the line of scrimmage for 10–15 yards and makes a 90 degree turn to the sideline.

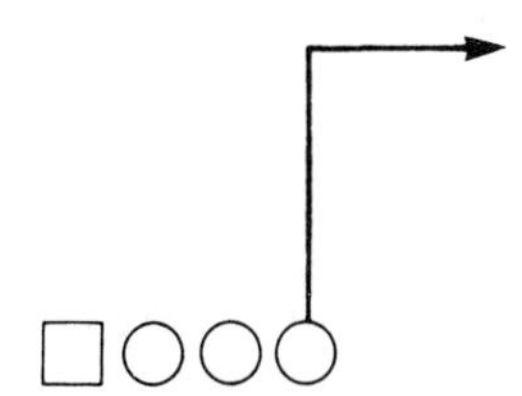

Pick — When one offensive receiver runs a pattern that impedes or draws the defender away from the primary receiver. If flagrant, it is illegal.

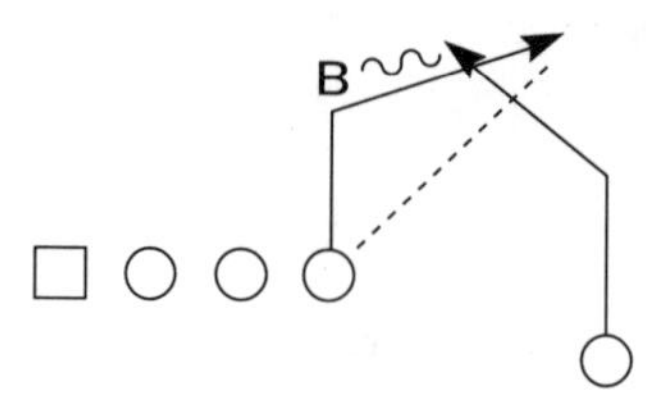

Pop — When an end drives off the line of scrimmage and immediately looks for a pass over his inside shoulder.

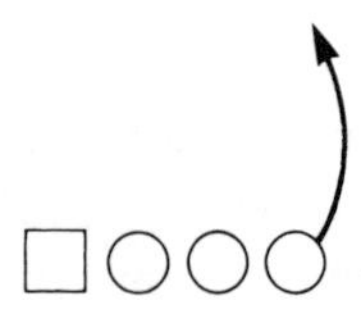

Post — Receiver makes inside break for goal posts after driving 10–12 yards downfield.

Release — The quick movement of an offensive pass receiver off the line of scrimmage and into his pass route.

Stalk Block — When a wide receiver releases off the line with speed to drive the defensive back off the line. As the DB releases his cushion, the wide receiver comes under control and maintains his position between DB and the ball carrier. The wide receiver must let DB support through him.

Streak — When a receiver attempts to get deep for a long pass.

Swing — When an end or running back releases laterally to the sideline.

PLAY TERMINOLOGY

Running Plays

Belly Option — When the QB rides the FB with the ball before continuing down the line of scrimmage on the option.

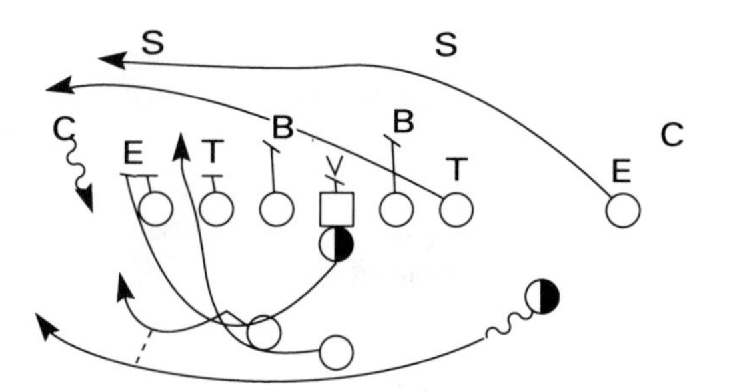

Counter

When the initial backfield flow is in one direction, but the play comes back to the opposite side.

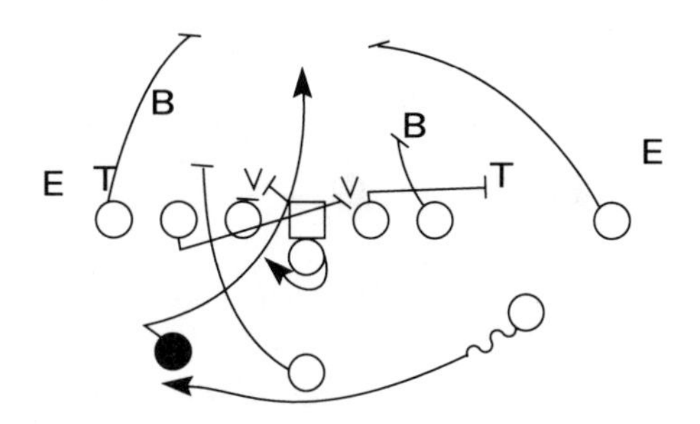

Counter Option

When the initial backfield flow is in one direction, but the QB comes back in the opposite direction with the option of keeping or pitching to a trail back.

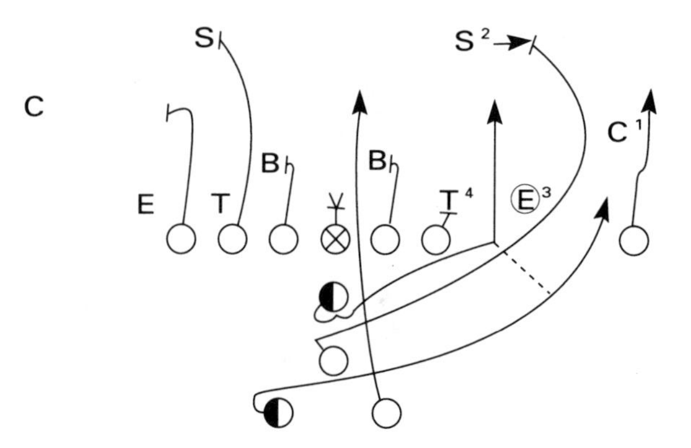

Dive — When a halfback explodes directly ahead into the line of scrimmage and receives the handoff from the QB.

Dive Option — When the QB fakes a dive and either runs with the ball or pitches to a trail back, depending on the movement of the defensive end or corner.

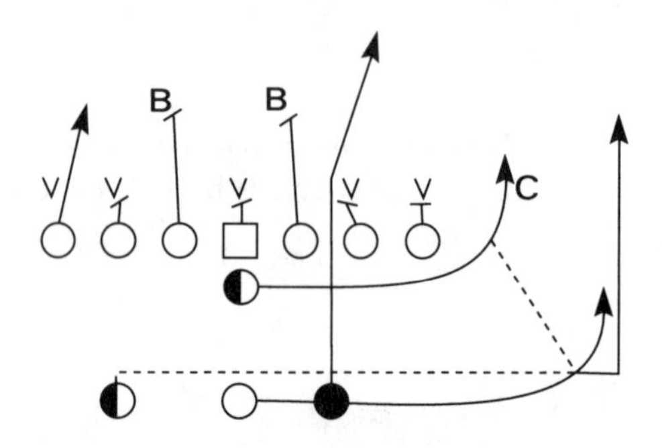

Draw — When the offensive linemen and backs set up as if the play is a pass, but the QB drops back and hands the ball off to a running back on a delayed run.

Isolation — When one back leads through the hole and blocks a linebacker, followed by a second back.

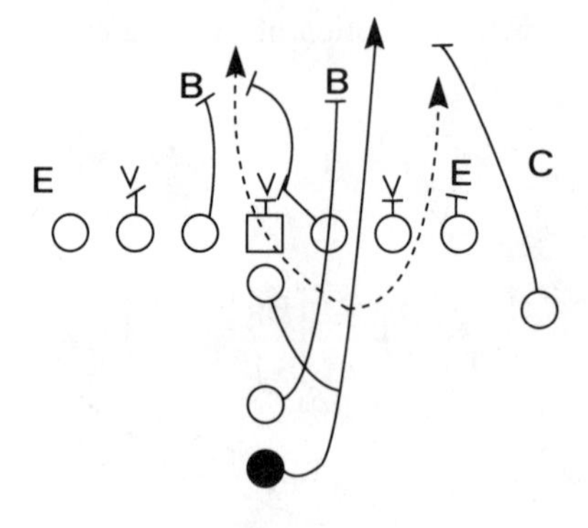

Power — Generally, a play off tackle with a post-lead block inside the hole and an inside-out block by a lead back or lineman outside the hole. A lineman generally leads the ball carrier through the hole.

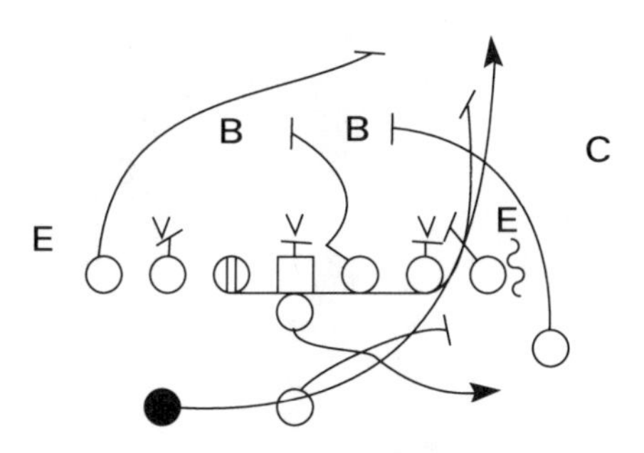

Reverse — Similar to a counter with flow being established in one direction, and the ball being carried in a direction opposite to its final destination.

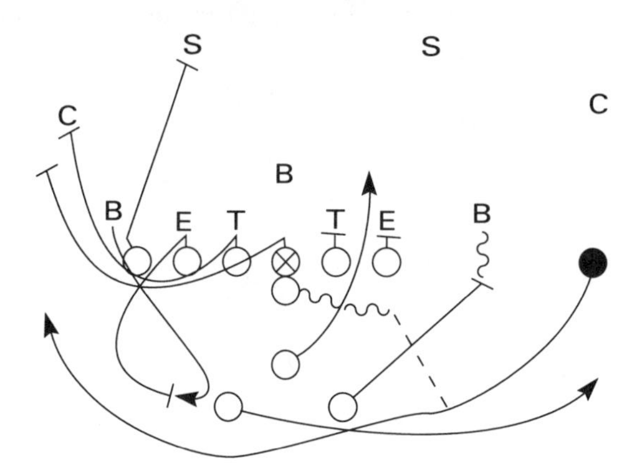

Sneak — When the QB keeps the ball and attempts to "sneak" past the defense, or he gets behind his blocking and "goes for the first down."

Sprint Option

The QB sprints directly down the line of scrimmage with no fake to a dive back and has the option of keeping or pitching to a trail back.

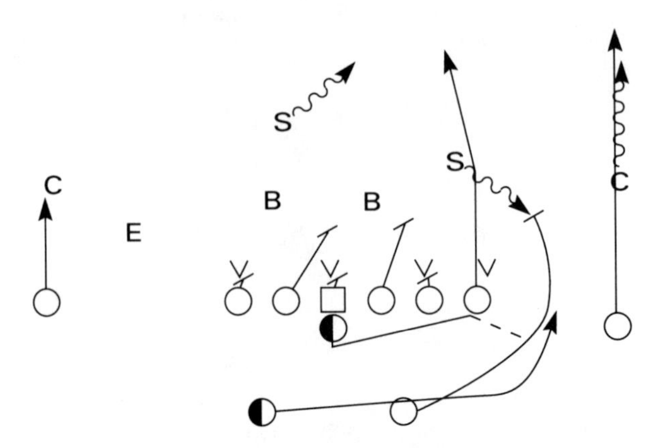

Sweep

On a sweep you pull one, sometimes both, guards and have a running back or QB (on pitch sweep) lead the play around the end.

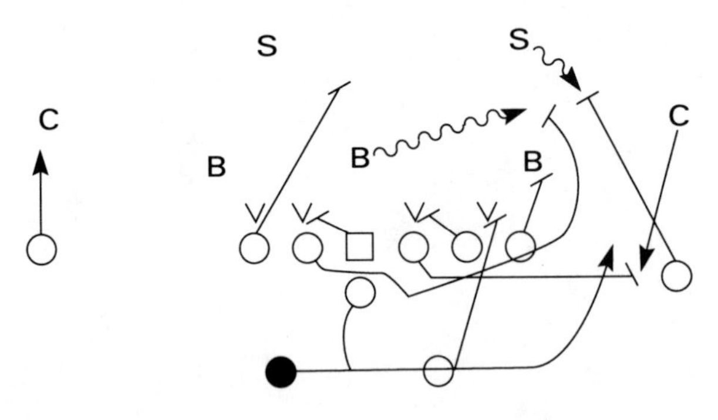

Toss (Quick Pitch) — A quick end run with the playside HB taking the pitch from the QB as he goes around the end on which he is initially lined up.

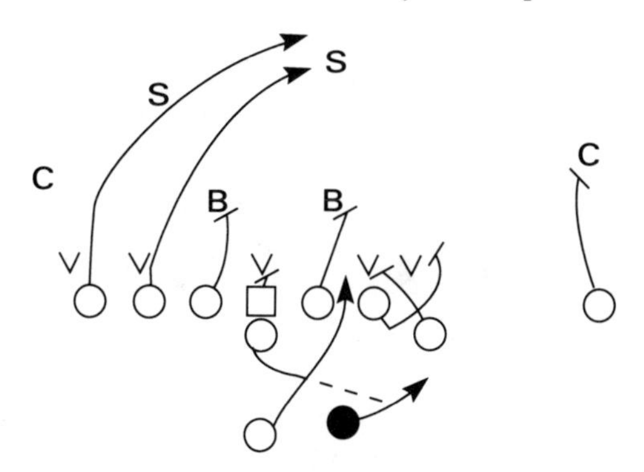

Trap — When the ball carrier takes the handoff and runs behind the block of a lineman who has executed a short pull and blocked the defensive lineman out of the hole.

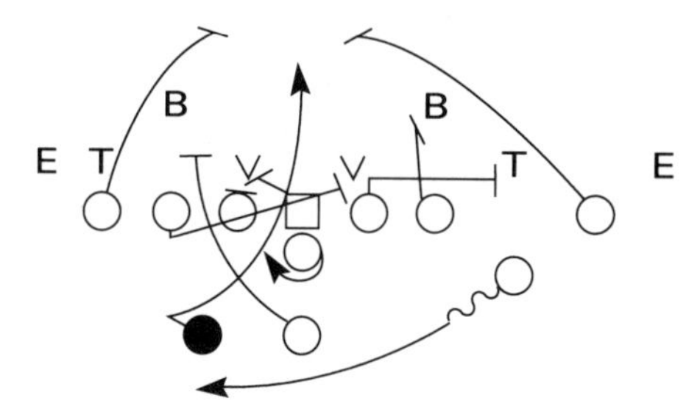

Trap Option

When the QB fakes the trap, then reverses his direction and comes down the line of scrimmage with the option to run or pitch.

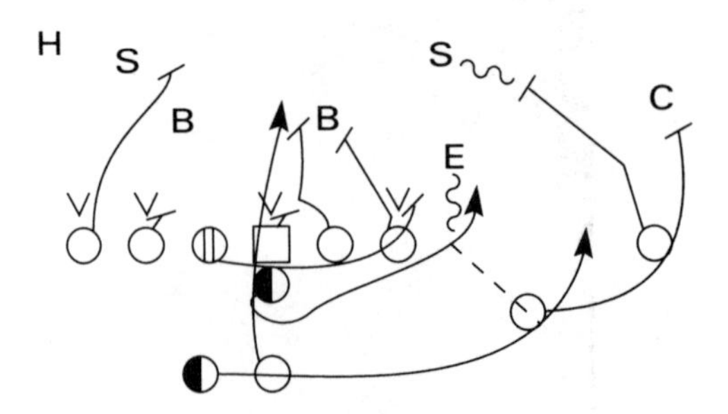

Triple Option

When any one of three backs can be the ball carrier *after* the ball has been snapped. Two defensive linemen at the point of attack are generally not blocked.

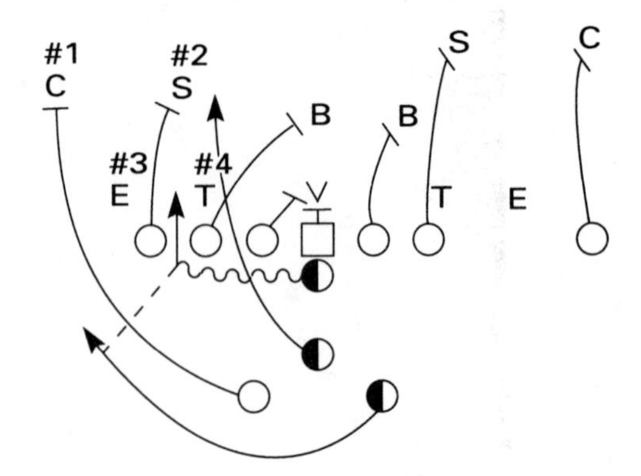

Passing Plays

Bootleg

On a play action pass when the flow of the backfield is in one direction, while the QB reverses and runs or throws back "against the grain."

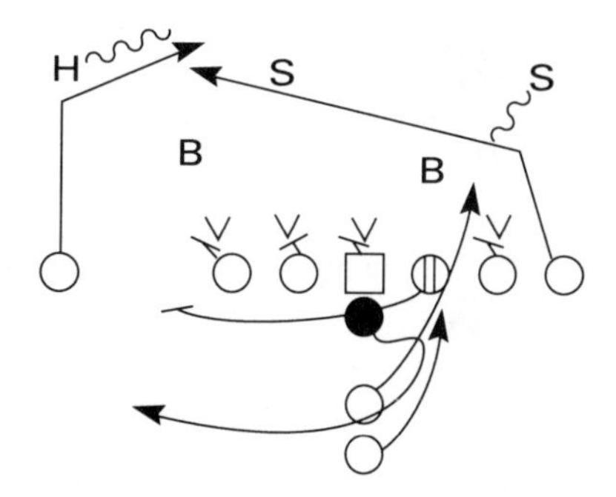

Dropback	When the QB sprints back to a spot approximately five to seven yards behind the center and sets up to pass.
Play Action	When there is a running play fake before the pass.
Roll Out	When the QB reverse pivots, often with a token hand fake, before setting up beyond the offensive tackle to pass.
Screen	When the offensive linemen show pass and the QB drops back encouraging the defensive linemen to rush and the linebackers to drop back before the ball is passed to an end or back with a "screen" of blockers in front of him.

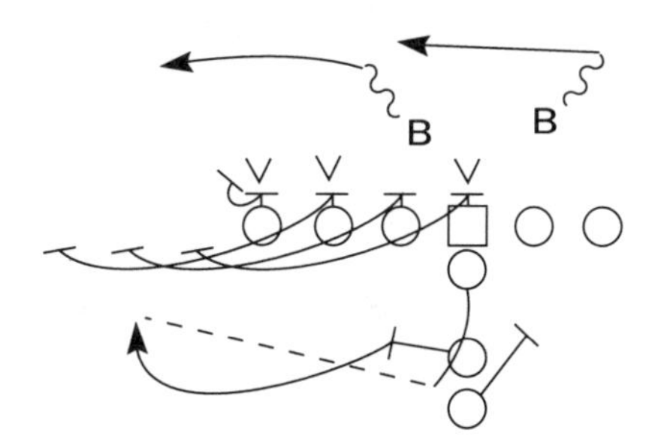

Sprint Out	When the QB doesn't reverse pivot but sprints out directly to a point wider than the offensive tackle before setting up.
Waggle	Bootleg play with guard(s) pulling opposite the offensive call, protecting QB.

FORMATION TERMINOLOGY

Presented in Figure 5.1 are the most popular offensive formations.

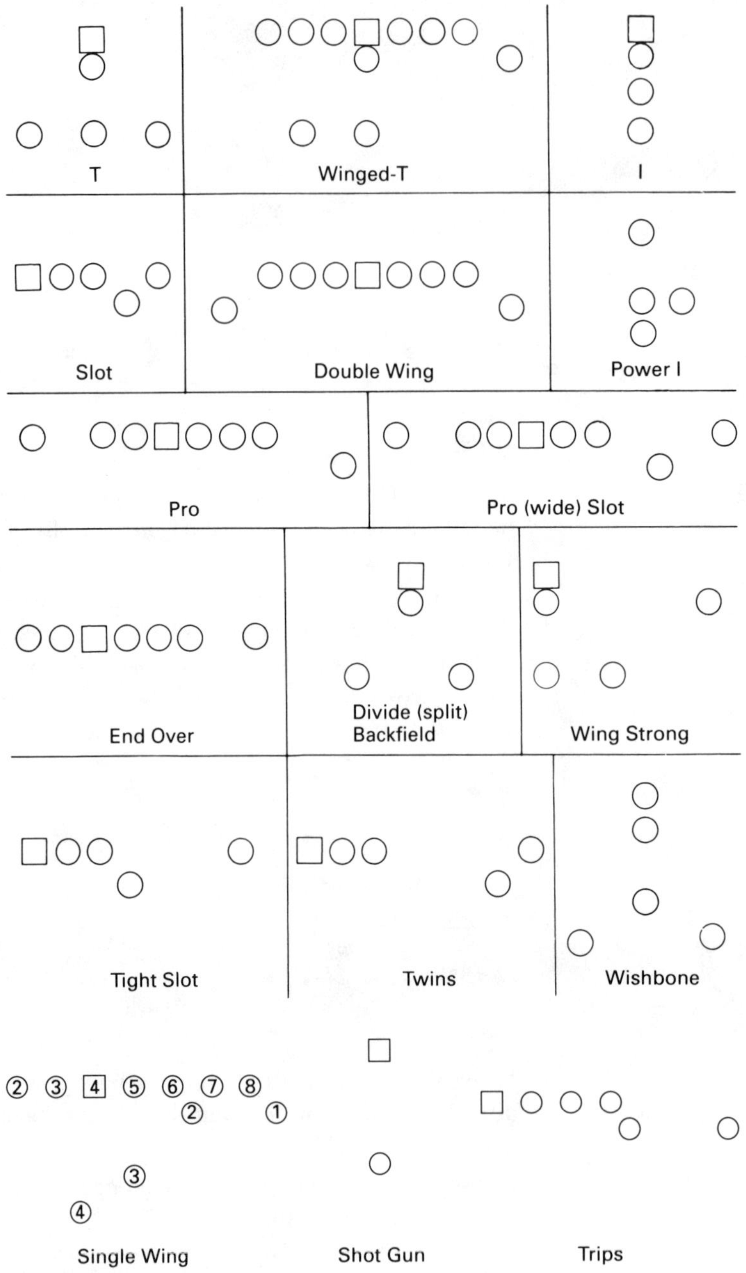

T

Winged-T

I

Slot

Double Wing

Power I

Pro

Pro (wide) Slot

End Over

Divide (split) Backfield

Wing Strong

Tight Slot

Twins

Wishbone

② ③ 4 ⑤ ⑥ ⑦ ⑧
② ①
③
④

Single Wing

Shot Gun

Trips

▶ **Figure 5.1** Offensive Formation

6

Position Requirements and Offensive Skills

POSITION REQUIREMENTS

The requirements and skills outlined in this chapter are those of ideal players. No coach is going to find eleven men perfectly suited to play each position. Certain offensive systems require different skills at the same position. The qualifications that follow are generalizations that would be true in most offenses.

Two characteristics must mark today's offensive football player. He must be *mentally sharp* and *physically quick*. With stunting defenses, the lineman who becomes paralyzed mentally when he sees movement in front of him or is just beginning to come out of his stance when the defensive man angles by him, cannot play.

Center

Size can be an additional attribute for the center in that it makes it easier for the quarterback to settle in behind him. The center must be a self-confident person. The huddle, spacing, and alignment at the line of scrimmage are initiated by him. He must know the starting count and be able to bring the ball up to the quarterback with authority. Agility is important since the center has to snap the football and then perform most of the blocks expected of other linemen.

Interior Linemen (Guards and Tackles)

The ideal requirements for guards and tackles will depend on the offense. Size and strength will be an asset in successful performance. If the offense pulls guards, they will need quickness and speed to aid them in leading the ball carrier. If the guards don't pull often, as is the case in most triple-option attacks, they will need the same size as the tackles. If a team runs an angling, penetrating, pursuit-oriented defense, the quicker big men will be put on defense. If, however, a read defense is used, the offensive line coach may be fortunate enough to get some quicker athletes on the offensive line.

Size and strength alone are no guarantee of success at this position. Interior linemen must master a variety of blocks, often in concert with other linemen, and be ready to change assignments at the last instant.

Tight End

The tight end must be a gifted athlete. He can be described as a tackle who must catch a forward pass. Speed is a bonus. More importantly, the tight end must be able to block and catch the football, often in crucial situations and in traffic. A tight end who can't block consistently severely hampers a running attack to his side.

Wide Receivers

Wide receivers must have good hands and good speed. They must be in excellent condition since they will have to run on every play as if they are the primary receiver. They must then hustle back to the huddle. Courage is an important factor since wide receivers must turn and jump to catch many passes, all the time knowing that they will be hit hard the instant they touch the ball.

Quarterback

The quarterback is the offensive leader. In any offense he must be a good ball handler. He must take the snap confidently from the center and mesh with his running backs. Good faking begins with the QB.

If a team passes a lot, the QB must have a strong, accurate arm and, while under pressure, be able to drop back quickly, get set, pick out his target, and release quickly and accurately.

If the offense requires the quarterback to run, he must be agile. On the option play he must make quick, correct decisions and be able to turn upfield sharply without undue loss of momentum.

All quarterbacks must have above average intelligence. Ideally, the QB should know everybody's blocking assignment on every play. Height can help him see over charging linemen. He must be willing to take charge, and he must be respected by his teammates.

Running Backs

The talents of running backs vary. Some rely on sheer speed; others use power combined with a solid base plus balance. Different offenses require different qualities. All running backs must have quick acceleration, and they *can't be prone to fumble.* In most offensive schemes they will have to block a moving target while running at top speed. Running backs must be rugged, since they will take a lot of hard hits during the course of a ball game. In the modern game, running backs must be able to catch the football. If the offensive system has one back carrying the ball more than the others, he should be the better ball carrier. Oftentimes the other backs complement him by being a better blocker or pass receiver.

FUNDAMENTAL SKILLS FOR LINEMEN

Proper fundamentals are at the heart of successful offensive football. The beginning coach is tempted to spend less time on the fundamentals so that he can get into his offensive attack and elaborate blocking schemes. This is a big mistake. At the younger ages especially, boys need work on the fundamentals, not razzle-dazzle plays.

Stance

Everything begins from a correct stance, therefore it must be taught from the very beginning. A skill that has been learned incorrectly and is repeated as often as a stance, is very difficult to correct.

Interior linemen will assume either a three-point or a four-point stance. The three-point is the most common. On occasion, coaches will have linemen fire out from a two-point stance. This is done to surprise the defense and catch them unprepared or in the middle of a shift.

As the offensive lineman comes to the line of scrimmage, he should immediately check his spacing and set his feet in the correct position. Most coaches state that the feet should be anywhere from hip width to shoulder width apart. If a lineman is moving straight ahead, a narrower width would be better, but not so narrow that he loses lateral stability. If he has to pull and trap a lot, a lineman must widen the base of support. Many young linemen have far too wide a base of support. The stance should not be too staggered. A lineman must be able to step off with either foot. A toe-instep relationship should not be exceeded. Feet should be perpendicular to the line of scrimmage. This will force the knees to be in the correct position. If the feet aren't perpendicular to the line of scrimmage, it throws the knees out of line and there is no possibility for a vigorous thrust into a block. The back should be parallel to the ground, but leg length will vary this somewhat.

There should not be too much weight on the hand or hands, but this also will vary depending on each individual's assignment. The shoulders should be level. The hand of the rear foot (in a staggered stance) is placed directly below the eyes with either the finger tips or knuckles placed on the ground.

The center's feet should be aligned at least shoulder width apart. The feet must be wide enough to allow a smooth snap to the quarterback, but not so wide that they limit mobility. The feet should be parallel and pointed straight ahead; the ankles and knees should be flexed; the hips should be elevated slightly so that the quarterback can receive the football easily.

Center Exchange

Before the center leaves the huddle he must be sure of the play and the snap count. He should get up to the line of scrimmage and get set quickly, since alignment begins with the center. There are two techniques used in the center-quarterback exchange.

The quarter-turn snap is the most frequently used technique. The laces should be up. The left hand carries the weight and should be on the left side of the ball with the base of the thumb at the back of the laces. The right hand is placed at the top of the laces but rolled under slightly. On the snap count, the center vigorously lifts the ball. As he lifts it, he applies a quarter turn to the football and delivers it to the waiting hands of the quarterback. The center steps out as he brings the ball up. It is the quarterback's responsibility to ride his arm forward with the snap.

In the half-turn snap the laces are on the right side. The right hand is spread out and on top of the ball. The top seam is visible between the middle and index fingers. The left hand is placed palm up and under the rear of the ball, which has been elevated to a height of not more than 45 degrees. On the snap count, the center executes a swift perpendicular swing with a half turn-over and places the ball into the quarterback's hands.

One-on-One (Drive or Base) Block

This is the most basic block in football and some time should be spent in every practice working on it. There are two schools of thought when it comes to teaching this block. Some coaches use the shoulder block exclusively. The blocking surface extends from the sternoclavicular joint, across the front of the shoulder, down the upper arm, and back along the forearm to the fist, which is placed near the chest.

In the teaching progression, start with the linemen on "all sixes" (knees, feet, hands). On command they explode at a dummy. The linemen then will freeze in position while coaches check to see that: 1) there is a good neck-shoulder squeeze effect, 2) the buttocks are lower than the shoulder, and 3) the back is arched and eyes are up. After this position has been checked several times, linemen explode at the dummy on command. Finally, the linemen assume their offensive stance and drive the sled or dummy.

The shoulder block emphasizes *horizontal thrust,* especially during the teaching phase. Direction of thrust is largely determined by the relationship of the center of gravity (the hips) to the base of support (the feet). If the hips are well out in front of the feet, there is a lot of horizontal thrust but less vertical lift. If the hips are above the feet, there is maximum vertical lift but minimal horizontal thrust.

Other coaches emphasize the *vertical action of the forearms* or a punch technique, with the base of the palms, as the blocker attempts to lift his opponent. The importance of keeping the center of gravity over the base of support is stressed.

These coaches begin with the offensive linemen's feet and knees on the ground similar to the position they are in for the shoulder block. But the shoulders and head are centered above the lower legs, and the hips and forearms roll *up* into the block or the base of the palms rip up through the opponent's chest region. The words "dip and rip" are the most frequently used to illustrate the action. When linemen are on the two-man or seven-man sled they are lifting it vertically and digging their feet as hard as they can. The blocker must be low with his feet underneath him at contact, not sprawled out behind. Horizontal thrust is sacrificed at contact in anticipation of achieving two alternate ingredients—vertical lift and sustaining potential.

A blocker must not overextend himself. Any lateral movement or a step backwards on the part of the defensive man and contact will be lost. Against an angling defense, a blocker cannot overextend in this fashion. The line of thrust must be more vertical. The player must keep his feet more directly under him and adjust to any change of direction by the defensive man.

The question every offensive line coach asks himself, either consciously or unconsciously, is which emphasis is best. Certain blocking techniques favor horizontal thrust, while others favor vertical lift. Most coaches who emphasize the shoulder block communicate to their linemen the concept of lunging. This is done from the first day when they tell their offensive linemen to dig their toes into the turf, get on their hands and knees, and explode *out* at the dummy. The word "drive" is used frequently to emphasize the action. When the linemen are on the two-man or seven-man sled they are driving it horizontally as hard as they can.

In either blocking progression you eventually want the offensive linemen to move their defensive men out of the hole. The danger of the shoulder block is that while they lunge out, agile defensive linemen will angle by them. The danger of the forearm lift or base-of-palm technique is that explosive defensive linemen may charge and bowl them over, since they haven't generated as much momentum.

Recent rule changes that dramatically liberalize the use of the hands by offensive linemen, have forced offensive line coaches to rethink blocking techniques. In the I-formation, where a talented tailback "runs to daylight" picking his hole after the snap of the ball, blockers must sustain their blocks much longer and can take the defensive man in any direction. This offense necessitates the forearm lift or punch technique of blocking. In the Delaware Wing-T attack, however, the shoulder block is used. The hole is more defined and the blocker seldom drive blocks a man directly over him. Even if he does block the man directly over him, the path of the ball carrier is usually predetermined.

Line Splits

Line splits vary considerably from team to team and offense to offense. The speed of the backs, location of the play, relative quickness of offensive and defensive linemen, defensive stunting, down and distance, and position on the field are factors that influence the amount of split between linemen.

If a team is firing the gaps, linemen will have to tighten down. If a trap play is called up the middle and the defense is lining up on the offense, splits should be increased. When throwing the football, minimum splits will give a charging defense less room to penetrate. Tight splits make the corner closer on sweep plays. As a general rule, splits will vary from 12 inches to a maximum of 42 inches.

Area Block

In the area block the blocker does not know who he will block as the ball is snapped. He could come off the ball for one step with his inside foot and then bring his outside foot up and parallel. His center of gravity must be low and his feet about shoulder width apart. This position should be held for two counts while the player blocks anyone who tries to come through his area. After two counts, the player can take off and block anyone in front of him.

Pulling

Certain offenses require a greater degree of pulling, but it is a skill that is good for *all* linemen to master. Pulling is a good agility drill. The stance must be virtually identical to the one taken when firing out. If possible, shift the weight back slightly without being detected. A three-point stance is better than a four-point stance for this purpose. On the snap count, the weight is shifted back and slightly in the direction of the intended motion. Weight transfer is crucial. Otherwise it is impossible to move the feet in the desired direction. Once the weight has been transferred in the proper direction, it is easy to make the first step with the lead foot about six inches back and six inches in the intended direction. Coaching points are: 1) shift weight; 2) step slightly back and in the intended direction; 3) drive lead elbow into back pocket and thrust the near arm forward; 4) push off trail foot; 5) point lead foot in the desired direction; 6) elevate body gradually, don't "pop up"; 7) keep a fairly wide running stance for purposes of stability.

The playside guard should run a "half-moon" route and the far guard should run a "sickle" path. This route will let the guard clear the center-quarterback exchange zone before he dips into the backfield. The precise route that is run on any given play is very important. Movements must mesh with a blocking back, if there is one, and the ball carrier. If the pulling lineman is going to log the defensive man, he must get outside leverage on him by delivering a blow with his inside shoulder or forearm through the outside hip of the defensive man. As he explodes through the defensive man's outside hip, he should swing his hips in order to drive upfield.

Trap Block

The initial movement on a trap block takes the lineman on a "sickle" path. The lineman does not need to shift his weight back as much since his route is flatter to the line of scrimmage. It is important that he stays flat. The center and guards must practice their routes often so they can pass as close to each other as possible. The blocker should stay low and aim for the upfield side of the person he intends to block. In this way he can pick up a stunting linebacker or a tackle taking a flat angling route. In any case, more tackles are made because the man that is being trapped slides off the block on the upfield side.

Down, Gap, or Angle Block

This is a block in the inside area (away from the hole) using a one-on-one blocking technique. If the blocker anticipates that the assigned man will be penetrating, he may have to reduce his split. The weight is shifted in the desired direction and the first step must be with the nearest leg. Seal off the gap first and then turn upfield, if necessary, for the block.

Reach-Out Block

The initial step on a reach-out block should be almost like a short trap. The line of scrimmage must be sealed. The head is aimed to the outside of the defensive man. This is a very difficult block because it requires the blocker to block a man that is lined up between him and the intended path of the ball carrier. The technique is the same as the log block noted under "Pulling."

Scramble Block

Opinions differ on whether this should be a basic block. Some coaches teach that it should be used only when the blocker senses that he is losing his man on a drive block. Other coaches teach it as a basic block. When the defensive man starts to slip off the block, lunge forward onto your hands and bring your feet and buttocks up quickly. Assume a crab-type position and pinch the defensive man between the thigh and upper arm. Keep scrambling with him as he attempts to free himself. The blocker's arm must not encircle the defensive man's leg, or holding may be called.

Fold Block

These are essential blocks against many defenses. Timing between the two men involved must be precise and considerable time should be spent practicing it. The uncovered lineman goes first and takes a route to the defensive man that does not allow penetration. Don't go to where the man is, but to where he will charge. The first step should be with the foot nearest the man to be blocked. The blocker folding behind must mesh closely. He should not loop too deep, but take a jab step slightly back and in the direction of the block. He then turns up to the linebacker as quickly as possible.

Cross Block

The execution of the cross block is similar to the fold block. The blocks are executed on two defensive linemen. If one lineman is uncovered, he goes first. If both are covered, the lineman farthest from the center goes first.

Post-Lead Block

A post-lead block is a double-team block on a defensive man. The offensive man with the defensive man on him is called the post blocker. The adjacent lineman that is assisting on the block is called the lead blocker.

The technique of the post blocker is identical to the one-on-one block. He drives straight up and through the man and attempts to immobilize his charge. The post blocker is aware of the direction from which he will receive help but should block the man as if he is blocking him alone.

It is the lead blocker's responsibility to close the seam. His first step must be with the foot nearest the post blocker. It is his fault if the defensive man splits the gap between them. He must get hip to hip with the post blocker and ride the defensive man out of the hole.

Bounce Block

Oftentimes a post-lead block will develop into a bounce block. This will happen frequently against stunting defenses. The lead blocker must come down expecting the defensive man to be coming at him, but if he angles away, the blocker must immediately bounce off to the far linebacker.

Crossfield Block

Any lineman who does not have a specific assignment on a play should pick the correct angle to the running lane and meet the defensive backs who may be converging for the tackle. Once the lineman meets the defensive back, some coaches will have him gather and rip right through the man with the one-on-one block. Others suggest a high cross body block thrown at the last second and followed up with an extended roll.

Influence Block

In an influence block the blocker is attempting to decoy the opponent into thinking that something other than the intended action is going to happen. This is especially effective against well coached, head defensive linemen and linebackers.

Reverse Shoulder Block

Generally, on any block, the head should be on the side of the hole. In a reverse shoulder block it is not. An example of when the block is used is on a down block when the defensive man is charging hard across the line of scrimmage. In order to prevent penetration, the head should be thrown across the hole and the reverse shoulder used.

The following six techniques are used in passing situations.

Basic Pass Protection Block

Without effective pass protection blocking, any passing attack is doomed before it gets off the drawing board. The single most important aspect of effective pass protection blocking is *position.* Following are some key points: 1) don't let the man get an inside route (establish an *outside* foot-to-crotch relationship); 2) "hit and 'git' low"; 3) wait until he comes and explode *up* and through him with the base of palms under his shoulder pads; 4) don't overextend; 5) recoil after every hit; 6) don't let the rusher get his hands on the blocker; 7) know where the quarterback is setting up; 8) keep or regain separation as much as possible.

Play-Action Pass Protection Block

In play-action pass protection, the play should look as much like a running play as possible. This type of pass is most effective in running situations. In theory, the play should be blocked just like the running play from which the pass originates. This is not always possible, but the blocker should not set up in a pass protection position immediately after the ball is snapped.

Quick (Cut Down) Block

This block is used on all quick passes. Explode out and high at the man to be blocked. When he reacts, change your body direction and block him low. Follow through on the block and get the defensive man's hands down as he attempts to extricate himself. In this way the hands will not be in the quarterback's face as he steps up in a shallow pocket.

Screen Block

Every team will have at least one form of screen pass. The exact timing, distance the linemen travel laterally, and actions will vary. The screen is intended to get the defensive linemen charging at the quarterback who is dropping back, and the linebackers moving back to their areas of pass responsibility. The quarterback will drop the ball off to a receiver who has a wall of blockers in front of him. On this block, the linemen want to create the impression that this is a typical drop back pass. They set up in pass protection, block for two seconds, and then release to their new position. The lead blockers must not block the same person, and one blocker, usually the center, will turn back and pick up a reacting lineman.

Backside Protection

Some offensive lineman is generally assigned backside protection on play-action or roll-out passes. The blocker positions himself between potential rushers and the quarterback. Use the basic pass protection technique.

Draw Blocking

This play usually comes from pass action. A set-up influence block is used and the man is blocked away from the point of attack. If nobody shows, the blocker continues downfield and blocks a halfback.

FUNDAMENTAL SKILLS FOR BACKS

Stance

The basic principles described in the linemen's stance apply. The exact stance will depend on the requirements of the position in a given offense. For example, the fullback in the wishbone attack has his feet parallel, since he must run to the right and left creases with equal quickness. He also has a fairly wide stance since he will be hit from the side often and hard. If a back sprints forward most of the time, he can get into a sprinter's stance with his feet hip-width apart and his weight well forward. If he must move laterally most of the time, he carries little weight on his hand. Some coaches who utilize a tailback like to have him in a two-point stance. Acceleration is not appreciably slower. In fact, some research indicates that a standing start may be the fastest.

Position

The position of the backs depends on the offense. In the wishbone attack, it is generally 13 feet from the line of scrimmage to the fullback's feet and 15 feet to the halfback's feet. There are 18 inches between the inside foot of the halfback and the near foot of the fullback.

An I-formation will generally have the tailback five yards and the fullback three and one-half yards from the line of scrimmage. A wingback's position can vary, but he is normally one yard deeper than the linemen and between one to two yards outside the end. A halfback in a winged-T is as deep as the fullback and lined up behind the offensive tackle, approximately three and one-half to four yards off the line of scrimmage.

Movement

When a running back moves forward, he rolls his weight forward and vigorously extends the trail leg (if in a staggered stance). His lead or power leg is now at an ideal angle to continue the forward thrust. The arms must act in opposition to the legs. He must continue driving with the arms until the exchange zone is reached.

When moving laterally a running back can utilize the same mechanics as the pulling guard (note fundamental line skills), or he can use a cross-step. In a cross-step technique, the back pivots on the foot in the direction of lateral movement, while the trail foot crosses over the front and the weight shifts in the direction of movement. Most research indicates that a cross-step is faster when the distance to be covered is greater than five feet.

Ball Handling

It is the quarterback's responsibility to get the ball to the ball carrier. A back cannot look for the ball. He must be watching the hole as it develops in front of him. As he nears the exchange zone, the ball carrier simply raises the near arm on the side of the quarterback and gets the inside elbow at eye level. The forearm should be parallel to the ground with the fingers spread and bent. The palm of the far arm is facing up, with the forearm about three to six inches from the body. Some coaches state that the ball should be placed firmly on the far hip of the receiver while others feel that the ball should be laid softly against the belly as if it were an egg that you don't want to break. The runner should guide the ball into place with the upper hand as his lower arm wraps around it. A firm grip is kept on the ball and the ball is not shifted around until the line of scrimmage has been well-cleared.

Faking

The ball carrier must mesh with the quarterback, stay low, and drive through the assigned hole. Fakes are continued until he is five yards beyond the line of scrimmage or tackled. Faking is just as important as ball carrying.

Blocking

The most important blocks for backs to master are the one-on-one (drive) block on a moving target and the pass protection block. On the one-on-one block the back must "gather" or "coil" just before contact and strike *up* and *through* the opponent. The basic pass protection blocking technique is no different than for the linemen. Inside protection is established and the attacker is prevented from getting to the QB.

Ball Carrying

A ball carrier can't be a fumbler. He must hang onto the football. As a general rule, the football is carried away from the initial center of formation. Most hits are received from the inside. Many young, inexperienced backs run laterally too much. They should move upfield as soon as possible and use lateral movement for specific reasons, such as dodging, setting up blockers, or outflanking a slower opponent. Skills that ball carriers must work on are changing direction while running at top speed, when to drop the shoulder and attempt to overrun an opponent, and setting up the defense for offensive blockers.

FUNDAMENTAL SKILLS FOR RECEIVERS

Stance

Receivers use either a two-point or three-point stance. With an upright stance a receiver can "read" coverages more effectively.

Release and Routes

A tight end must work hard at getting off the line of scrimmage. A head and shoulder fake in one direction as the weight is shifted to the opposite side often will get an end by the line of scrimmage. If this doesn't work, he can try a drive block directly at a linebacker lined up on him. Before the linebacker recovers, the tight end can drive by him. If the area is really congested, a tight end may have to scramble on all fours, get under the defense's arms, return to a running stride, and get into the prescribed pass route.

Wide receivers should utilize an outside release. This opens a larger area in which to run patterns. One exception to this is when the initial position is close to the sideline. Then a wide receiver should not take as large a split.

Receivers must be consistent in their routes. In this way quarterbacks know what to expect. Quick passes normally require cuts at four yards. Sprint-out passes require cuts at eight yards and drop back and play-action passes at twelve yards. Wide receivers must learn correct depths and routes. Defenders have weaknesses and these will be spotted by good receivers. Good receivers run just as hard when they're not the primary receiver.

Receiving the Football

A receiver should stay in his normal running position until the last second and only then reach for the football. If he doesn't, speed is lost. After receiving the football, a receiver normally drops the shoulder and turns upfield. Be a runner.

It takes a certain amount of natural ability to be a receiver. The proverbial "stone hands" are more than a myth. The three "C's" certainly are necessary ingredients. These are confidence, courage, and concentration. A receiver has to believe that the quarterback will get him the football. The quarterback has to have confidence in the receiver. They are a team and must spend hours together working on their movements. Receivers will take some of the hardest hits of anyone on a football team. These hits often occur as they are gathering in the football and are often from a blind side. It goes without saying that a good receiver must watch the ball into his hands. He must focus on the ball, not the person that is about to tackle him.

There are two opinions on how to catch the football. Some coaches say that the ball is caught with the hands and then brought in to the body. They argue that the hands are softer and can absorb the force more effectively. Other coaches tell receivers to catch the football with arms and body whenever possible. Leap into the air, if necessary, to catch it this way. In this technique the hands are under the football. The shoulders bend and form a pocket for the ball. This technique screens the defensive back more effectively, allows the body to aid in force absorption, and results in less passes being knocked loose when the defensive man's hit occurs.

FUNDAMENTAL SKILLS FOR QUARTERBACKS

Center Exchange and Stance

In the quarter-turn exchange, the throwing hand is placed under the center so that the hyperextended wrist of the throwing hand conforms to the curve of the center's buttocks. Bury the hand to the wrist. The middle finger should be along the crease of the buttocks with the tip at the crotch. The elbows should be bent so the quarterback can ride forward with the center's charge without having to step forward.

In the half turn-over exchange, the quarterback's hands are with the thumbs side by side and the hands spread out. His hands will naturally conform to the curvature of the center's inside thighs and crotch.

Quarterback's stances vary. Some are fairly wide and staggered and some are narrow and parallel. Since a quarterback must move quickly in both directions, it is mechanically most efficient to have the feet hip-width apart and parallel. If, however, a team runs to pro-type offense with a lot of drop back passing, it would be advantageous to have the throwing leg back.

Body positions vary also. Some quarterbacks are hunched over the center; others do all the bending at the knees and the back is perfectly straight and perpendicular to the ground. The knees are bent. It is impossible to move from a stiff-legged position. Much depends on the offense, the demands placed on the quarterback, and the body build and disposition of the quarterback himself.

Movement and Ball Handling

The center of gravity of the quarterback must be near the point of his base to which he moves most frequently. If he drop back passes often, his weight should be back on his heels. If it is forward on the balls of his feet, it has to travel that much farther. The fastest way to get back seven yards is to begin with the weight on the heels, sit back, vigorously turn, and sprint. On a quarterback sneak, shift the center of gravity as far forward as possible. Obviously, these shifts of weight can't be so obvious that they telegraph the quarterback's intentions.

As soon as the quarterback gets the ball, he must bring it in to his navel. This serves two purposes. It protects the ball from pulling guards and crossing backs and hides it more effectively from the other team. It is interesting to note that the quarter-turn exchange has the ball in a better position for passing, but the half turn-over exchange is better for handing off.

The exact movements of the quarterback will depend on the offense, but in any offense the quarterback should not take big steps. The weight should be centered and under control.

Throwing the Football

Most coaches have some idea of the mechanics of throwing a baseball and assume incorrectly that throwing a football must be similar. It is not. Pitchers take a very long stride in the direction of home plate, quarterbacks must not; a pitcher can take as much time as he wants provided nobody is on base, a quarterback cannot. Shortstops often take a skip step prior to throwing to first base, quarterbacks dare not; and lastly, a pitcher combines significant linear motion with rotary motion, a quarterback should utilize primarily rotary motion. By wheeling the body around in a circle instead of moving the weight forward and whipping the ball with the arm, a quarterback can generate velocity and spiral without the obvious dangers noted in the previous sentence.

In the rotary throwing motion that will be summarized here, the following points must be observed. Assume that the quarterback is right-handed.

1. When setting to throw, the weight is on the right foot, but the center of gravity must be forward.
2. The body is turned with the chin over the left shoulder.
3. The left leg steps to the left of the target, not in the direction of the intended throw.
4. As the left leg steps, the ball is raised from the chest to alongside the head.
5. The hips begin to open before the left shoulder pulls away from the intended flight line of the ball.
6. The body weight is transferred from right to left, not back to front, as the left arm pulls around.

7. The hip whip and shoulder rotation naturally pulls the ball away from the ear. The ball is not consciously whipped out.
8. The wrist snaps forward with the throw but doesn't rotate (pronate) as it does in pitching.
9. The body rotation finishes with the weight on the left foot, exposing the quarterback's right side and back to the charging linemen.

This throwing motion, which is mechanically sound, has several advantages over a more traditional pitching-type motion. They are: 1) the quarterback isn't stepping *up* into the pocket and is, therefore, closer to the rushing linemen; 2) the ball can be released much more quickly (.5 second); 3) the weight can be kept under control more easily since the feet aren't being moved as far; and 4) upon completion, the quarterback is stepping out to the side and around, thus avoiding a head-on collision.

7

Elements of a Successful Offense

THE COACHING STAFF

In the first chapter of this book the personal qualities and attitudes of a successful coach were discussed. Certainly a successful offense begins here.

The coaching staff must be flexible. The offense must suit the personnel. When personnel changes, the offense might have to change. It is impossible to run an I-formation without a hard-nosed fullback and a rugged, talented tailback. A split-T offense requires explosive linemen and backs. If a coach doesn't have a gifted passer and talented receivers, it would be foolish to run a pro attack.

Successful coaches all have a desire to learn. The coach who runs the offense he ran in college because he has never taken the time to learn anything else will soon become obsolete. Knowledge in itself is not enough, however. A coach must be able to communicate that knowledge. Good coaches must be effective teachers.

Finally, the successful coach must be able to motivate his players to perform to their maximum. Every coach must be true to his own personality, but without enthusiasm toward his profession and his players, it is unlikely that any coach will successfully motivate athletes to maximum performance.

STRESS THE FUNDAMENTALS

A coaching staff must have an excellent grasp of the basic fundamentals of offensive football and the ability to teach them to their personnel. Many coaches have noted that the fundamentals of offensive football often deteriorate during the course of the season. If a coach isn't vigilant, he may find himself with twice as many offensive plays in late October, but without the skills needed to execute them. A coach must never neglect the ABCs of the game. Some time in *every* practice must be spent exclusively on fundamentals.

TEAM STRENGTH

This aspect of a football program was developed in Chapter 3. Teams that have established winning traditions continually work on strength development. It should be stressed during the season as well as in the off-season. Studies have shown that there can be considerable strength loss from the beginning to the end of the season. It was once erroneously thought that large muscles meant slow muscles. It is now realized that strength is an absolutely essential aspect of speed. Many of the most successful teams have what are called "strength coaches."

CONSISTENCY—DON'T BEAT YOURSELF

A team cannot sustain a consistent attack if it has an excessive number of fumbles, interceptions, penalties, and broken plays. This is especially true in a ball control type offense. It is tempting to overcoach. Many young coaches are so eager to get all the offense in by the first game that they neglect the fundamentals in order to do so. This is a big mistake. It is much better to run five plays well than run ten in a less confident manner. An occasional "trick" play for a key ball game is not necessarily bad, but a successful coach knows that he doesn't win consistently with them.

UNDERSTAND AND EVALUATE DEFENSES

A successful offensive coach must spend much time studying and analyzing defensive alignments, theories, and trends. Modern defenses are highly sophisticated. There are a number of defenses that a team can utilize with numerous stunts and secondary coverages. It would be a good exercise for a coach and a student of football to diagram all the basic football defenses against various formations and list the basic theories, strengths, and weaknesses of each alignment. This is covered in Chapter 15.

KNOW EACH OPPONENT

The successful offensive coach must know more than just what defense an opponent runs. He must make use of every legitimate means at his disposal to learn everything he can about each opponent. Films, scouting reports, and other coaches are three obvious sources of information. File information from previous years. Organization is essential. While there are personnel changes from year to year, offensive tendencies, theories, and attitudes remain fairly consistent with coaching staffs.

SCOUT YOURSELF—KNOW YOUR TENDENCIES

Some coaches receive a lot of statistical data and other information about their opponents but fail to analyze their own tendencies. The coach who is aware of the scouting information and data that other staffs are compiling on his football team is better able to anticipate what opposing coaches might do in given situations.

KEY FOR THE BIG GAMES

There are certain games on a schedule that a coach realizes are must games. Point for these games. A team cannot get "sky-high" for every game. A coach cannot be dishonest with his team. They know if they are obviously better. The coach who misleads his team about how tough an opponent is will not be believed the next time. The wise coach will look at the entire schedule before the season starts and begin to formulate a plan of how to approach each game with the players in order to get a maximum effort.

DEFENSE DICTATES OFFENSE

If a team's defense gave up an average of five points a game the previous season and all personnel are returning, this will have a bearing on offensive philosophy. If the defense allows the offense to begin most drives at midfield, it gives the offense much more flexibility than if it is constantly beginning drives deep in its own territory. Before the season begins, the offensive coaches must realistically look at the defense, attempt to project its strengths and weaknesses, and consider this when determining offensive philosophy.

PLAYER EVALUATION

In Chapter 3 player evaluation was discussed. Each offensive player should receive objective feedback on his performance. Some teams with large coaching staffs have elaborate grading schemes. Other coaches will make a few comments at Monday afternoon's practice. Criticism must be constructive, and positive aspects of performance should be noted as well.

SIMPLE BLOCKING PATTERNS

Blocking systems are the subject of Chapter 8. The key to consistency in offensive football is to minimize breakdowns at the line of scrimmage. A coaching staff must spend a great deal of time going through all of their plays against every conceivable defensive alignment to make sure that blocking assignments hold up.

INCENTIVES AND GOALS

Some coaches do a lot more in this area than others, and there is disagreement as to the value of incentives and goals. Goals must be realistic. To go undefeated is something every coach strives for, but if the first game is lost and no other goals have been set, a coach will have a morale problem on his hands! Effective goal setting begins in the off-season. This was discussed in Chapters 1 and 3. When the head coach talks with each athlete about next season, they can mutually establish goals for the player. The coach can also share his goals for the team and get feedback. Some of these might be: 1) to score when inside the 10-yard line (improve by a certain amount on last year's percentage), 2) to convert a greater percentage of third-down plays and state a target percentage, 3) to cut down on turnovers and state a target amount, 4) to improve on drives—the average position that the ball is given up (state a yard line), 5) to reduce penalties, 6) to score more per game, 7) to gain more first downs, and 8) to improve on quarterback sacks relative to the number of passes thrown. In this way the athletes are made aware of areas of concern for the coaching staff.

PASSING AND RUNNING ATTACK

Time must be spent on both aspects of offensive football. A team can go along for several games with a strong ground attack, but if they fail to develop their passing game, it will ultimately come back to haunt them. In the crucial game, when the quarterback has to throw the football, the ability to do so effectively will not be there. A team can put on an "aerial circus" for one or two games but, if that is their entire offense, it will not get them through an entire season.

SHORT-YARDAGE OFFENSE

A team has to believe that they can score when they get inside the five yard line, and that they can convert crucial third-and-two situations into first downs. Time must be set aside every week to work on these situations. Certain basic plays that have solid blocking against stacked defenses must be explained and practiced. An elaboration of offenses for these situations is included in Chapter 11.

THE GAME PLAN

The earlier the coaching staff can decide on the game plan for a ball game, the better. Some decisions that should be made by Monday afternoon's practice are: 1) plays to work on (pass and run), 2) blocking scheme, and 3) personnel. Some minor adjustments can be made later in the week, but major changes should be avoided.

COMPLETE AND CONSISTENT OFFENSE

On the face of it this recommendation may sound obvious. It is amazing how often coaches violate it. Many coaches tend to add plays in a rather piecemeal fashion as they go through the season. Before they know it, their offense is a strange mixture of formations and maneuvers. A coach must be sure that he can attack all along the defensive front from every formation that he runs, and that he *actually does*. It's surprising how often coaches slip into the readily detectable trap of shifting to this formation for these plays and point of attack and to that formation to attack at this location.

TWO-MINUTE OFFENSE

This element of the offense must be practiced. Coaches must determine the most effective techniques to use in speeding up the offense and in wasting time, depending on which is necessary. Games have been lost because a team unnecessarily scored too quickly, leaving the opposition time to come back and win. Some considerations are discussed in Chapter 11.

CONSISTENT TERMINOLOGY

A clear, concise offensive vocabulary must be developed. This should be written down and included in the playbook. Vocabulary should be developed for all formation alignments, plays, personnel, defenses, and blocks. These should be short but descriptive.

8

Blocking Systems

INTRODUCTION

The development of a blocking system that is easy to understand, but at the same time complete and adaptable, is the single most important element in offensive football. A large part of the offensive staff's time will be spent checking the blocking patterns of all plays against every defensive alignment.

Once blocking assignments have been decided, the best way of communicating them to the players must be determined. Some athletes with greater conceptual abilities will profit from a more theoretical development of the offense; others will not. Everyone learns differently. Memorization of one's position assignments by rote does not make for permanent learning; yet for certain people this is the best approach. Other athletes want to know why a particular offense was selected, the philosophy behind it, and the rationale behind every play. Coaches must be willing to provide this.

In practical terms, this means that a coaching staff should begin each season by explaining to the players why a particular offense has been chosen; and if it has been changed, the reasons for the change. When position coaches present the plays, the entire play should be presented before individual assignments are covered. This ideally can be done in a classroom setting. If the use of a classroom is not practical, it can be done on the field. A veteran offense can line up on the ball and one by one give their assignments to the rest of the team.

People learn at different rates and for this reason a playbook is a valuable tool. Some athletes will know their assignments after the coach has put a play on the backboard once, but others will need frequent review. For these athletes, a playbook that they can take home and review on their own is a valuable learning aid.

Outlined below are several blocking systems that have been used successfully. The basic blocks explained and diagrammed in Chapter 6 should be reviewed before reading this chapter.

BY DEFENSE

In this system, every play in the offense is diagrammed against every defense that a team anticipates seeing. They are drawn up by one of the offensive coaches, duplicated, and distributed to the team.

COUNT SYSTEM

In a typical count system the defensive men along the line of scrimmage are assigned numbers. If a man is directly on the center, he is not numbered and is blocked by the center. Every player memorizes the number of the man he blocks for every play. A "227 Dive" would look like the top play diagrammed in Figure 8.1. (Numbering systems are covered in Chapter 9.)

Count systems may include secondary personnel and be numbered from the outside in. This is how blocking assignments are often determined in the popular wishbone attack. (Note the bottom two diagrams in Figure 8.1.)

RULE SYSTEM

Rule blocking became popular with the advent of split-T, tight slot, and winged-T attacks.

One-on-One (Split-T) Blocking

In this blocking scheme, holes are numbered *over* the offensive men. The numbers assigned are immaterial as long as everyone understands them. For the sake of example, the numbering system in Figure 8.2 will be used.

A 27 Dive would be over left tackle. The rule for the lineman *at* the hole, in this case the left tackle, is over, inside, outside, LB. For the first lineman *inside* the hole, his rule is over, outside, LB. For the first lineman *outside* the hole, his rule is over, inside, LB. It takes practice and communication on the part of the offensive linemen to insure that they interpret the location of defensive personnel

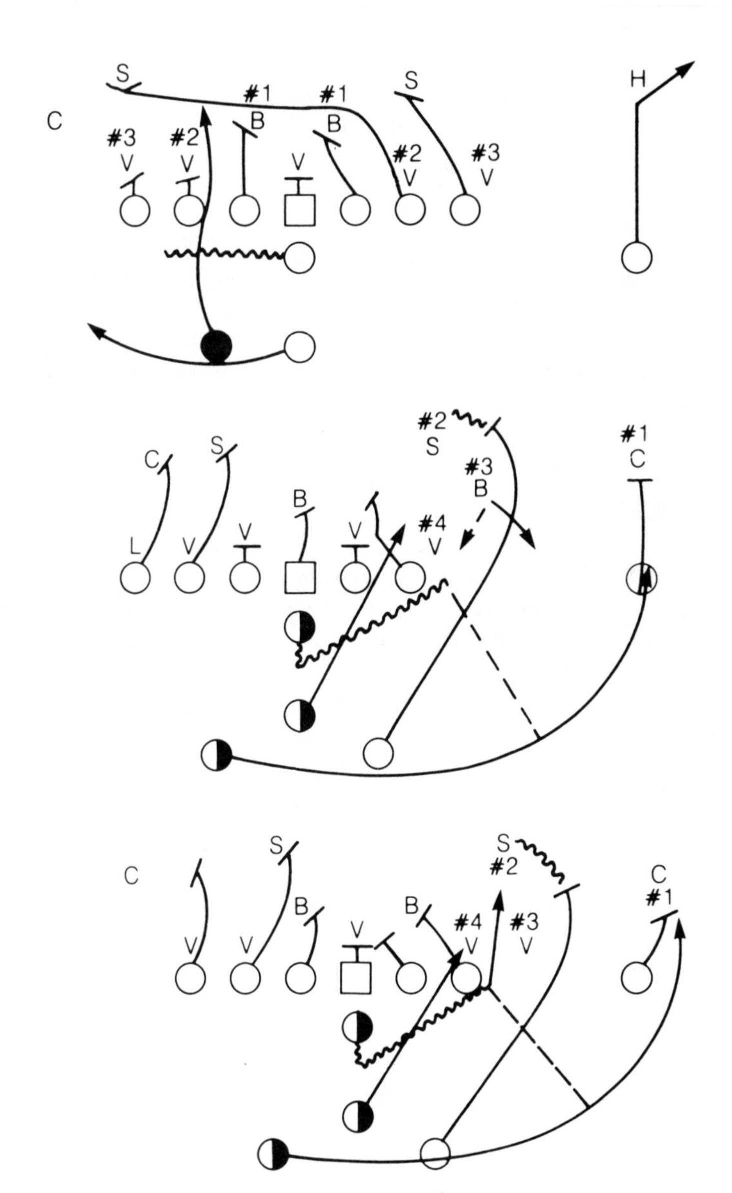

▶ **Figure 8.1** Count Blocking System

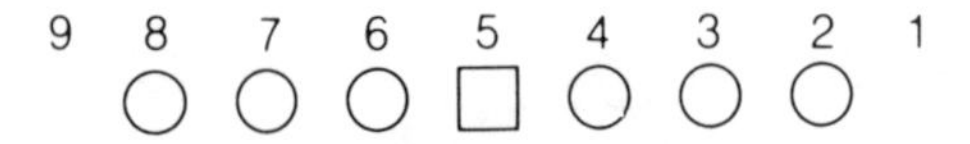

▶ **Figure 8.2** One Numbering System for Rule Blocking

consistently. Following are definitions to assist in interpretation: *Over*—if the defensive lineman's helmet would hit the offensive lineman's helmet if they moved straight ahead. *Inside*—if the defensive man is inside but not *over* the next lineman to the inside. *Outside*—if the defensive man is outside but not *over* the next lineman to the outside. If a lineman is not next to the hole man, his assignment is over, LB, cutoff.

Crossblocking

If a "27 Dive X" is called, it means a *crossblock* at the point of attack. A crossblock always involves the hole man, in this case the tackle, and the man inside him, in this case the guard. The uncovered lineman goes first and they simply switch assignments. The two linemen adjacent to the crossblockers must keep the next linemen away from closing down the hole. If there are no dangerous linemen, they get the most dangerous LB. The rules are consistent all across the line of scrimmage.

Post-Lead with Inside-Out Blocking

The fundamental idea of this blocking system is to get a double team or post-lead block on the lineman *inside* the hole and an inside-out block by a pulling lineman or back on the lineman *outside* the hole. The first lineman outside the hole will go *across to a LB,* and the next lineman to the outside or wingback will block the near LB. (Note Figure 8.3, top diagram.)

The rules have two parts for the offensive player at the hole, the *principle* rule and the *secondary* rule. His principle rule is lead (block), and his secondary rule is, if nobody to lead on, pull away. (Note Figures 8.3a and 8.3b.)

For the first lineman inside the hole, his principle rule is post (block); if no man on post, down block first man away from hole. (Note Figures 8.3c and 8.3d.)

The inside-out blocker blocks the first man to show *from the hole to the outside.* (Note Figures 8.3e and 8.3f.)

Rule blocking for a trap at the 3 hole (using the numbering system presented earlier) is diagrammed first in Figure 8.4. Rule blocking for a power play at the 2 hole would be similar except extended out one man. The center's rule becomes the right guard's rule, the right guard's rule becomes the right tackle's rule, etc., as in the right diagram in Figure 8.4.

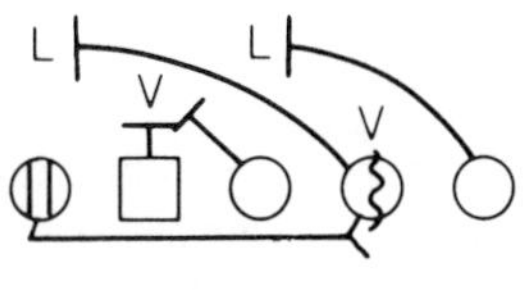

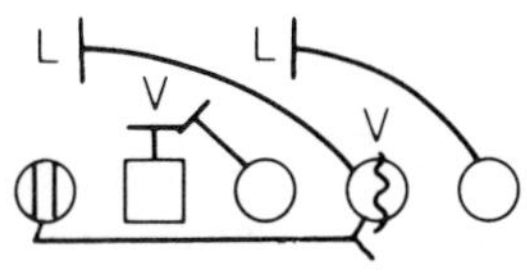

Principal Block

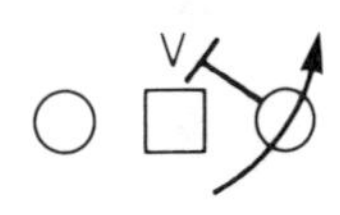

a

Secondary Block

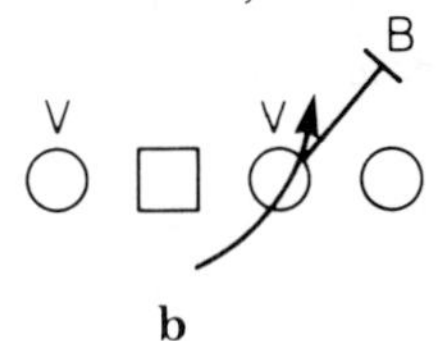

b

Principal Block

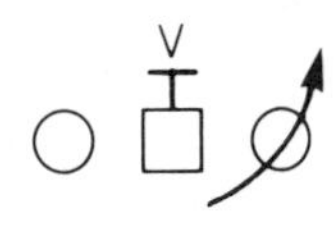

c

Secondary Block

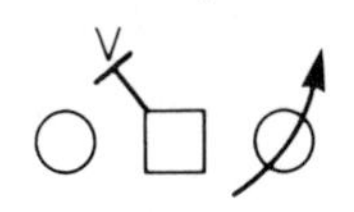

d

Inside-Out Block

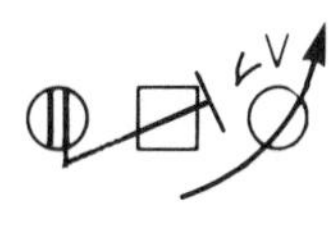

e

Inside-Out Block

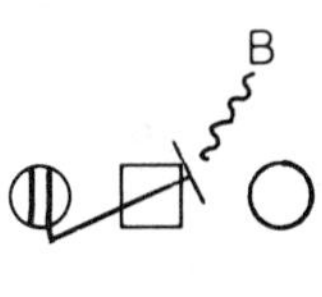

f

▶ **Figure 8.3** Post-Lead with Inside-Out Blocking

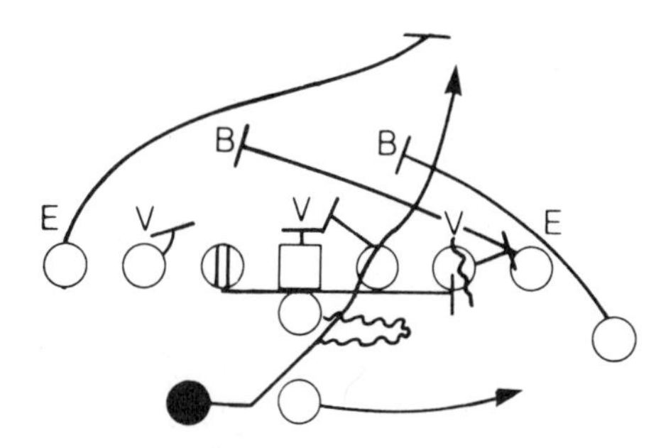

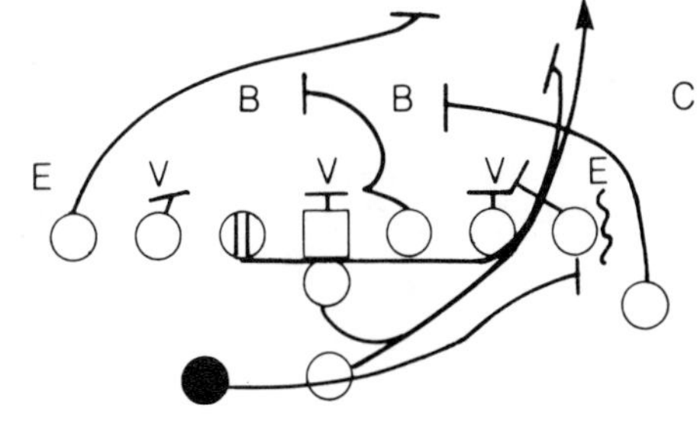

▶ **Figure 8.4** Rule Blocking for Trap Play at 3 Hole and Off-Tackle Play at 2 Hole

TECHNIQUE SYSTEM

The technique blocking system is really a combination of the count and rule blocking systems. The count system tells you *whom* to block. This system adds an additional element. It tells you *how* to block. The 24 Dive outlined under the technique system would look like this. The technique listed first is the primary assignment. If this is impossible due to the position or shift of the defense, the next assignment is executed.

TE: drive, reach
ST: drive, angle
SG: drive, angle
C: drive, angle
QG: drive, reach
QT: drive, crossfield

A 28 Pitch Sweep would look like this:

TE: drive, angle
ST: drive, angle
SG: pull, lead, block color
C: reach, drive
QG: pull, lead, seal
QT: reach, crossfield

With this system it is essential that the offensive coaches check and double-check techniques against all possible defensive alignments and be sure that they are sound. Backfield assignments should be listed the same way.

A lot of time must be spent making sure that all offensive personnel understand all of the techniques. Various techniques that are basic to any attack were outlined in Chapter 6. Some of these should be practiced every day. Concentrate on those that are going to be crucial in the next ball game.

With this system it would be possible to put your entire offense on one page![1]

[1]Ralston, *Coaching Today's Athlete,* p. 262.

Assignment Sheet

Play	*TE*	*ST*	*SG*	*C*	*QG*	*QT*
41 (21) Sweep	Angle	Angle	Pull Hook 2	Drive Strong	Pull Seal 2	Pull Seal 5
33 Opt.	Drive	Drive	Drive	Drive Strong	Cut Off	Cut off
42 (22)	Lead, inf. Cross to LB	Drive (Post)	Drive	Drive Strong	Drive (C.O.)	Drive (C.O.)
33	Drive	Drive	Drive	Drive Strong	Drive (C.O.)	Drive (C.O.)
23 Bl.	Drive #3 inf.	Blast Lead	Lead, Pull Trap 2	Drive Strong	Drive (C.O)	Cut off
44 Tackle Trap	Near LB Safety	Near LB Inf.	Lead, inf. Cross to LB	Post Lead	Drive	Pull Trap 4
36 Trap	Near Safety	Inside	Pull Trap 6	Post Lead	Lead, inf. Cross to LB	Near LB

GAP SYSTEM

One of the most difficult tasks for offensive coaches and players is blocking a defense that runs a variety of stunts and effectively disguises them until the last possible moment. Some teams stunt frequently and offensive coaches must consider *gap* blocking. Gap blocking is based on the assumption that stunting defenses try to penetrate gaps all along the line of scrimmage, but especially at the anticipated point of attack.

When a team is stunting with regularity, the offense must plug the gaps with angle, reach, or wedge blocking techniques.

If the offense is using a trap block or a lead back in front of the ball carrier on a particular play, angle blocking should be used. The defensive man outside the hole is left for the trap blocker or lead back, and the lineman over this man either down or influence blocks.

If the lead back is getting the ball, then either wedge or reach blocking must be used.

These calls can be made at the line of scrimmage.

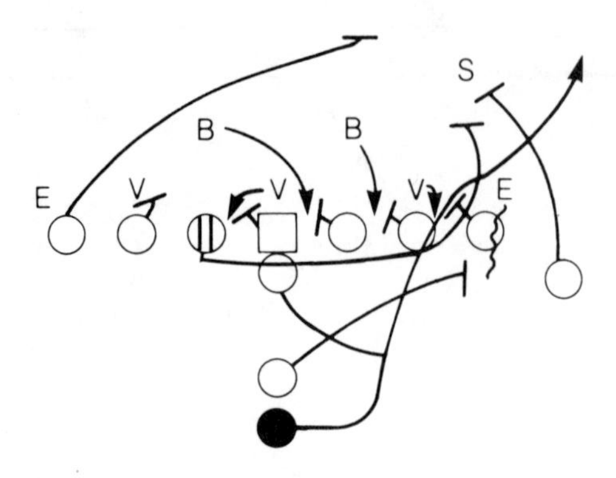

▶ **Figure 8.5** Gap System with Down Blocking

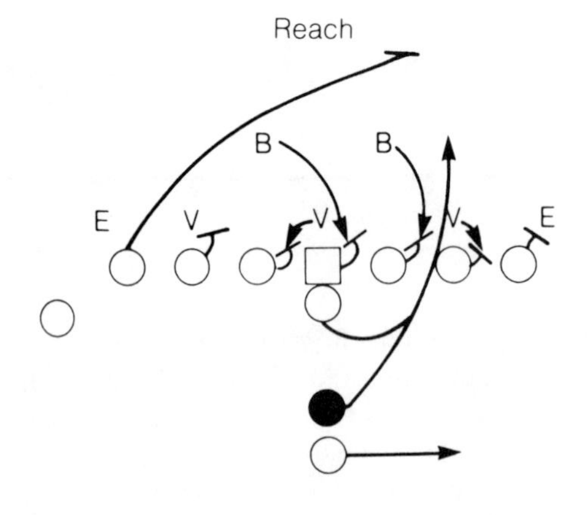

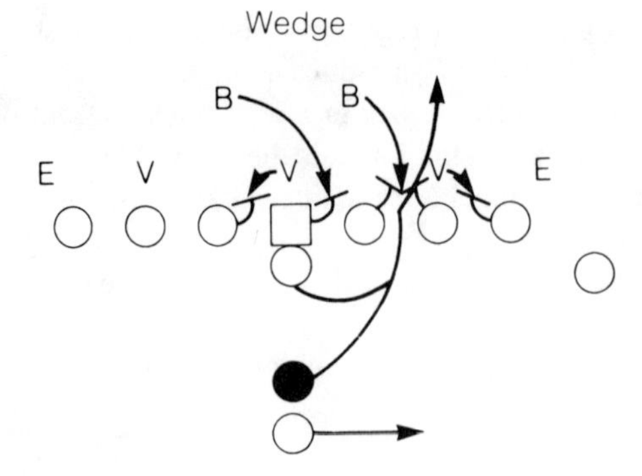

▶ **Figure 8.6** Gap System with Reach and Wedge Blocking

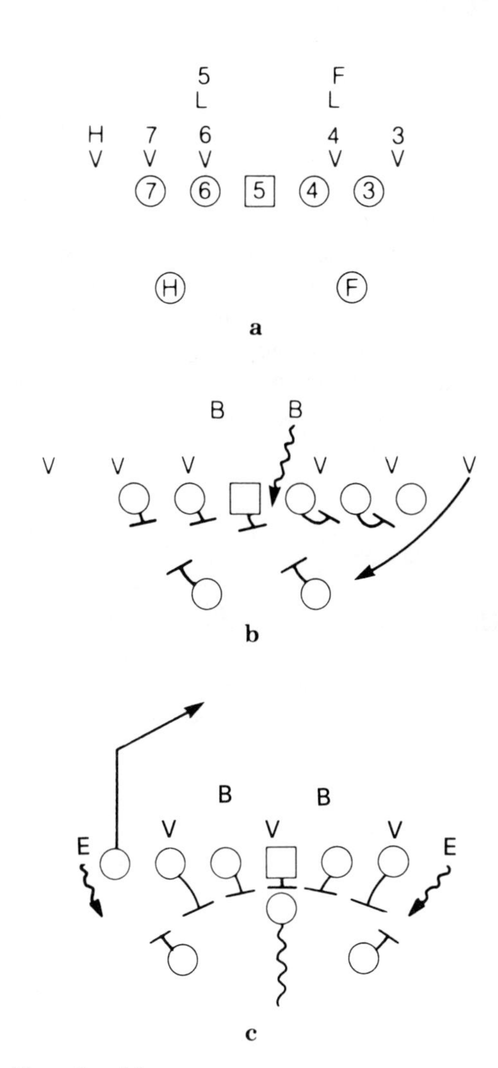

▶ **Figure 8.7** Man-for-Man and Area Pass Protection Blocking

PASS PROTECTION

Man-for-Man[2]

In this system every available lineman and back is assigned a defensive person to block. Assignments are memorized for every defense. This system makes assignments very clear. However, if a team blitzes one of the four defensive men not numbered as a likely pass rusher, he may get through. Any offensive blocker whose man doesn't come must immediately look for one of these rushers. It is also vulnerable to defensive pass rush stunts. (Note Figure 8.7b.)

Area (Zone)

In this system offensive personnel are assigned an area to defend. The interior linemen and blocking backs create a wall and don't allow penetration. Adjustments must be made when the defense overloads an area. (Note Figure 8.7c.) If a team has one great rusher, a back may be added to help in an area. For example, if a team has a great nose tackle, the center and a back may be assigned to him. If the nose tackle slips off, he will be "chipped" by the back, giving the center time to recover.

[2]Ralston, *Coaching Today's Athlete,* p. 248.

9

Presenting the Offense

Offensive information and procedures must be organized in such a way that they quickly and clearly communicate to the players. A quarterback cannot come into the huddle and make lengthy, wordy calls. A series of numbers indicating various functions is the quickest means of communication. Some words may have to be used, but coaches must work at keeping play calling *brief.* The quarterback will have to communicate all or some of the following elements in his play call: 1) hole, 2) ball carrier, 3) formation, 4) series, 5) shift, 6) motion, 7) snap count, and 8) break huddle signal. There are many ways in which this can be done. The following is one excellent way.

PLAY CALLING

Hole

Each point of attack along the line of scrimmage should be assigned a number. How they are numbered is immaterial as long as everyone understands the numbering system. Some coaches number offensive players, while others prefer to number the holes *between* offensive players.

Ball Carrier

Each backfield person should be assigned a number.

Formations

Each formation should be assigned a number. Some coaches use colors.

1. (Blue) I-wing right
2. (Red) I-wing left
3. (Green) Winged-T right
4. (Black) Winged-T left
5. (Gray) Pro right
6. (Brown) Pro left
7. (Purple) Divide, wing right
8. (White) Divide, wing left

These three essential numbers (hole, ball carrier, formation) can be combined into a number between 111 and 999 that readily indicates all three functions. The formation could be the hundreds number, the ball carrier the tens number, and the hole the units number. Then 324 would mean a play run from the 300 formation, by the 2 back at the 4 hole.

If the second (tens) digit is higher than four (not a back number), it designates a passing series. Five (5) could mean drop back, six (6) sprint out, seven (7) screen, and so on. The third number, rather than designating the hole, would indicate pass routes. The number 654 could mean a drop-back pass from the 600 formation with everyone hooking.

Series

Most teams will attack a hole with a given back in more than one manner. Therefore, a word is added either before or after the three numbers indicating the type of play. For example: power, trap, slant, or blast.

Shift

In order to confuse defenses, many teams like to shift prior to final alignment. This could easily be indicated by a number preceding the play. For example, 5–324 Trap might mean that the team would initially line up in a 500 formation, shift to the 300 formation on signal, and then run the play.

Motion

Letters of the alphabet can indicate types of motion. A flanker in long motion could be called "x"; a wing in short motion could be called "y"; a TB in motion strong could be called "z." This letter would follow a shift call, but precede the play.

Snap Count

This is designated by the QB in the huddle. Some teams utilize a system whereby the ball carrier's number is always the one on which the ball is snapped. This can eliminate one call by the QB in the huddle but prevents the QB from using delayed and quick calls when advisable.

Break

A team should break from the middle uniformly and with enthusiasm. This is best accomplished by having the QB give a break signal, at which time everyone claps his hands, yells "break," and moves to the line of scrimmage.

To review the sequence of a play call:

1st	Number indicating pre-shift formation
2nd	Letter indicating motion
3rd	Hundreds number indicating formation
4th	Tens number indicating ball carrier
5th	Units number indicating the hole
6th	Word indicating series
7th	Snap count
8th	Break signal

Example: "4z 427x on 2, ready, go"

HUDDLE AND BREAK

There are many forms of huddles. Whatever their formation, it is important that all team members can hear the call, that the opposition can't hear the call, and that the huddle facilitates rapid release to the line of scrimmage.

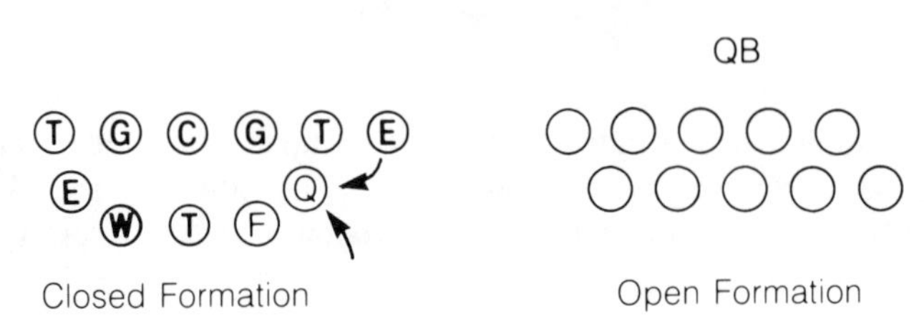

▶ **Figure 9.1** The Huddle

The center forms the huddle. He should get in a position seven to ten yards behind the spot where the referee has placed the ball. The huddle should look orderly. Football is a game that requires precision and this begins in the huddle.

Some teams allow the center and wide receivers to leave the huddle early after they have picked up all necessary information. The center must take his position quickly since other linemen get their splits and position from him. Wide receivers have farther to go. Everyone must break from the huddle quickly since getting the football snapped as fast as possible helps the total offense.

SEQUENCE AT LINE OF SCRIMMAGE

Taking Stance

Some coaches have players take their offensive stance on their own, while others have players assume a pre-shift stance and go into their offensive stance on a signal from the QB. The pre-shift stance is usually a two-point stance with hands or elbows on knees. If a team does a lot of shifting prior to the snap, it is probably better to have them go down as a unit after the shifting has been completed. Once the hand has been placed down, it cannot be lifted until the ball is snapped.

A team can run a play from a pre-shift position on first sound, and this can be an effective surprise element.

Rhythmic Versus Nonrhythmic Cadence

The sequence of sounds uttered by the QB can be either rhythmic or non-rhythmic. Proponents of a rhythmic sequence feel that offensive personnel can anticipate the snap count and get off more uniformly and quickly. Some coaches will even have the center delay the snap slightly to allow the offense to get an additional edge. Other coaches feel that a nonrhythmic cadence gives the edge to the offense. Through voice inflections and varied spacing of snap counts, the QB can get the defense off balance and overextended when the ball is actually snapped.

Sounds

Various series of sounds are used. Some examples are: 1) "Down, set, hut, hut . . .", 2) "Set, go, go . . .", 3) "Down, red 34, set, hike, hike. . . ." A touch snap signal can be used occasionally. This is a nonverbal signal, with the football being snapped when the QB exerts pressure on the center's crotch.

Automatics

A very common system for changing plays at the line of scrimmage is through the use of a "live" color. A team's normal cadence might be "Down, (a color), (a number), hike, hike." Certain colors will be designated as "live" colors for a particular game. When the QB calls out one of these colors after "Down," all players know that the play is changed to the number that follows. For example, if the "live" colors for a game are white and black and the call at the line of scrimmage is "Down, black, 37, hike," the players know that the play called in the huddle is changed to 37.

Motion

It is the QB's responsibility to coordinate the length of motion with the snap. This can be done in one of two ways. Motion can begin on a certain sound prior to the snap or with a foot signal from the QB. The QB lifts his heel in the direction of the back that is to go in motion.

10

Offensive Systems

Offensive systems, strategies, and formations are constantly undergoing change. The successful coach is one with a basic knowledge of all current offensive systems. The coach who refuses to take advantage of innovative trends most likely will not be successful.

Coaches should stay current with modern day football by reading, visiting, and talking with coaching staffs at schools with proven records, and by attending clinics.

In this chapter a brief examination of various offensive systems is presented. Entire books have been written on each system and references are made to them in footnotes.

It is amazing, however, how completely ignorant some coaches are of offensive systems that they didn't play as an athlete or coach. This chapter will provide an historical, progressive, and logical look at the evolution of offensive systems in American football.

FROM SOCCER TO AMERICAN FOOTBALL

In 1823, during a soccer game at Rugby School, an English schoolboy by the name of William W. Ellis defied all the rules of his day by picking up the soccer ball and running with it! The "handling game," as it was often called, became a controversial issue in English schools. Young gentlemen at Eton and Harrow were issued white gloves prior to each soccer match, and the penalty was severe for any young man caught with soiled gloves at the end of the contest! Other schools, however, gladly adopted this innovative idea, and rugby began to emerge. Rules of a more definitive nature were formulated in 1871. Rugby began to take hold in the United States after the Civil War, and in 1876 the Intercollegiate Football (Rugby) Association was formed.

The first "football" game in the United States was said to be between Princeton and Rutgers in 1869, but it looked much more like a combination of soccer and a little rugby than American football. Running and throwing the football were not allowed, twenty five players were on each side, there was no protective equipment, and scoring was only by field goals, which were knee-kicked over the bar, often on the run!

Space will not allow a complete listing of rule changes, personalities, and humorous and major events that shaped American football, but the following sample will aid the reader in understanding the key changes that led up to the current game.

1874—The rugby-style dead ball was placed between the two teams for a scrummage. Harvard and Yale claim to play the first "real" game where running with the ball was included.

1875—Harvard played McGill in a "football" contest. Actually, it was more like two contests—soccer for one half, rugby for the other half.

1876—The American Intercollegiate Football Association (Harvard, Yale, Princeton, Columbia) was formed.

1880—The field size was reduced from 500 by 300 feet to 110 by 53 yards. Rugby-style play was adopted with the ball being "heeled" back to a "quarterback" to begin play. Team size was reduced from rugby's fifteen to eleven. Rugby scrum was replaced with a line of scrimmage.

1882—Walter Camp ("Father of American Football") convinced the Football Association to adopt a rule permitting three downs to gain five yards (four downs to advance 10 yards didn't come until 1912). Striped fields, therefore, appeared for the first time. Positions received names—seven forwards, one quarterback, two halfbacks, and one fullback. Running games replaced kicking games at most colleges.

1884—Walter Camp devised the first numerical scoring system: field goal—five points; touchdown (when runner crosses the goal line and touches the ball down on the turf)—two points: try-after-touchdown—four points; safety—one point. A safety was upped to two points after the 1884 season.

1886—Harvard's faculty prohibited the school from playing football until a rule was adopted placing more severe penalties on slugging. A rule change in 1886 prohibited slugging.

1890—Centers were allowed to snap the ball back with the hands instead of the heel of the foot.

1894—No more than three men were allowed in motion before the ball was snapped, and they had to be within five yards of the "line of scrimmage." This reduced the injuries caused by the "flying wedge" and mass momentum interference tactics. Amos Alonzo Stagg ("Grand Old Man of American Football") became the first paid college coach with faculty status at the University of Chicago where he coached for 41 years. He was a great innovator introducing end-arounds, reverses, criss-cross backfield action, double handoffs, onside kicks, and man-in-motion.

1896—At least five men were required on the line of scrimmage when the ball was snapped. A touchdown was increased to five points and a point-after-touchdown was reduced to one.

1901—Michigan defeated Stanford in the first Rose Bowl (granddaddy of all the bowls) game 49–0.

1904—The forward pass was legalized, but with severe limitations. The pass could only be thrown over the middle of the line in a five-yard lateral zone on either side of the center. There was no such thing as pass interference. If the ball was not caught, it passed to the defense! Passing restrictions required a football field to be chalked off in five-yard squares, hence the name "gridiron." The field goal was reduced from five to four points.

1905—Eighteen players were killed in college games and President Teddy Roosevelt threatened to abolish football.

1906—The American Intercollegiate Football Rules Committee was established. Requiring the offense to gain ten yards in three tries for the first down encouraged more wide open play with end runs and passes, and discouraged battering, straight ahead wedges that were the cause of many injuries.

1907—Iowa State kicked a field goal that bounced over the goal post earning them a 13–10 victory over Nebraska! Nebraska appealed the validity of the field goal to Walter Camp. Since nothing in the rule book at the time said it couldn't bounce over, Iowa State won! The rule was changed, but the Nebraska Cornhuskers still register the game in their record books as a 10–9 victory!

1910—Seven men were required on the line of scrimmage. Gridiron appearance disappeared with the removal of lengthwise stripes since passes were no longer restricted in a lateral direction. Pass interference on the defense was instituted for the first time.

1912—The field was reduced from 110 to 100 yards with an end zone behind each goal line. A team was given four rather than three downs to make a first down. A pass caught in the end zone was no longer a touchback with the other team getting the ball, but a touchdown.

1917—At Georgia Tech, John Heisman coached the team that defeated Cumberland College 222–0 and went into the *Guiness Book of World Records.*

1918—Knute Rockne became head coach at Notre Dame, the first in a prestigious line of coaches at this football powerhouse.

1922—Point-after-touchdown tries were centered on the goal posts. Wide-angled kicks taken from the point the touchdown was scored were eliminated.

1923–24—The "Four Horsemen" of Notre Dame (Miller, Layden, Crowley, and Stuhldreher) galloped into immortality using a controversial, shifting single-wing box formation.

1925—Red Grange, the "galloping ghost" of the University of Illinois, signed on with the Chicago Bears and personally received a percentage of all gate receipts. He was the first player to have his number retired by a college.

1926—Forward passing was discouraged by a five-yard penalty and loss of down for two incompletes in the same series of downs.

1927—Goal posts were taken off the goal line and placed at the rear of the end zone.

1930—In an attempt to encourage passing, the ball was made slimmer and the 1926 loss-of-down rule for two incomplete passes was eliminated.

1939—A ball exploded in midair on an extra point try, enabling Washington and Jefferson to defeat Geneva.

1957—Notre Dame broke Oklahoma's win string of 47 games with a 7–0 victory.

1958—Rule makers added the two-point conversion, the first scoring change in 46 years. Bear Bryant became the head coach at Alabama. (Career record 1958–82, 323–85–17.)

1959—The Rules Committee, under the chairmanship of Fritz Crisler, decided to widen the goal posts from 18.5 feet to 24 feet to encourage field goals. But, a last minute call from a lumberman friend of Crisler's informing him that the longest two-by-fours were 24 feet caused a last minute ruling that limited the width to 23 feet 4 inches, its current width.

Both football and rugby continued to be played in the United States into the twentieth century, but the American version of football, with its more clearly defined rules and structure, became much more popular. However, in recent years there appears to be a resurgence of interest in rugby. The cost is minimal, the action is constant, and play can be enjoyed beyond the high school and college years.

SINGLE-WING ATTACK

Football in these early years was a rough and rugged sport that mirrored the values most popular in American society. The only "manly" way to move the football was on the ground and yardage made by skirting around the end was even questionable!

Pop Warner, one of football's great coaches in the first half of the century had this to say on the subject.

> "I think passing should be illegal. Something should be done to curtail the wild, promiscuous, glorified football that some teams now indulge in. They throw long forward passes and figure on a percentage basis that if one of these connects, they will fluke a touchdown and win the game. That's what I'm against. I think a game of football should be strictly on a merit basis."

Since helmets were flimsy to nonexistent, blocking and tackling were done with the shoulder or side of the body. Everybody played both offense and defense, and it was a personal affront to be taken out of the game.

The formation that pitted offense against defense in classic confrontation was the so-called "single wing." Linemen were shoulder to shoulder and when the ball was snapped, the runner was not so much tackled as he was smothered under a mass of humanity. Glenn (Pop) Warner is credited with inventing the single wing.

The rules and configuration of the game conspired against passing. The forward pass became legal in 1906, but the ball was still shaped like a rugby ball (which is much fatter) and a pass had to be thrown five yards behind the line of scrimmage.

Although the single wing is not an offensive system of any major school today, the influence of single-wing principles and techniques is certainly still present. The use of wingback, double-team blocking, trap blocking, unbalanced lines, tailback run-pass, flip-flop of personnel, and much terminology (wingback, tailback, strongside guards, etc.) all have their origin in single-wing football.

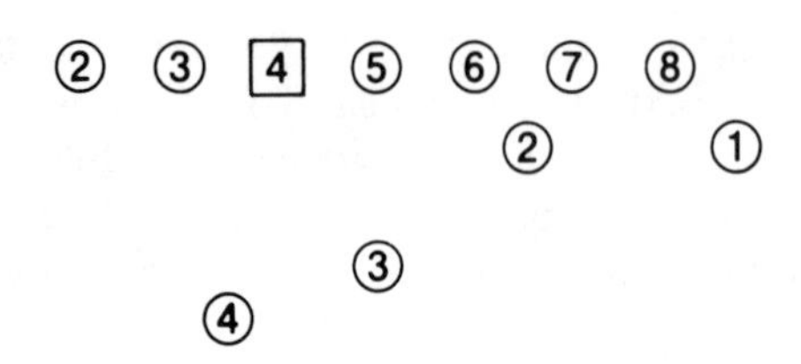

▶ Figure 10.1 One Popular Single-Wing Offensive Formation

It is unlikely that today's student of football will ever coach the single wing, but a brief review of it is included here because of its historical importance and influence on the modern game.

The most common names for the various single-wing positions are:

Offensive Linemen	*Offensive Backs*
2 weakside or shortside end	1 wingback
3 weakside or shortside guard	2 QB or blocking back
4 center	3 fullback
5 inside tackle	4 tailback
6 outside tackle	
7 strongside or longside guard	
8 strongside or longside end	

The play from the formation that embodied plain, hard-nosed football with no faking or razzle-dazzle was the off-tackle play. It was basic football. The philosophy of the play was to get to the point of attack with the most men and just mow the defenders down. The defensive line was weakest between the tackle and the end since defensive ends had to cover the occasional sweep. This base play easily develops into a sweep by having the wingback hook the end while the blocking back and fullback lead the play. An inside reverse was soon introduced, with the wingback taking an inside handoff from the tailback with the inside tackle and longside guard leading.

Many people felt that the inadequacy of a passing attack brought about the demise of the single wing, but a revived interest in the "shotgun" formation indicates the advantages in allowing a QB to immediately spot receivers and secondary rotations.

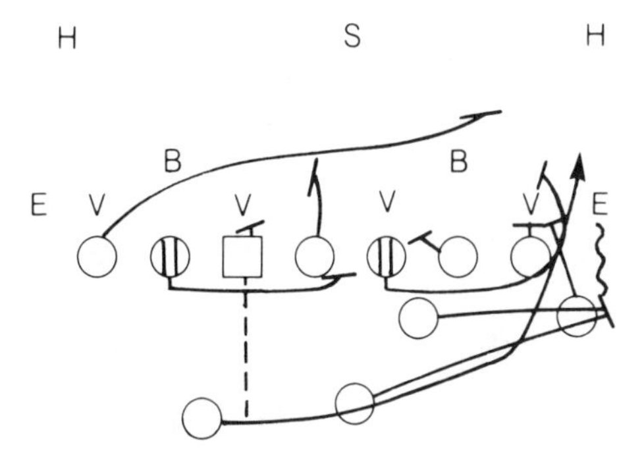

▶ **Figure 10.2** Single Wing Off-Tackle Play

The punt was crucial in those days since territory was hard to acquire. Teams punted regularly and waited for the other team to make a mistake, hopefully in its own territory. The single wing was and is an ideal formation from which to quick kick.

AN INTERESTING INTERLUDE

Many football coaches and fans are unaware of an interesting interlude in offensive football that became especially evident in the professional game in the midthirties.

The ponderous confrontations of the single wing gave way to the T-formation during World War II, but not until several teams experienced success with a wide open brand of football surprisingly similar to today. Two of these teams were the Green Bay Packers with the legendary Don Hutson and the Washington Redskins with a "slinging" Sammy Baugh. (Note Figures 10.3 and 10.4.)

A favorite play of Green Bay was to fake a run (play action passes are not new), isolate Hutson on one defender (defenses in those days never dropped back more than three men), and let him fake the defender out of position.

By looking at Figure 10.4, it's not hard to see why Baugh threw for so many yards. This double-wing formation allowed four receivers to get into the defensive secondary quickly, making it impossible for their defenders to adequately cover the territory.[1]

[1]Bob Oates, Jr., editor, *The First Fifty Years, The Story of the National Football League* (New York: A Ridge Press/Benjamin Company Book, Simon & Schuster distributors, 1974), 137, 139.

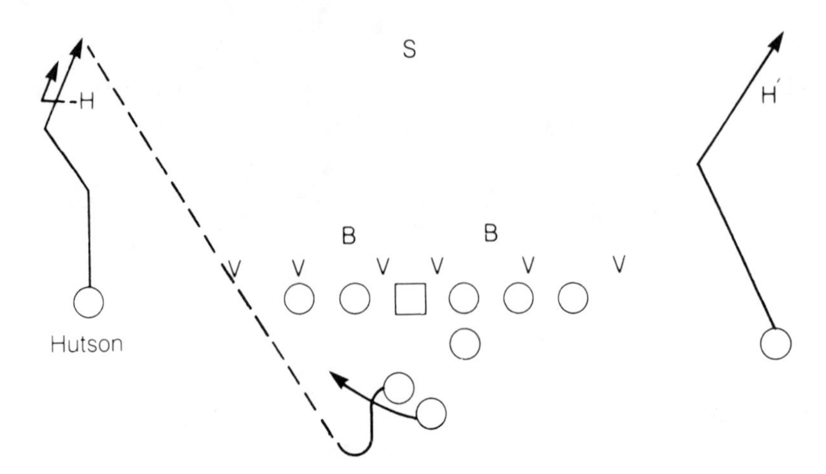

▶ **Figure 10.3** Single Coverage

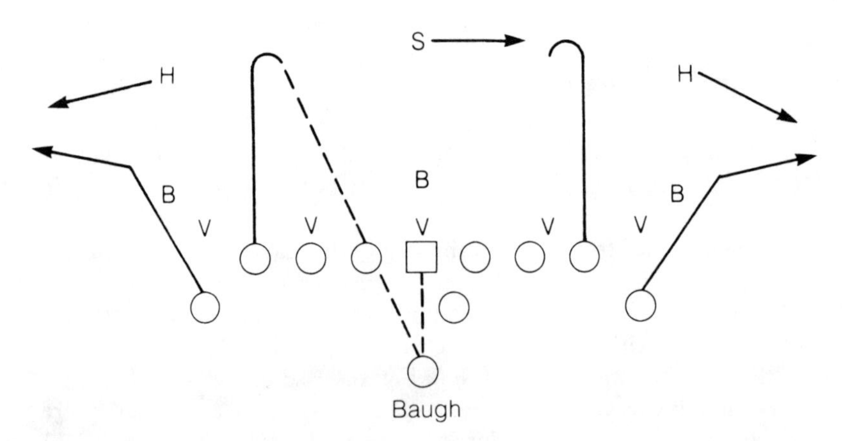

▶ **Figure 10.4** Four-on-Three

T-FORMATION

December 8, 1940, is a day to be remembered for it was on this day that the Chicago Bears, underdogs to a team that had beaten them in the regular season, piled up eleven touchdowns and thrashed the Washington Redskins 73–0!

George Halas had been dabbling with variations of a T-formation since 1920, but on this Sunday afternoon it was run to perfection. Within five years most teams in the country—high school, college, and professional—were using some version of it.

Many individuals contributed to the development of T-formation football and heated arguments can follow if one credits the "wrong" person! George Halas of the Chicago Bears, Bud Wilkinson of the University of Oklahoma, Don Farout of the University of Missouri, and Jim Tatum at Maryland often receive credit.

No single individual deserves more credit, however, than Clark Shaughnessy. He was the offensive architect of that amazing game on December 8, 1940.[2]

Shaughnessy replaced Stagg as coach at the University of Chicago, and during the years 1933–1939 developed a close friendship with George Halas, owner-coach of the Chicago Bears. Shaughnessy never claimed that he invented the T-formation. What he did was simply rejuvenate it, dust it off, and counterattack the single and double wing formations. The University of Chicago abandoned football after the 1939 season. Not surprising, when their chancellor Dr. Robert Hutchins was purported to have said that whenever he got the urge to exercise, he laid down until it went away! In 1940 Shaughnessy went on to coach Stanford, who had won only one game in 1939, to an 11–0 season and won Coach of the Year honors.

The T-formation was a dramatic shift from the single wing. The tailback in the single wing had to be a master of everything—power inside runner, fast outside runner, and passer. The T-formation naturally divided these responsibilities. The QB became the passer; the FB provided the inside power; the halfbacks were utilized for quick hitting dives and speed to the outside.

The single-wing attack requires hard-nosed runners, effective double-team blockers, and a good blocking back; the split-T requires explosiveness, one-on-one blocking, runners capable of quickly "popping" into the open areas, and deception.

The split-T offense, featuring wider spaced linemen, a shuttling quarterback, and the option play was introduced by Don Farout in 1941, and popularized principally by Bud Wilkinson's Oklahoma dynasty from 1947–63.

[2]Oates, *The First Fifty Years,* 139.

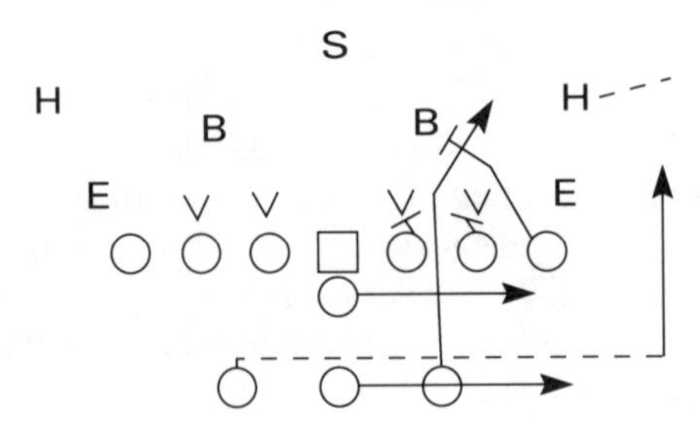

▶ **Figure 10.5** Split-T Dive (Dive Option)

Line splits are significantly increased. Three feet between linemen is not unusual. Double-team blocking is not used as frequently. Everyone in the backfield becomes a potential ball carrier. The split-T allows a team to make good use of quick, fast-charging linemen and a good running quarterback.

The formation and the basic play from it are shown in Figure 10.5. The quick handoff to the diveback is the base play from this formation. The play set up after the dive threat is established is the QB option. This was, and still is, one of the most exciting plays in football. In essence, it allows a team to change a play *after* the ball has been snapped, which puts real pressure on the defense. Nobody blocks the defensive end or outside linebacker and his movement dictates whether or not the QB keeps or pitches.

TIGHT-SLOT ATTACK

Shortly after the split-T offense was becoming popular, the tight-slot attack began to be used. It combines the elements of split-T football to the "at home" halfback side, while retaining many aspects of single-wing football to the slot-back side. Much of this information is taken from Vince Dooley's book, *Developing A Superior Football-Control Attack.*[3]

It can readily be seen that, from this formation, the split-T quick handoff can be run to the left. By putting the slotback in motion, the QB option can be run. A hard-nosed power series with double-team blocking at the point of attack and a lead blocking back can be run to the right.

[3]Vincent J. Dooley, *Developing A Superior Football-Control Attack.* (West Nyack, New York: Parker Publishing Company, 1969), 228.

Since the nature of blocking assignments and techniques vary depending on whether a lineman is on the slotback or halfback side of the center, teams began designating linemen as either *strong*-side or *quick*-side linemen. Quick-side linemen always line up on the side of the halfback, while strong-side linemen always line up on the side of the slotback. The words are descriptive of the qualities needed to play on that side of the center. Quick-side linemen (QG, QT, and QE) are the linemen responsible for the blocking of the split-T series. Strong-side linemen are responsible for the power series plays.

This does not mean that teams always run split-T (quick hitting) plays to the defense's right and power (double-team with lead back) plays to the defense's left. When a team wants to run with the slotback to the defense's right, they "flip-flop" as they come out of the huddle.

Designating strong-side and quick-side linemen minimizes the number of blocking techniques that a lineman has to learn; it also minimizes the number of plays to be learned. For example, a ST never has to block a dive.

Backfield responsibilities also become more specialized. One back (HB) is always the dive back, one back (FB) specializes in blocking and bucking into the line between the defensive ends, and the slotback is primarily a blocker. In recent times, the role of the slotback as pass receiver has received greater importance.

Several series of plays will be diagrammed from this formation. Most of the series (with minor modifications) can be run from other formations.

Power-Sweep Series[4]

The off tackle power is the base play that was retained from the single wing to the slotback side. The play concentrates strength at the point of attack. The tight-slot attack must make this play function. The QG leads the play. The play puts five blockers at the point of attack in front of the ball carrier.

The wide power sweep becomes effective once the off tackle power has been established. As they develop, the plays look identical. When the end or corner defender crashes down to meet the block of the fullback, he is hook blocked instead, and the play sweeps outside of him.

A halfback trap also develops from the off tackle power. The FB runs at the defensive end and the HB takes two steps as if he is going to receive a pitch from the QB. The QB fakes the pitch and gives it back to the HB as he runs at the offensive center. See the three diagrams in Figure 10.6.

[4]Dooley, *Developing A Superior Football-Control Attack,* 15–16.

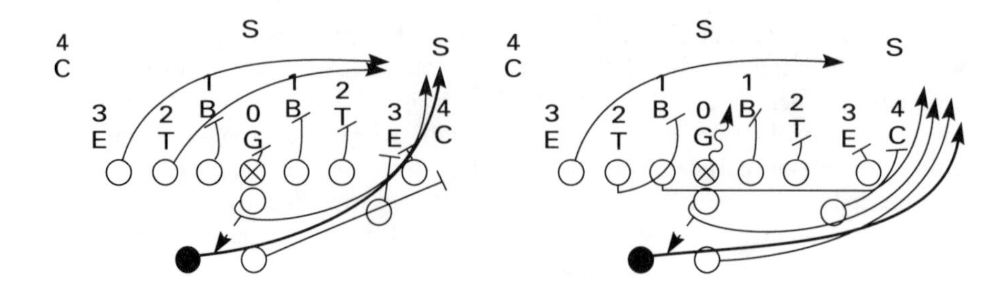

The Off-Tackle Power

The Wide Power Sweep

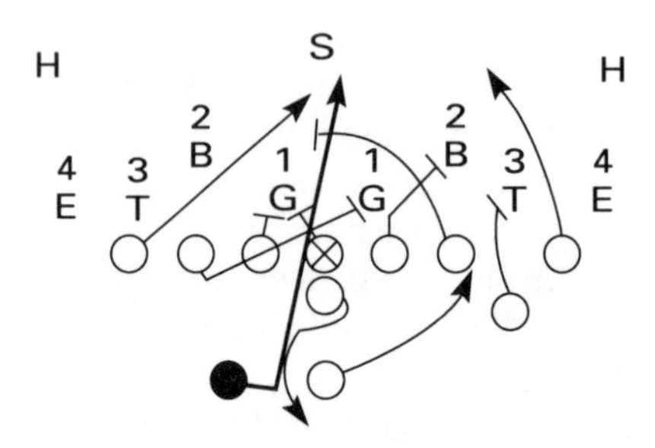

The Halfback Trap

▶ **Figure 10.6** Power-Sweep Series

Inside Belly Series[5]

The inside belly series has the fullback running inside tackle. If he receives the football it is with a lead back as a blocker. If he does not, his movement serves to establish flow and open the HB up on a trap or counter. Three plays are shown in Figure 10.7, the isolation play to the FB, another HB trap, and a counter trap.

Outside Belly Series[6]

The outside belly series is comprised of two plays: 1) FB off tackle and 2) option. The second builds on the first. Once the threat of the FB has been established off tackle, the QB can fake this play and have a nice option play open between him and the slotback who went in motion (note Figure 10.8).

[5]Dooley, *Developing A Superior Football-Control Attack,* 17.

[6]Dooley, *Developing A Superior Football-Control Attack,* 20.

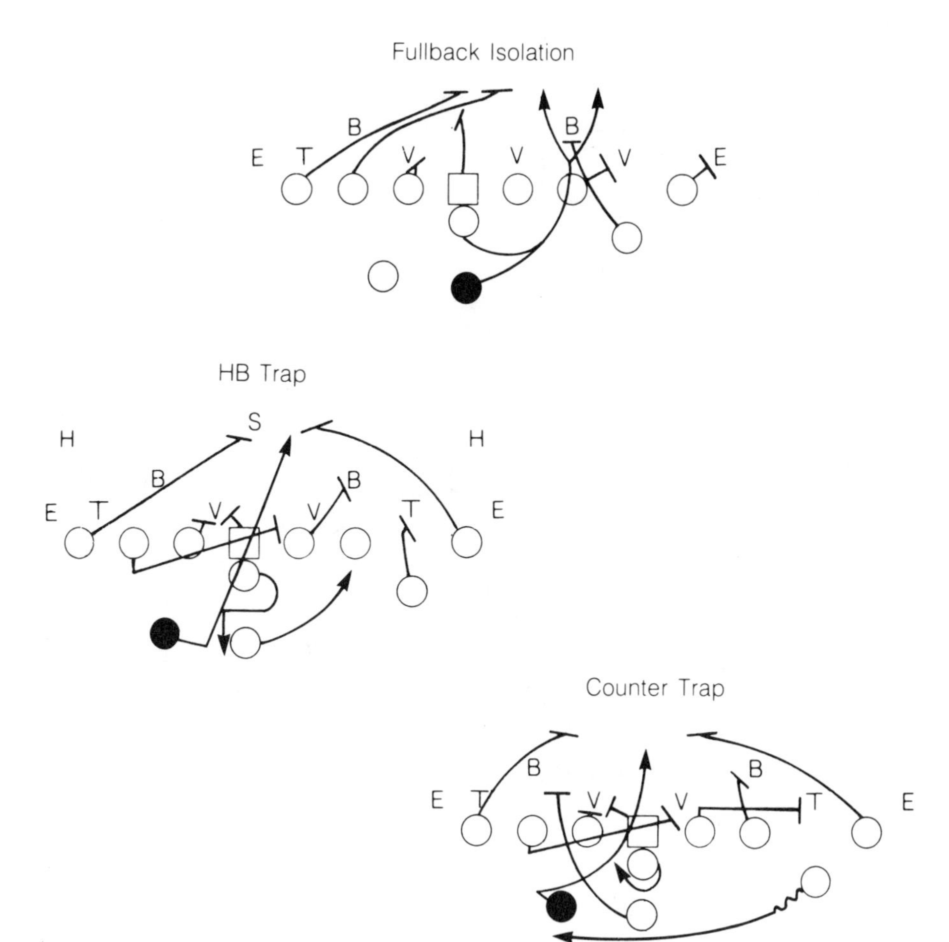

▶ **Figure 10.7** Inside Belly Series

If one looks at Figure 10.7 it can readily be seen that the slotback must be able to block. If he can't, he should be moved out to a wing or, better yet, a flanker position. This is called a winged-T formation.

WINGED-T ATTACK

Dave Nelson, former standout coach and athletic director at the University of Delaware, and for many years executive editor of NCAA Football Rules, devised an original winged-T formation used at Maine in 1950, and continued to this day

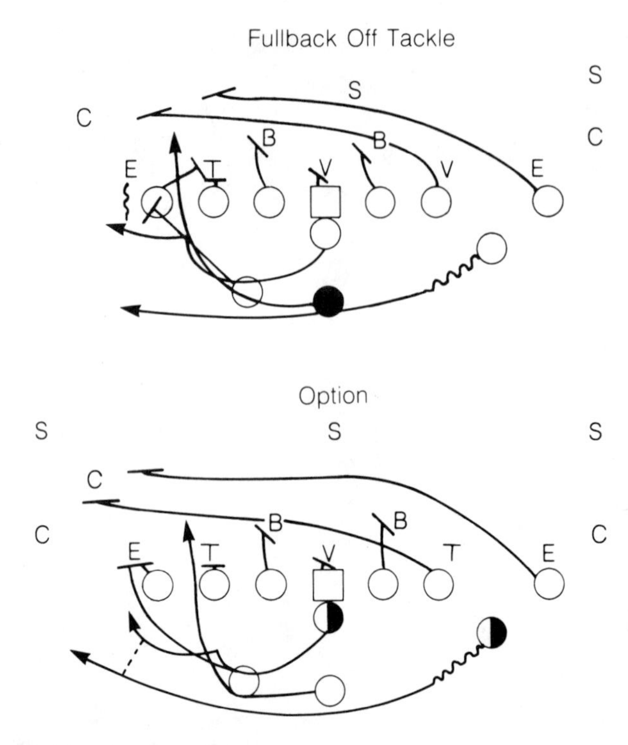

▶ **Figure 10.8** Outside Belly Series

under Harold (Tubby) Raymond. Forest Evashevski adopted the system now called the Delaware Wing-T at the University of Iowa, and produced championship Rose Bowl teams in 1956 and 1958.

Many teams put the slot in a winged position. This is done for several reasons. It enables the back to get into passing routes more easily, especially for deep patterns. This, of course, puts the strong end in a less advantageous position for passing but a better position for blocking. However, most of the TE's routes are shallow and often delayed. The post-lead block of the back and end is better from this position. The post blocker makes contact first.

Play-action passing also can be developed more readily from the wing as opposed to the slot. The slot (wing) back began to be used less as a blocker and more as a pass receiver. For these reasons the winged position is more popular today. Offensive philosophies also changed. The isolation play in which the slot-back blocked inside, usually on a linebacker, became less popular. One-on-one blocking similar to the quickside attack began to be used more.

Quick Trap Series[7]

One additional series that also can be run from the slot or T is the quick trap series. Three plays are diagrammed in Figure 10.9. They are the fullback trap, the counter trap, and the fake trap sweep. The FB trap is a quick hitting trap play. It is especially effective against an attacking, penetrating defense.

I-FORMATION

The I-formation, in which the quarterback, fullback, and halfback (tailback) line up one behind the other, was used by Northwestern as early as 1900, but today's version differs in its use of flankers and men in motion. Coach John McKay of the University of Southern California used the I-formation very effectively in the early 1970s with his legendary tailback O. J. Simpson. "Student body right" and "student body left," an unsophisticated name for pitching the ball to Simpson, who would run laterally along the line of scrimmage while the entire line pulled and blocked in front of him, was the key play in the University of Southern California's attack.

If a team has one running back who is definitely better than the others and is gifted at "running to daylight," the I-formation may be the best formation to run. This formation places the HB behind the FB, often in a two-point stance. From here he can run in either direction with equal effectiveness.

In this formation the FB must be a good blocker and inside runner. This is what he does almost all the time. The TB must have enough speed to get to the outside, but equally important is a knack for knowing where a hole will open up and then the ability to accelerate through it. The split-T concept of "popping" through a hole gives way to more lateral motion behind the line and then sensing when to cut upfield.

Proponents of the "I" like it because of the many ways it can be used to attack an opponent, particularly on the ground. The fullback can hit quickly and the tailback can hit from any angle.

[7]Dooley, *Developing A Superior Football-Control Attack,* 13.

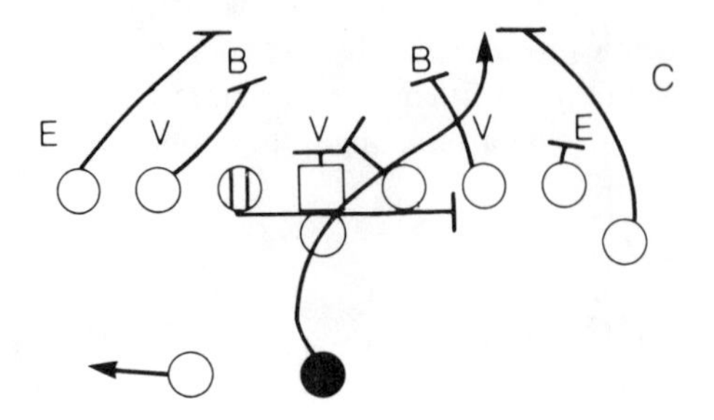

Fullback Trap

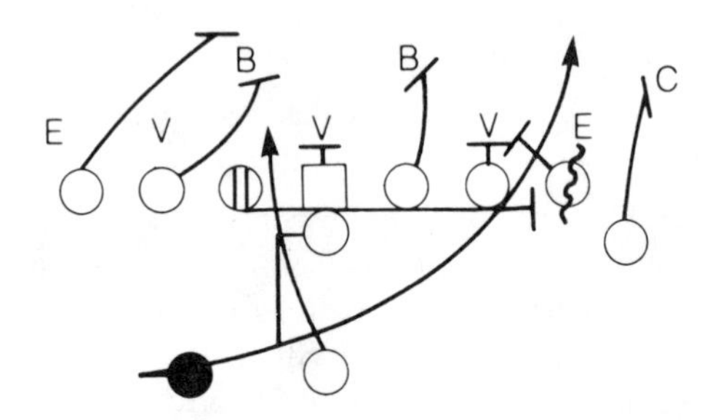

Counter Trap

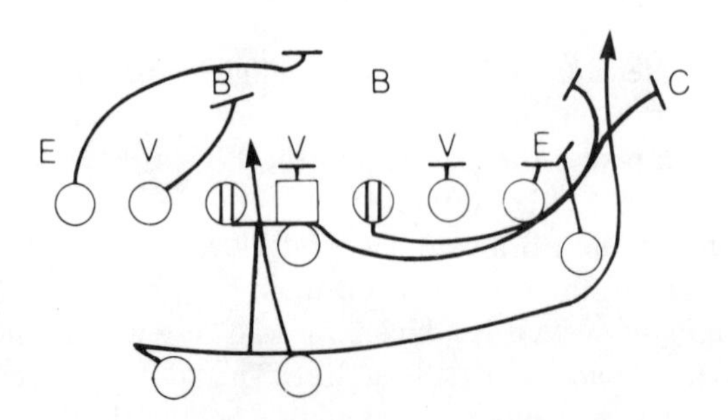

Fake Trap Sweep

▶ **Figure 10.9** Winged-T Trap Series

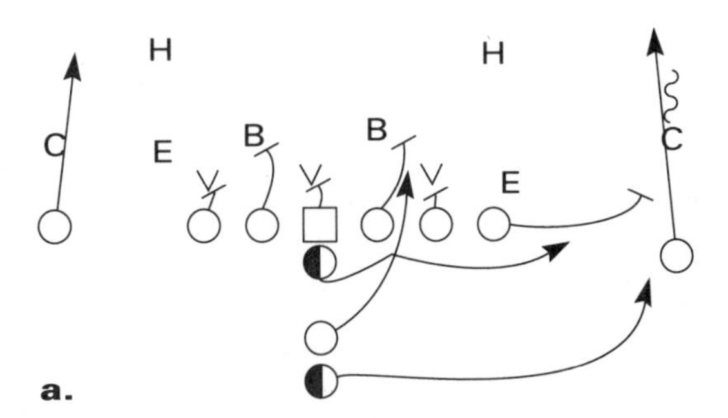

Fullback Dive Option

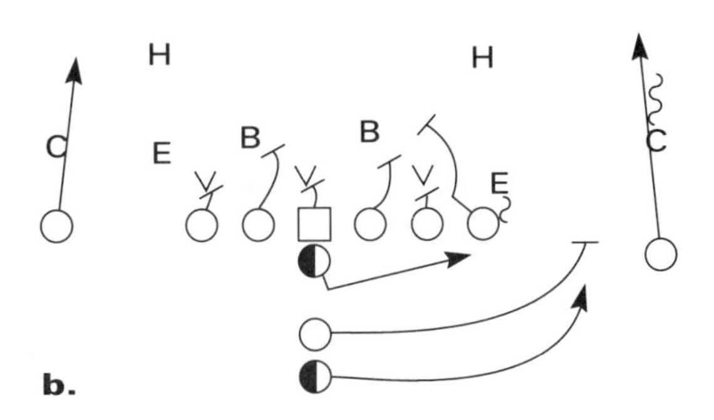

Sprint Option

▶ **Figure 10.10** a. Fullback Dive Option; b. Sprint Option

You can still run the option game with the QB riding the fullback, and then coming down the line for an option run-pitch to the tailback or a sprint option with the fullback leading the tailback as a blocker (Note Figure 10.10).

In addition, with a minimum amount of ball handling, every hole along the line can be hit, thereby cutting down on mistakes. The blocking is the same no matter to which side you run. Speed-wise, it's better to run a sweep from the "I" than from the pro set because the tailback can get to the flanks faster.

An effective passing game can be implemented from the "I." A ball fake to the tailback will certainly freeze the defensive linebackers and slow the charge of on-rushing linemen. The fullback can slide out into the flat or hook up in the middle after diving into the line. The tailback can become a viable receiver on a variety of patterns.

The power series is still very effective and can be run in either direction. All blockers have to sustain their blocks longer and every block is crucial since the TB often can cut back into an unexpected location.

The sprint-out series is very popular from the I-formation. The QB opens to the side of the play and sprints directly *at* the defensive end or corner man. The FB leads the TB as the TB keeps his pitch position with the QB.

Isolation plays are now run with the FB as the isolation blocker rather than the slot back. This is a basic running play of the I-formation. The linemen "drive" block, and the TB "runs to daylight." The QB should get back and give the ball to the TB early. If the defensive LBs begin keying the FB, assuming that the TB always goes in the same direction, misdirection is effective. (Note Figure 10.11.)

PRO FORMATION

As passing became a more common method of advancing the football, the pro formation was used more often. It splits an end out in one direction and uses a back as a flanker in the other. The flanker back also can be put on the same side as the split end. This is called a wide slot and can be effective when the ball is placed on a hash mark.

Many of the running and passing plays from the single-wing, T, wing-T, and I are run from the pro set. An example of this is the power sweep made famous by Vince Lombardi and the Green Bay Packers in the early 1960s. This powerful end run was actually a modern version of the old single-wing off-tackle play. Containing end runs were no longer the responsibility of the defensive end or even an outside linebacker. Since the pro formation was more spread out, a defensive back was assigned certain responsibility and would run up and force the play back to the inside.

This "three end" attack developed by Clark Shaughnessy, who had moved to Los Angeles as head coach, had Bob Waterfield and Norm Van Brocklin throwing the football to wide outs Elroy (Crazy Legs) Hirsch and Tom Fears and tight end Bob Shaw. Tight ends had to be more than a third tackle. They had to be able to catch the ball, often in traffic. This dual role added glamour to the position and soon some of the better athletes were gravitating to tight end in hopes of becoming a third receiver. The Rams won the western title in 1949, and in 1950 and 1951 set scoring and yardage totals that stood for over 20 years.

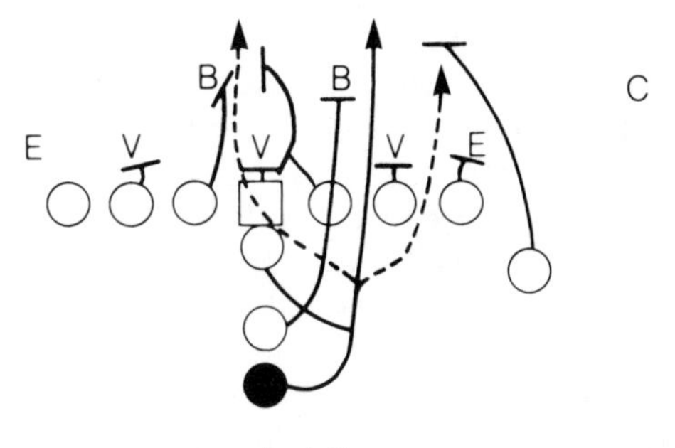

Isolation

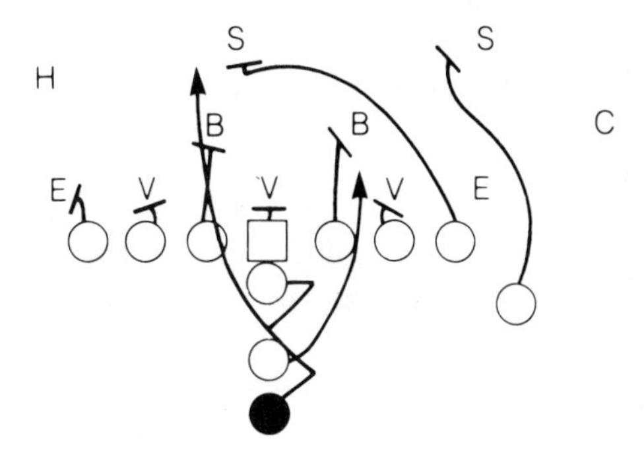

Misdirection

▶ **Figure 10.11** I-Formation Tailback Plays

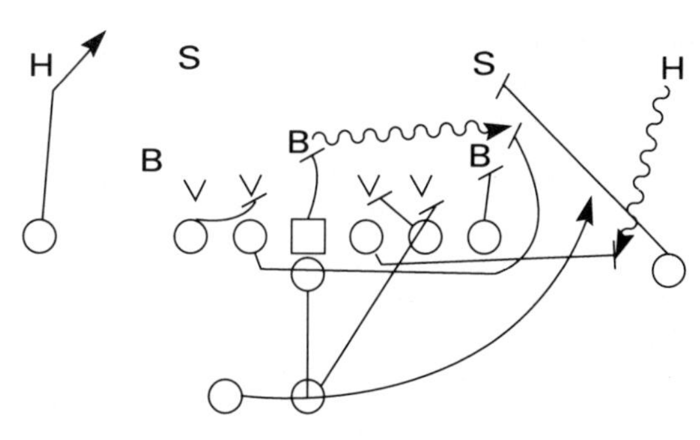

▶ **Figure 10.12** Pro-Formation Sweep

As defenses began to double cover elusive wide receivers and the tight end, coaches began to look at the two set backs as potential receivers. Not only did these running backs have to be quick and strong, but capable of catching the football as well. Passing plays were designed that had them as primary receivers.

In addition, the set backs were very effectively utilized in short passes called by a thousand names—the safety valve, outlet, check-swing, dump, flare, and flat. Quarterbacks about to be tackled would at the last second turn and lob the ball to a running back drifting into the flat and convert a sack into a respectable gain. Nobody executes the short passing game better than Joe Montana of the San Francisco 49ers. His average yardage per throw is not that high, but his pinpoint accuracy on short passes, often to backs out of the backfield, is very demoralizing to the opposition. Since set backs are the best runners, it is an excellent way to get them the football with some room to maneuver.

Of course, running backs can be sent on deep routes also. What team hasn't tried to split a two deep zone and then sneak a set back down the middle of the field for an easy touchdown?

The theory behind the pro formation is that if the offense can isolate one defensive back on a receiver of equal ability, a good QB should be able to get the ball to him, since the defensive man can only react to the wide receiver's maneuvers.

The pro look forced teams into many defensive adjustments. The 4–3 became the most widely accepted defense since three LBs were available to help out with the pass coverage. Their role becomes absolutely essential when teams go to double coverage on the wide receivers. Offensive linemen have to spend a lot of time on pass protection blocking since this is what they are doing most of the time.

VEER

Bill Yeoman at the University of Houston was the first coach at the major college level to utilize the veer. It, along with the wishbone, was probably the most radical departure from offenses of the day since the introduction of the T twenty years before. Interestingly enough, one element in them is surprisingly similar. The pure option play of the T-formation, in which the defensive end or corner man is not blocked, gives the offense two plays that can be run *after* the snap of the ball. It is still a basic play in most offenses.

With the advent of the veer, the point of attack and ball carrier can be any one of three different spots or players *after* the snap of the ball. The philosophy of the veer and wishbone attacks is similar. In this triple option not only is the defensive end not blocked, but often the next man to the inside is not blocked either.

In the inside veer, the quarterback takes the snap, pushes off his far foot and reads the defensive tackle. If he remains stationary or comes upfield, the QB gives the ball to the fullback. If the defensive tackle closes down, the QB removes the ball from the fullback's belly and runs a normal option on the next defender assigned to him. If this defender remains stationary or comes upfield, he keeps the ball and turns upfield. If he closes down, the QB steps upfield with his inside foot to induce the defender in before he leans outside to make the pitch.

Dive backs line up at a depth of four and one-half yards, directly behind or slightly wider than the offensive guards. On the snap the dive back slashes at the inside hip of the tackle. As he feels the ball, he puts a "soft squeeze" on it keeping his head up and his eyes open, watching the defensive tackle. If the QB gives him the football, he hits the soft spot in the defense, driving for as much yardage as possible. If the QB pulls the ball away, he makes sure he doesn't cause a fumble, and continues his fake.

The option back pushes off the foot away from the direction he intends to go, accelerates to the pitch position and maintains his pitch relationship with the quarterback. He must be aware and ready to receive an early pitch, should the defense close on the quarterback quickly.

In the outside veer, the quarterback's first read is the defensive end. This first read is possible because the defensive tackle is always blocked by the offensive tackle and also, under certain circumstances, the offensive guard or tight end. The offensive end does not release as he did on the inside veer, but steps down to the defensive tackle and either blocks him or scrapes off to the play side linebacker. The play side guard steps out to the tackle and blocks him if he angles down or continues to the play side linebacker. If the defensive end does not close with the dive back, he will get the football. If he does close, the quarterback will pull the ball back and sprint into the secondary. If the secondary force man chooses to defend him, he will pitch the football; if not, he will seat the ball in a good ball-carrying position and sprint upfield.

Most veer teams also have a predetermined hand-off dive to complement the inside and outside veer. It is necessary and effective when the linebackers are running, or when the nose guard is making the tackle on the inside veer hand off to the dive back. The quarterback will give the ball to the dive back deeper so that he can read "daylight" more easily and cut off his blocks.

These three similar looking but distinctively different plays are the guts of the veer attack. Other plays can be added to the offense to give it versatility, but are not integral nor unique to the offense.

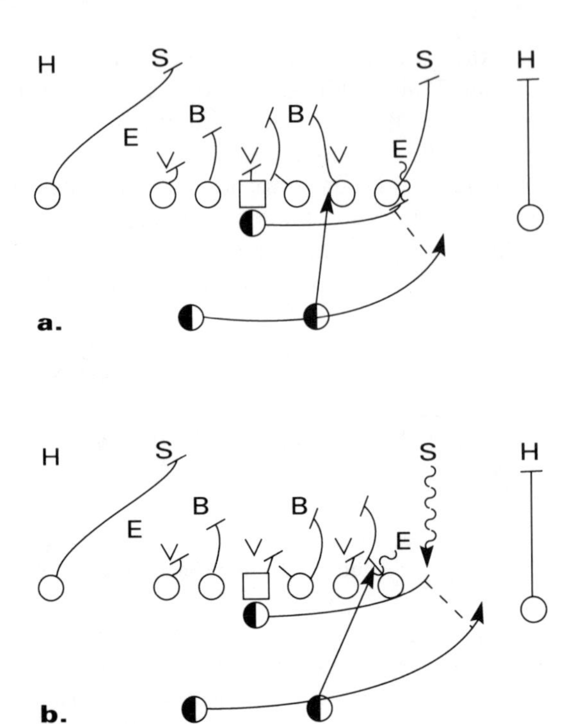

▶ **Figure 10.13** a. Inside Veer Triple Option; b. Outside Veer Triple Option

WISHBONE

Darrell Royal at the University of Texas was the first major college coach to run the wishbone. He introduced it at approximately the same time that Bill Yeoman began running the veer at Houston.

As already stated, the concept of the wishbone is very similar to the veer. It's triple option football. In this formation, however, all *four* backs must be able to carry the football. Rather than having two wide receivers in the initial formation, there is only a split end.

The wishbone is a consistent ball control offense. Only the fullback runs into the heart of the defense on the "triple" from this formation. In the veer, both running backs have to be able to dive and run outside for the pitch. The formation also provides a lead back in front of the pitch back.

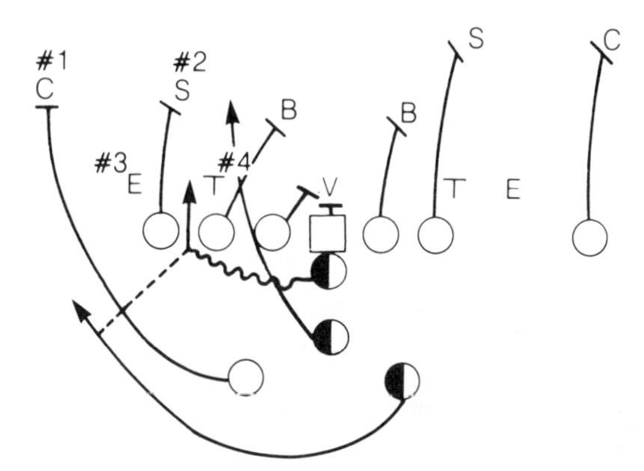

▶ **Figure 10.14** Wishbone Triple Option

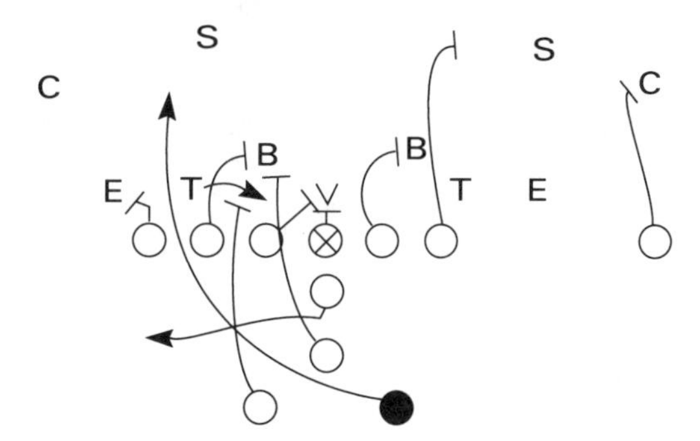

▶ **Figure 10.15** Belly Play Off Wishbone

The basic "triple" against a 5–2 defense appears in Figure 10.14. (Note: Blocking assignments are numbered from the outside in and *include* secondary personnel.) The "triple," with some variations in the blocking and predetermined ball carrier, can be an offense in itself.

All linemen, including the tight end, are usually in a four-point stance with the split end in a three-point stance. The fullback lines up directly behind the quarterback in a four-point stance with his heels about 13 feet from the tip of the football. The alignment needs to be exact so that there is a perfect mesh between the fullback and quarterback on the "ride" to the line of scrimmage. The halfbacks line up in a three-point stance 15 feet from the tip of the football, with 18 inches between them and the fullback.

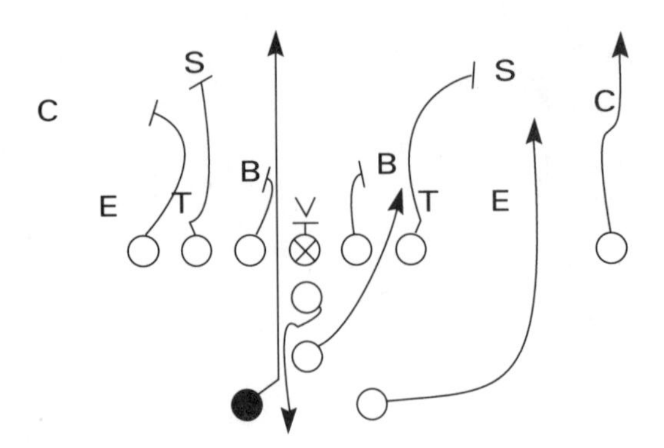

▶ **Figure 10.16** Halfback Counter Off Wishbone

The reads and keys on the basic triple option are similar to the veer and will not be restated here. Because of the three set backs, many plays from other formations can be run very effectively. A coach must be careful to teach the triple option carefully and thoroughly, but may want to add some other plays along the way. The belly play can be used to take advantage of a man who is consistently attacking the fullback on the triple option. There is a fake to the fullback, the lead halfback blocks the hand-off key man to the inside, and the far halfback carries the ball over the playside tackle's outside leg.

Both the veer and wishbone will have a counter and counter option play in their attack. They start out looking like the triple option, yet hit on the opposite side of the line of scrimmage. These plays should be run to take advantage of good defensive pursuit and fast-rotating secondaries. A halfback counter is presented in Figure 10.16.

The counter option has the quarterback opening away from the eventual direction of the play before turning and faking to the dive halfback with a short ride prior to continuing down the line of scrimmage. The fullback takes a jab step away from his eventual path before running parallel to the line of scrimmage. He then arcs up to block the outside secondary man, if the play is run to the tight end side, or the next man in, if play is run to the split end side. The trail halfback also executes a jab step fake before running parallel to the line of scrimmage, looking for the pitch and keeping a proper pitch relationship with the quarterback.

Although the veer and wishbone are primarily run-oriented formations, the quarterback must be able to pass. Most of the passes are thrown off the fake to the fullback veer play. The quarterback does not drop back very far after the fake and generally throws quick patterns. All manner of patterns can be run, but

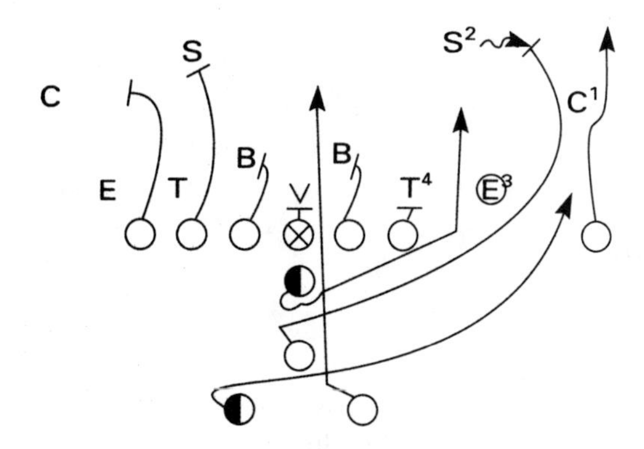

▶ Figure 10.17 Counter Option Off Wishbone

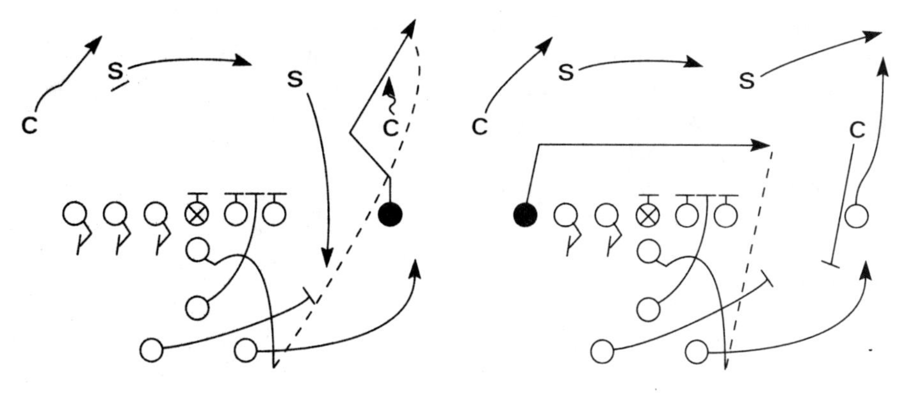

▶ Figure 10.18 Passes from Wishbone

generally the playside halfback runs a flare route, while the backside halfback crosses over to the playside and blocks the first defender outside the block of the playside tackle. The tight end and split end can run a variety of routes depending upon the contain responsibilities and rotations in the secondary.

PASSING ATTACKS

Pass defenses today are much more sophisticated than they were in the 1970s. Many more coverages are being used. It's very hard for the QB to know in advance who in the secondary will be responsible for what.

Six principles will be mentioned that must be considered in any passing attack.

Run Precise Patterns. Receivers cannot run sloppy patterns. They must be precise and consistent if the QB hopes to connect with consistency. Secondary receivers must run their patterns just as hard as primary receivers.

Pass Protection. No passing attack can be successful without pass protection. The best pass defense is the QB sack. If a team plans to throw the football, offensive linemen must spend a lot of time working on pass protection blocking.

Know Pass Coverages. Secondary pass coverages will be developed in Chapter 15. The offense must know what the other team is doing. Where are their weak personnel? How can we isolate one-on-one coverage? Careful scouting of the opposition's tendencies is crucial.

Straddling the Patterns. Offensive pass receivers should not all make their final breaks at the same time. If they do, the QB can only focus on the primary receiver at the proper time. If he is covered and the QB must shift his focus to a secondary receiver, it will occur after he has made his break and the defense will be back on him again before the ball can arrive. It is easiest for the QB if the breaks are made in sequence from left to right or right to left. In this way he can shift his gaze sequentially across the field. Having the final break on a sideline, when possible, allows the QB to throw the ball out-of-bounds without fear of an interception or intentional grounding call.

Develop Three-, Five-, and Seven-Step Drop Patterns. Versatility is crucial. The importance of the three-step passing game was vividly demonstrated by the San Francisco 49ers in their championship game against the Minnesota Vikings on January 7, 1990. The Vikings had the best pass rush in pro football, so Joe Montana basically threw nothing but three-step drop patterns all afternoon. Even though the field was muddy, Montana's jersey was clean at the end of the game. The three-step pass demands disciplined routes run the same every time. On seven-step patterns, receivers should read linebackers and maneuver into openings.

Pass on First Down. Don't isolate passing to a given down or distance. First down can be a very good time for a five-step, high percentage pass, followed by a running play and then a seven-step maneuvering pattern.

In recent years many teams have been going to the "shotgun" formation, especially in obvious passing situations. In the shotgun, the quarterback stands approximately five yards behind the line of scrimmage and takes a direct long snap from the center. Four, and sometimes all five, eligible pass receivers line up on or near the line of scrimmage. At the snap they scatter in various patterns like a load of buckshot, thus giving the formation its name.

As we have already seen, variations of the shotgun have been around since the earliest days of the game. It reemerged in 1960 in pro football. The San Francisco 49ers, with quarterback Y. A. Tittle and star running back Hugh McElhenny both injured, were 16-point underdogs to the Baltimore Colts. But the 49ers came out in a unique formation and upset the Colts 30–22. Sportscasters and writers covering the game didn't know what to call it and were left groping for the most descriptive title. The 49ers coach, Red Hickey, settled the discussion when, after the game, he said, "We call it our shotgun offense."

The following are some advantages to the formation: 1) An immobile or injured quarterback doesn't have to risk stumbling or reinjury as he releases from the center. 2) The quarterback can see the patterns developing all the way. 3) The coverages and pass rush can be picked up more quickly. 4) Screen passes work well since defensive linemen expect a pass and are charging hard.

Detractors of the formation make the following claims: 1) The defense knows you're going to pass so it can really tee off on the offensive linemen. 2) It's difficult to change the play at the line of scrimmage and if the stadium is noisy, it's more difficult to hear the quarterback's signals. 3) Quick pass routes are difficult to throw. 4) The center must learn to master a snap when he snaps blind and is still expected to pass protect. 5) A play action pass is difficult to execute.

11

Special Attacks

HURRY-UP OFFENSE

Many football games are won or lost in the waning moments of the first or second half. Coaches need to give more than lip service to the importance of these minutes and actually devote practice time to them. The key is *speed*. Everything must be done quickly. There can be no wasted time getting back to or leaving the huddle. Utilize time-outs wisely. A field goal that is scored too early when additional time could have been taken off the clock may allow the opponent time to come back. Every team must have an automatic (audible) system that allows them to run plays without huddling.

Coaches and QBs must know what situations stop the clock and call plays accordingly. Five of these are: 1) measurement, 2) first down (until the ball is re-marked), 3) out-of-bounds play, 4) penalty, and 5) incomplete pass.

In their book, *Coaching Today's Athlete,* Ralston and White present a checklist for saving or wasting time on the clock.[1] For saving the clock:

1. Hustle at all times
2. Use QB preplanned option strategy
3. Down rolling punts quickly
4. Use preplanned touchdown series
5. Punt out of bounds
6. Request measurements when ball is close

[1]Ralston, *Coaching Today's Athlete,* p. 186.

7. Space time-outs intelligently
8. Hustle to huddle after the tackle
9. Eliminate the huddle if possible
10. Use quick snap counts
11. Throw sideline or out-of-bounds passes

For wasting the clock:

1. Break the huddle slowly
2. Use long signal count
3. Unpile slowly after the tackle
4. Get back to the huddle slowly when on offense
5. Run wide but stay in bounds
6. Eliminate pass
7. Never call time-out
8. Take full allotted time to place the ball in play
9. Eliminate penalties that may stop the clock
10. Keep the ball within bounds

AUTOMATICS (AUDIBLES)

A play called at the line of scrimmage is an audible. Audibles were mentioned in Chapter 9, but since they are an essential part of a hurry-up offense and can be used for an entire game, they will be elaborated on here. Audibles give the QB the freedom to change a call at the line of scrimmage. The "live" color concept was covered in Chapter 9. The QB can also indicate "check with me" in the huddle and call the play at the line of scrimmage. A series of offensive plays or even an entire game could be called without a huddle. If time must be saved on the clock or the defense is tiring, this should be done. A coach must have confidence in his QB. If the coach calls the plays the entire game, it is unlikely that the QB will call intelligent audibles in the waning moments. The offensive coaches must spend a lot of time with the quarterbacks explaining various pass coverages, defensive line stunts, and potential weaknesses.

SHORT-YARDAGE AND GOAL-LINE OFFENSE

Some offenses, like the Wishbone and Power I, need little or no adjustment when confronted with a short yardage or goal-line situation. Others, like a passing attack or a team with several split receivers, will have to make adjustments.

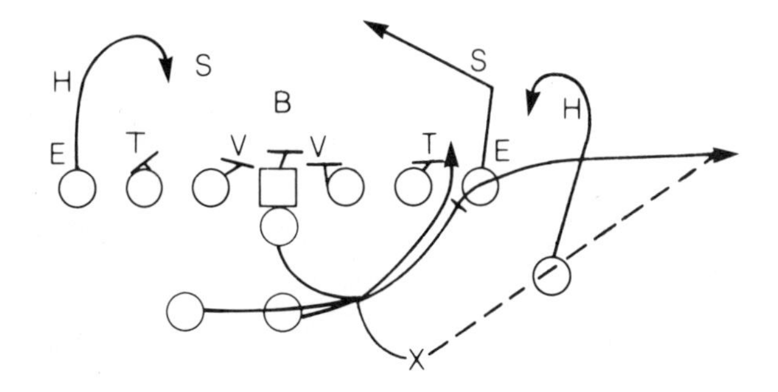

▶ Figure 11.1 Fullback Flat Pass

More teams are going with a double tight end offense in these situations. It provides a maximum number of blockers to stop the heavy rush and at the same time allows for play action passes.

If running against a gap defense, the offense should run plays that utilize down blocking with an inside out block by a lead back. Care should be taken in pulling a lineman. If a lineman does pull, be sure the adjacent lineman away from the play executes a reach block.

Cross blocking is also a possibility, provided the lineman to the side of the cross block can reach out and prevent penetration by the man in his gap.

The 6–5 is a very common goal line defense. (This defense is discussed in Chapter 16.) Misdirection plays are effective against it in that they can fool the MLB, whose job it is to roam free and meet any running play at the hole. The off-tackle power is still solid. Play action passes are good. One that can be especially effective is a FB flat pattern. Boot passes can also draw an overanxious secondary in the wrong direction while a dangerous receiver cuts back against their movement.

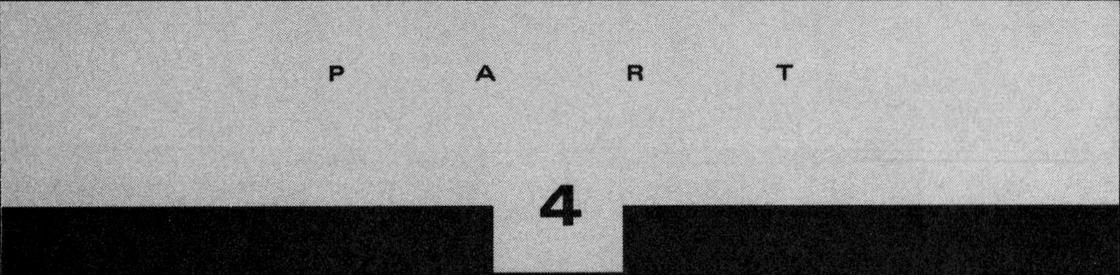

P A R T

4

12

Defensive Terminology

Defensive terminology does not have quite the same consistency as offensive terminology. Each team has a few more terms that would be meaningless to another coach unless defined. A defensive player and coach must understand many aspects of offensive terminology, since it is the offense that he is defensing. In this chapter, key offensive terminology is reviewed, but the reader would do well to reread Chapter 5. The defensive terms and illustrations are presented in the following five sections: 1) Positions, 2) Key offensive terminology, 3) Techniques (linemen, linebackers, secondary), 4) Defensive numbering/lettering scheme, and 5) Formations.

POSITIONS

Middle Guard or Nose Guard (MG) (N)	The defensive lineman who lines up on the center of the offensive formation.
Tackle (T)	The defensive lineman not lined up on the center but inside the defensive ends.
Linebacker (LB)	Defensive players who initially line up anywhere from on the line of scrimmage to four yards back. Linebackers support the linemen against rushing attempts and usually drop back and help the secondary on passing situations.
Strong Halfback (SH)	The halfback that is positioned to the strong side of the offensive formation.

Cornerback (CB)	A halfback that has rotated up closer to the line of scrimmage. He generally has contain responsibility if flow comes to him and backside third if flow goes away.

KEY OFFENSIVE TERMINOLOGY

Offensive Formations

Review the following offensive formations: T, Winged-T, I, Slot, Power I, Double Wing, Pro Slot, End Over, Set Strong, Split (Divide), Twins, and Trips (triplets).

Pass Routes

Review the following pass route information: Screen, Swing, Check Swing, Cross, Delay, Flag, Flare, Flat, Hitch, Hook, Out, Pop, Post, and Streak.

Additional Terms

Bootleg	When the QB rolls away from the flow.
Contain	Responsibility given to defender whose job it is to maintain outside leverage, forcing play back to the inside.
Crack	Call used to alert inside support that a receiver is blocking down.
End (E)	The defensive lineman immediately outside the tackle. Defensive ends normally line up in the vicinity of the offensive end, but their responsibility varies greatly from plugging the off-tackle hole, to containment, to pass protection.
Safety (S)	The last line of defense. The middle person in the three-deep secondary responsible for pass protection in the middle one-third of the field.
Halfback (HB)	Secondary personnel on either side of the safety(ies). Halfbacks are responsible for pass protection on the outside two-thirds of the field in a three-deep secondary.

Strong Safety (SS)	In a four-deep secondary, the safety that positions himself to the *strength* of the offensive formation.
Free Safety (FS)	In a four-deep secondary, the safety that is not given a zone or man to defend. He is "free" to assist where needed.
Weak Safety (WS)	In a four-deep secondary, the safety that positions himself to the weak side of the offensive formation. The WS is often a "free" safety.
Downfield	Refers to play on defensive side of line of scrimmage.
Dropback	When the QB drops directly back from the center.
Fill	Responsibility given to defender to step up at the point of attack and make the tackle.
Flow	The direction that the majority of offensive backs or a designated back move.
Leak	Pass action through the line by an offensive back.
Motion	When an offensive back moves laterally prior to the snap of the ball.
In	When motion takes a back toward the center, but not beyond the set.
Long	When a wingback or flanker goes across the formation immediately behind the QB to the opposite side of the formation.
Out	When motion takes a back away from the center.
Short (fly)	When a wing or slot back takes three or four steps in the direction of the tailback position.
Yo-yo	When motion goes one way and then reverses before the snap.
Play Action	When the offense fakes a running play before passing.
Roll Out	When the QB reverse pivots, gives a minimal fake, and sets up to pass outside the offensive tackle.

Seam	The area between zone-defense coverages.
Shift	Pre-snap movement by the offensive that changes the formation.
Split Flow	Offensive backfield action in which backs go in opposite directions.
Sprint Out	When the QB runs directly to a position outside tackle with the intention of either running or passing.
Stalk	When a wide receiver releases off the line and attempts to block a defensive back by continually keeping his body between the defensive back and the ball carrier.
Stem	When backs shift positions prior to the snap of the ball.
Stunt	Change in charge after the snap of the ball where linemen and linebackers exchange responsibilities.
Upfield	Refers to play on offensive side of line of scrimmage.

TECHNIQUES

Linemen

Attack (Penetrate)	When interior linemen move immediately on the snap of the ball to a predesignated location without regard for offensive keys.
Chase, Spin Out Fight Back	Three techniques that defensive linemen can execute after their initial movement.

Chase

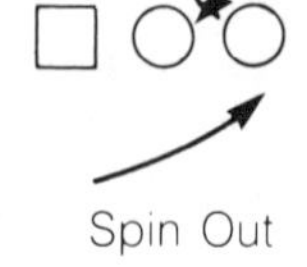

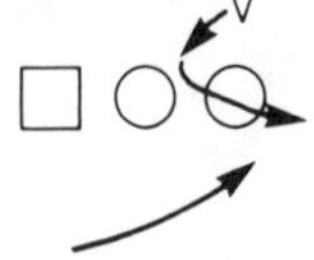

Games	Change in charge after snap of ball where linemen exchange responsibilities.

Loop — When a defensive lineman takes an arcing path, usually from a man to a gap, in an attempt to foil blocking patterns.

Pursuit — Picking the correct path in an attempt to tackle the ball carrier.

Read — When interior linemen position themselves in a head up position slightly off the ball and base their movements on keys presented by the offense.

Reduce — When the defensive tackle and end slide down toward the nose guard when the offensive end splits out.

Slant — When a defensive lineman takes a direct path to a gap or man other than the one he is lined up on.

Submarine — When a defensive lineman lines up on all fours with his shoulders close to the ground and penetrates into the backfield on the snap of the ball. This is a common technique when the defense is backed up on their goal line.

Linebackers

Blitz (Dog, Red Dog) — Penetrating *through* a gap in front of you on the snap of the ball.

Chase — When a LB and down lineman penetrate gaps to their right or left.

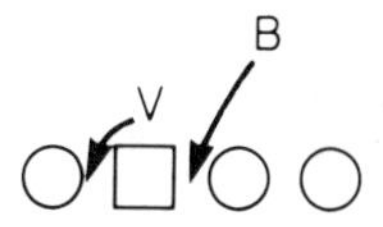

Couple — Two linebackers covering two running backs according to release.

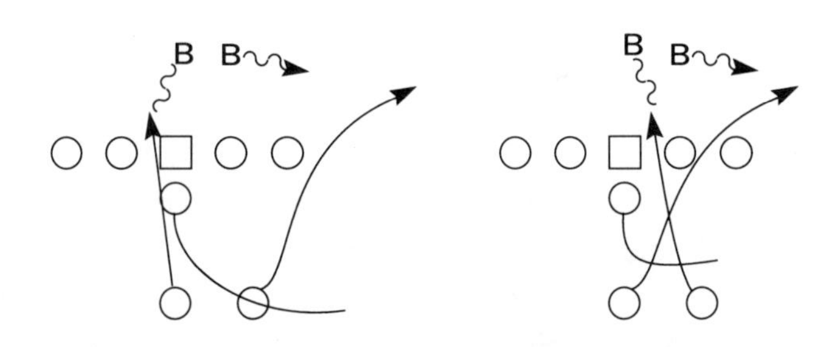

Disengage	The ability to "get rid of" an offensive blocker who is blocking you.
Drop	Getting back into your assigned pass protection area when the offense shows pass.
Over Pursue	Opposite of the stall. A common error of linebackers.

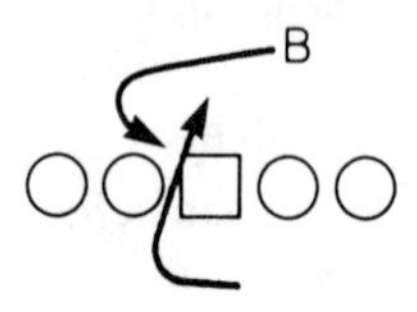

Read	When a LB bases his movement on keys presented by the offense.
Scrape Off	When a LB loops off the angle of a down lineman.

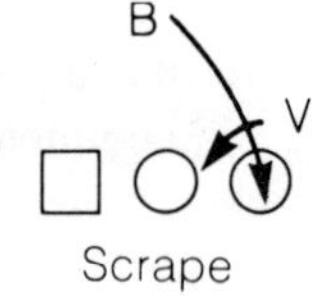

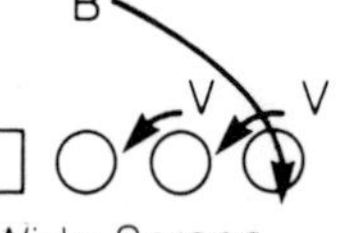

Skate	The ability to stay square on your feet and keep the ball moving laterally in front of you.
Stall	Staying behind the ball and checking for cutback.

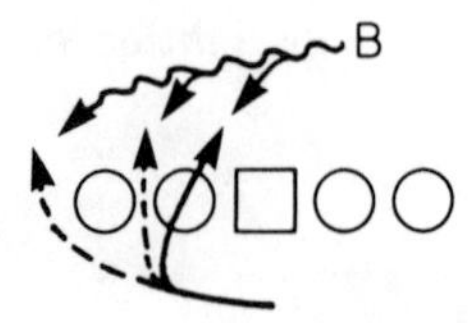

"X"	When a LB and down lineman penetrate the gaps opposite the points of initial alignment.

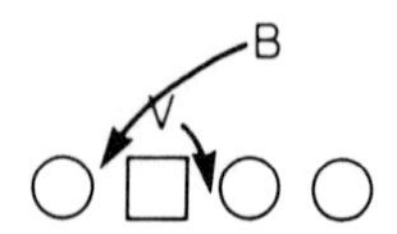

Secondary

Bracket	Man-to-man coverage determined by release and path of offensive receivers (note "couple").
Combination Defense	A defense that combines elements of man-to-man and zone coverage.
"Combo"	When pass defense personnel utilize either man-to-man or zone-pass coverage depending on the action of the pass receivers.
Cushion	Separation between receiver and coverage man. To "close the cushion" would be to come directly up on the receiver.
Funnel	To physically reroute a receiver to the inside. Opposite of jam.
Invert	Pass coverage in the four-deep secondary in which the inside safety covers the flat area and the HB backs up to cover the deep third.
Jam	To physically reroute a receiver to the outside. Opposite of funnel.
Man-to-Man Defense	When pass defense personnel are assigned specific men and stay with them wherever they go.
Numbering Receivers	Pass defense personnel must always be aware of where the eligible receivers are. It can be valuable to number them from one side of the formation to the other and note how many are on each side of the formation.
Pre-Rotate	When a four-deep secondary rotates *prior to* the snap of the ball.
Press	When a LB or HB lines up head-on a receiver on or near the line of scrimmage.
Rotate (wheel)	Pass coverage in which the outside HB comes up to the flat and the adjacent safety covers the outside behind him.

Safety Blitz	When a safety rushes the QB in a passing situation.
Slide	When defensive backs exchange coverage alignments (responsibilities) with motion.
Zone Defense	When pass defense personnel are responsible for areas of the field.

DEFENSIVE NUMBERING/LETTERING

Just as offenses number holes differently, defenses have a variety of ways of communicating assignments to the defensive personnel. The following method of designating responsibilities is used by many teams and is said to have been originated by Paul (Bear) Bryant at Alabama. If linemen or linebackers are assigned to gaps, they are identified by the letters A, B, C, D. If an even number is called, this is a head-up technique. If an odd number is called, this is an off-set assignment (note figure 12.1).

If no word or words are assigned after the numbers/letters are called, the linemen would carry through on their assignment with a read technique. If a game or stunt was called, the linemen and linebackers involved would carry out the assignment.

Defensive secondary and linebacker pass coverages can also use numbers. "Cover 10" for many teams means the free safety is the lone zone protector in the deep middle and all underneath coverage is man-to-man, while "cover 1" would mean there is still only one back in the middle zone, but underneath coverage is all zone also. "Cover 2" would mean a two-deep zone protection with underneath coverage in zone protection, while "Cover 20" would put underneath coverage in man-to-man. "Cover 3" and "Cover 30" would follow the same logic. "Cover 0" would be completely man-to-man coverage and "Cover 4" would have a four deep zone protection with the zone coverage underneath also (note figure 12.2).

FORMATIONS

There are many defensive schemes in football. Each defensive scheme makes adjustments to various offensive sets. Figure 12.3 presents the *basic look* of several defenses in a seven-man front, eight-man front, and goal line.

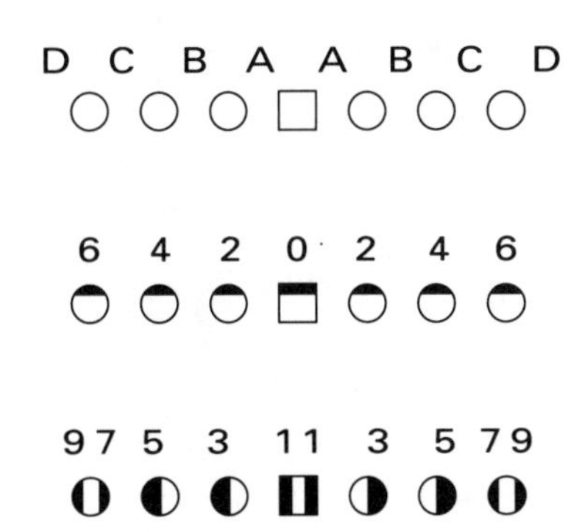

▶ **Figure 12.1**

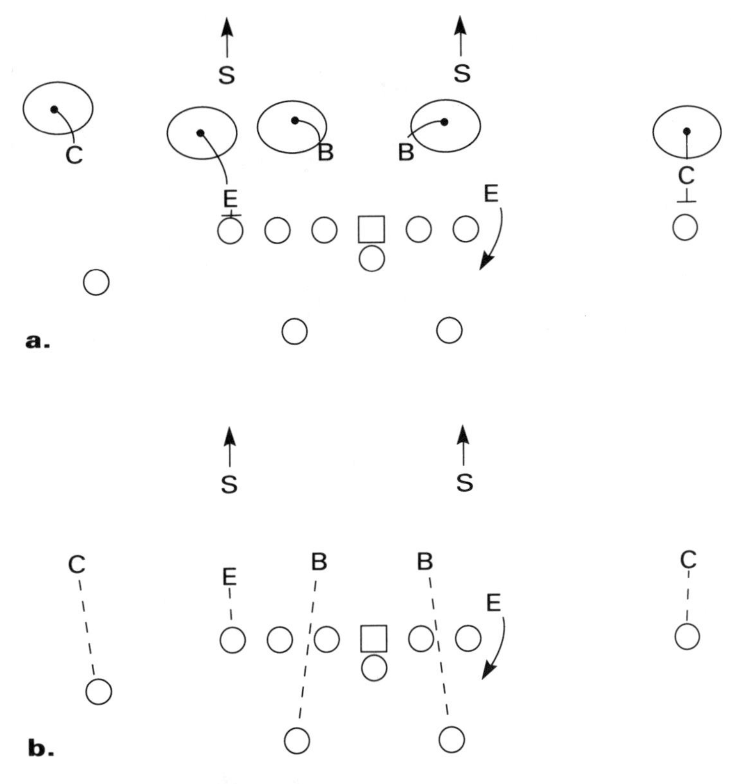

▶ **Figure 12.2** a. ''Cover 2'' (All Zone); b. ''Cover 20'' (Underneath Man-to-Man)

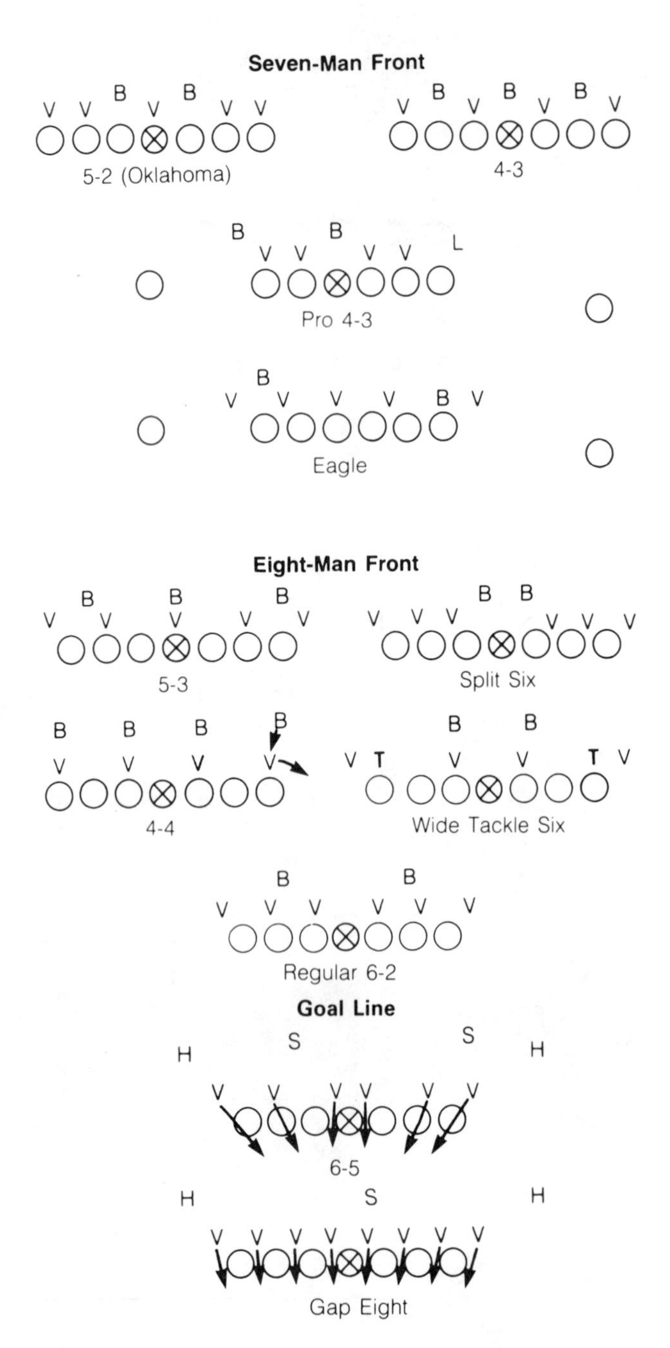

▶ **Figure 12.3** Basic Defenses

13

Position Requirements and Defensive Skills

POSITION REQUIREMENTS

The qualities that defensive personnel should possess will depend to a large extent on the defensive scheme being employed. For example, linemen in a read defense need more size and strength than linemen in an angle defense. The following information should be used as a general guide in evaluating and placing personnel.

All football players, including those on defense, must be quick. The agility drills noted in Chapter 4 should be used and the results noted. Strength is an obvious asset, but if an athlete can't mobilize that strength into explosive bursts of movement, it will do him little good.

Defensive football players must enjoy hitting people. Contact is what the game is all about. An athlete can have many assets, but if he shies away from contact, he can't play football. This in no way is a reflection on his manhood; it just means that football is not the game for him.

Middle Guard

A middle guard must be a gifted athlete. This is no place for the six foot, 260-pound boy with a 50-inch waist. He must be one of the quickest and most agile people in the entire defense. If he reads a lot, size and strength become more important. Most defensive schemes angle or loop the middle guard on the snap of the ball. When flow goes away from this initial loop, he is usually required to come back and assist, and thus the ability to change direction rapidly and accurately is important. Because of his central alignment on the field, the MG will be involved in many plays. He must have good football sense and be able to sort out the probable play from backfield actions.

Tackles

Defensive tackles that loop and angle most of the time must have good reaction and movement time. Most defenses that have tackles angling, have a LB filling in behind them, so agility is not as important as it is for the MG. Speed is more important than size for tackles since they frequently chase down plays going in the direction of their initial angle or loop. LBs will cover if the play comes back in the opposite direction. A 5–2 or 4–3 read tackle must be stronger because he must immobilize the charge of the offensive guard or tackle while reading his keys.

Strong-Side End

If a defensive end has an offensive tight end facing him, he must possess different abilities than a defensive end who does not. A strong side end must be one of the most rugged individuals in the defense. In a pure 5–2 angle defense, for example, he is the only person required to meet a one-on-one block and defeat it. He must also be able to hold his ground against a post-lead block and defeat inside-out blocks. There are other times, however, when the strong-side end has to contain, so he must have the necessary agility and quickness.

Weak-Side End

Since most teams split an offensive end, his assignments vary. He must be flexible and possess many of the qualities of a LB. He must be able to rush the passer effectively, crash down over the OT, drop back and cover the flat, and contain a bootlegging QB. An undisciplined weak-side end will oftentimes allow the offense a big play.

Linebackers

Many coaches feel this is the most crucial position of all and therefore linebackers should be spotted and coached immediately. They must be leaders, since they usually call defensive signals. They must be sure tacklers and be able to both rush the passer and drop back into pass protection. Costly defensive breakdowns often revolve around incorrect LB play.

Gene Ellenson in his excellent book, *Coaching Linebackers and the Perimeter Defense,* lists several qualities that he feels LBs must possess, including: 1) quickness, 2) football smarts, 3) shuffle (skating) ability, 4) aggressiveness in game situations, and 5) inquisitiveness. Linebackers also are 6) short striders, and 7) have a football nose.[1] Some athletes just seem to sense where the play is going and can make tackles. Other athletes look great in drills but don't show up in ball games. LBs must be game-type people who make tackles.

Halfbacks

Along with the safeties, halfbacks must be gifted athletes. Oftentimes they play other sports. They must not wilt under pressure since their errors are obvious even to the most untrained eye. Some of the qualities halfbacks must possess are: agility, jumping ability, good hands, speed, and a nose for the football.

Strong Safety (Monster)

The SS or monster must combine elements of the LB with the qualities of a HB. He must often come up and make tackles at the line of scrimmage, but he can't be up when his keys indicate that he should be covering the deep middle third. The SS should be the hardest hitter in the secondary.

Free (Weak) Safety

The free safety is the "center fielder." He must have good range, sense where passes will be thrown, and get there. Once he is there, the free safety must have the ability to intercept. He must be a sure tackler since often he is the last line of defense.

FUNDAMENTAL DEFENSIVE SKILLS

Many coaches make the statement that you win with defense. If the other team doesn't score, a team can't lose. All too often, however, these verbal statements are not backed up with a realistic allotment of practice time. The brief practice time given to defense is often spent reviewing overall defensive strategy and special stunts rather than on fundamental skills. At the younger ages especially, but also throughout a football player's career, time must be spent on fundamentals such as tackling, pass rush, and pass defense.

The two skills of tackling and block protection must be practiced by all defensive personnel. The specific aspects of each will vary depending on the defensive position played, but the fundamentals are similar.

[1]Gene Ellenson, *Coaching Linebackers and the Perimeter Defense* (West Nyack, N.Y.: Parker Publishing Company, 1972), 21–24.

Tackling

Surprisingly little has been written on how to tackle. In actuality, it is very similar to blocking. In Chapter 6 and in the coach's manual there is a lengthy discussion on the forearm lift and shoulder drive block techniques. Coaches teach the one-on-one tackle using the same techniques. In fact, many of the same drills are used. The basic one-on-one blocking drill is also a basic tackling drill. The tackler must be in the same crouched, coiled position and must rip up through the ball carrier's numbers whenever possible. It would be well if the reader reread the sections on blocking in Chapter 6 while thinking of them as tackling suggestions and drills. The helmet cannot be used as a weapon and initial contact cannot be made with it. Officials call this more closely on tackling than they do on blocking.

Many coaches teach tacklers to drive the forehead portion of the helmet through the ball. Since most ball carriers are coached to put the ball in the arm away from the point of expected contact, this is probably a good target point. Whenever possible, tackles should be made with the helmet between the ball carrier and the goal line. Even the contain man tries for an outside head position since it is his responsibility to keep the ball carrier inside him.

The tackler uncoils, drives *through* the ball carrier, and *wraps* his arms firmly around him. The legs should continue to drive as the tackler finishes the tackle. The basic difference between a block and a tackle is in the use of the arms. Some tacklers get into the bad habit of not wrapping firmly with their arms on all tackles. Blockers go to a scramble block as a last resort; similarly, tacklers leave their feet when tackling only when necessary. The head must be up with the eyes fixed on the target.

Gang Tackling. Tacklers can generally expect to receive help. This is one reason why the use of the arms is so important. Even if the initial hit doesn't bring the ball carrier down, help is on the way. This is where gang tackling and correct pursuit angles become so important. Great defensive teams always gang tackle. Athletes on the defensive unit cannot assume that the play is dead or that the ball carrier has been brought down until the whistle blows. Ball carriers who get hit by several people on every play lose their enthusiasm and spirit more quickly.

Pursuit. Gang tackling requires proper pursuit angles. Many athletes instinctively pursue at the correct angle, while others seem to constantly try to chase plays down from behind. This must be coached and emphasized in all scrimmages. The basic principle is logical. The farther a defender is from the ball carrier, the flatter or deeper to the defense's goal line the route must be. A pursuing football player should never follow a jersey his own color.

Block Protection

Some athletes have the ability to stay on their feet while others seem to get "chopped down" at the slightest contact. This is a skill that must be practiced. The most basic principle for any defensive player is not to let a blocker get underneath his arms and into his legs, trunk, or chest. If a defender lets a good blocker get underneath his protection, he will be upended. After being told this, however, many aspiring defensive players place their arms in a catching position. This is no better. It is impossible, unless you are much stronger, to get rid of the blocker with arm strength alone. By the time the arms are freed, the ball carrier will be gone. There are three basic ways of fending off the blocker. Depending on the defensive position played, each will be used to varying degrees. Defensive linemen most frequently will use a shoulder shiver. Linebackers often will use a single or double forearm shiver, while secondary men with more room to maneuver often will resort to a hand shiver.

Shoulder Shiver. The defensive lineman cannot let the blocker get underneath his protection. He also cannot get so low that the blocker can pin him to the ground. When the drive, trap, or angle block comes at him, he must meet mass with mass. The shoulder pads make initial contact. After the initial stalemate, the battle will be won by the player who follows up with hard forearm lift and driving legs. It is executed like the shoulder block.

Forearm Shiver. Linebackers can use a shoulder shiver but once they have committed themselves to this degree, it limits their mobility. If a LB's responsibility is to play a specific hole, the shoulder shiver is fine. If, however, he is skating behind the line of scrimmage, the forearm or hand shiver would be much better.

In the forearm shiver, the initial movement is very similar to a shoulder shiver except that contact is made with the forearm(s) rather than the shoulder pads. It is executed just like the forearm lift blocking technique.

Hand Shiver. The hand shiver is executed by striking up and out with the heels of the hands. It is used frequently on the open field when the defender has time to step back or shuffle away.

FUNDAMENTAL SKILLS FOR DOWN LINEMEN

Stance

Some coaches advocate a three-point stance, while others strongly favor the four-point stance. Rationale and position are similar to that for offensive linemen. If horizontal thrust and penetration are key factors, the four-point stance is fine. If the defender must loop and slant a lot, the three-point stance may be better. It also may free an inside arm more quickly for a forearm shiver. More important than the number of hands touching the ground is the weight displacement on the hands and feet. For driving straight ahead, the ideal location of the center of gravity is as far forward as possible. If lateral movement is required, the weight cannot be on the hands. Coaches must analyze the requirements for each down lineman and then decide on the best stance.

Depth

The initial distance of the interior linemen from the line of scrimmage also will depend on the nature of their assignments. For example, if a defensive tackle normally lines up on the offensive tackle and as close to him as possible, he may have to adjust somewhat if his assignment is to prevent the offensive guard from getting to the LB. If a defensive tackle is to explode into the offensive backfield, he will want to crowd the line of scrimmage.

Looping linemen, especially MGs, often like to crowd the line of scrimmage, since their initial movement is to push the helmet of the blocker as they shuffle their feet in the looping action.

Basic defensive philosophy also will dictate the ideal depth. Many coaches subscribe to a philosophy that "first downs don't appear on the scoreboard," so "give them three." They will align all defensive personnel at least three feet off the line of scrimmage and count on offensive mistakes, gang tackling, and pursuit to create opportunities. Other coaches feel that a "2nd and 13" situation is what they want, and this is accomplished through an attacking, penetrating defense. They will fire individuals through any line split that is too large and attempt to disrupt backfield actions on every first down.

Alignment

In addition to depth of alignment, down linemen can be situated in one of three locations. They can be directly *over* an offensive player, *offset* to one side, or in a *gap*. These alignments can be taken to confuse the blockers or to assist the down linemen in carrying out their assignments.

Read

When a defensive lineman has a read technique, he should take his stance with a heads up position and slightly off the ball. His actions are determined by the actions of the man over him. Three examples follow. If a defender is lined up on offensive guard and the guard pulls behind the center, he must move with him. The center may be blocking him on a middle trap, the tackle may be attempting a reach block on a sweep, or the center may be blocking him on an off-tackle play. In a second example, if the guard attempts a reach block, he may be protecting for a sprint out pass or cut off blocking for a power or sweep. In either case, the defender must move out with the blocker.

If the blocker drive blocks, the defender must use a shoulder shiver, immobilize his charge, and look for the ball.

Many coaches erroneously assume that a read defense is an easy defense to teach and learn. The opposite is true. Stunted defenses are easier to both teach and learn since defensive personnel know their assignment *before* the ball is snapped.

Angle or Slant

When the defensive lineman has an angle technique, he is usually lined up on the blocker. When the ball is snapped or when the hand of the blocker moves, the defender must drive off the opposite foot of the intended slant and explode through the gap or down to the next offensive lineman, depending on his assignment. He can't do this slowly, and can't be overly concerned about flow in the opposite direction. He must carry out his assignment first and then play football. Linemen who slant half-heartedly create breakdowns at other locations. An angling lineman should be a backside chaser first and a spinout artist second.

As the lineman angles down or out, the near arm must be ready to make a vigorous forearm shiver on the blocker, while the far arm is free to strike the lineman to whom he is angling. If contact is to be avoided, he should line up a bit deeper or cheat a little in the direction of the slant.

Loop

A loop is a more controlled movement than the angle, and as the name implies, the movement describes an arc as opposed to a direct path. On the snap of the ball or on the movement of the hand of the lineman across from him, the defender shuffles the foot away from the direction of the loop alongside the near foot as the near foot moves laterally at least 18 inches. He then drives off the foot in the direction of the loop and fires into the gap. This is a common technique for a defensive tackle on a 5–2 defense when he is going out. As he moves into the gap, he must stay low and be ready to meet a double-team block by the T and E. If the tackle is going down, the defensive tackle must be ready to close down. In this way the loop is more controlled than the angle. The spin-out technique is an important skill for looping linemen to master.

Pass Rush

Pass rushing techniques are covered under defensive end play.

FUNDAMENTAL SKILLS FOR ENDS

Stance

The stance will vary with the assignment. If a defensive end is playing over a tight end and always has a safety or HB with contain responsibility, he should be in a three-point stance. From this position he can more effectively explode into the offensive end and be tough at the off-tackle hole. If the offensive end is split on his side, he should be in a two-point stance. If the defender does assume a two-point stance over an offensive end, the inside foot should be back. When his assignment is to hit the offensive end, he should step in with his inside foot while delivering a hard forearm shiver. If a wingback is present, he must be conscious of him.

Alignment

Defensive end alignment and responsibilities vary considerably. If their main responsibility is off-tackle, they may line up inside the offensive end. When the end is split, they may be in a walk-away position. If there is a slot or wing, the defender can line up over the slot, in the gap, or on the outside man and either crash down, hit straight ahead, or angle out.

Pass Rush

With the increased use of the pro formation and passing QBs, the pass rush has become a skill that must be taught and practiced. Ralston and White state, "We believe it probably is the poorest taught fundamental at both the high school and college level."[2]

[2]Ralston, *Coaching Today's Athlete,* 332.

A popular phrase with defensive backfield coaches is that the best pass defense is a good pass rush. Tackling QBs for a big loss is a favorite pursuit of all defensive linemen and LBs. The crowd loves it too! When a QB is harassed and can't set up, his normal rhythm is disturbed, pass routes break down, and the secondary personnel can engage in their favorite pastime—intercepting the football and maybe even scoring a touchdown!

A basic technique to employ in any pass rush is to tackle the QB from the top down. The arms should be raised high, hopefully forcing a high throw or one that must go through the defender's arms. Rushers must stay on their feet since the QB may scramble.

There are three ways of getting to a passing QB. A rusher can take an outside route, inside route, or go straight through the blocker. Defensive ends normally take the outside route. When a defensive end's job is to contain the QB with his pass rush, he *must* not let him get outside. There is nothing that puts more pressure on the secondary and hurts the overall defensive effort more.

Outside. The end can attempt to beat the blocker with sheer acceleration and speed as he goes wide and attacks the QB. A second alternative is for the rusher to force the blocker deep with a quick charge, make an outside fake, and use the blocker's momentum to throw him as he rushes the QB.

Inside. These techniques are more frequently used by interior linemen. A rushing lineman usually will engage the blocker immediately with a hard shoulder or forearm shiver and then get rid of him with a fake followed by a grab and throw or a butt and throw.

Power Rush. If a blocker senses that a pass rusher is always attempting to go around him in one direction or the other, his job is a bit easier. He won't have to uncoil at the rusher as vigorously. For this reason the rush should go straight through the blocker on occasion. Unload on the blocker with all the momentum possible. This should drive him back as the rusher goes right over the top at the QB. This is a dangerous route if the rusher has contain responsibility.

Contain

Contain techniques are covered under secondary play.

FUNDAMENTAL SKILLS FOR LINEBACKERS

Stance

The basic stance for most linebackers is with the knees bent, feet slightly wider than shoulder width apart, head up, back tilted forward but straight, and arms hanging at the side but ready to deliver a forearm shiver. This is called the football "breakdown" position.

LBs in a 5–2 normally have the outside foot back. In a 6–2, the inside foot is back, and a MLB normally has no stagger. OLBs over ends have more flex in the knees in anticipation of uncoiling on the OE.

Depth

Depths vary depending on the defense and attitudes of the coaching staff. If a LB has to scrape off an angling lineman or skate behind the line of scrimmage, he can't be so close that he gets tangled up in the linemen's feet. Inside linebackers (ILBs) are normally 2½ to 3½ yards off the ball. Outside linebackers (OLBs) can be on the line of scrimmage over an OE or several yards off in a walk-away position.

Alignments

This obviously depends on the defense. LBs can be located anywhere along the scrimmage line. Examples of various alignments appear in Chapter 15.

Dog

"Dog," "Red Dog," "Fire," or "Blitz" are words most commonly given to a LB who charges through the gap or shoulder of an offensive lineman he is over in an attempt to penetrate into the offensive backfield. This can be done on the snap of the ball or after the LB has read flow. The LB must be careful to not telegraph his intentions. It is better to be a bit late than to tip off the offensive line. A LB cannot assume that he will get through without being hit. When he charges, he must have a solid base with his forearms low and ready to deliver a blow. The objective is to penetrate, however, so the LB must not unnecessarily make contact with offensive linemen. As he penetrates, he assesses backfield action and gets to the football.

Scrape Off

This technique is sometimes called a "strike" action. It is when the LB runs an arcing path behind the angle of a down lineman. This also can be executed on the snap of the ball or once flow has been established. The biggest mistake that LBs make is to arc too wide. When this is done, the offense can split the angling lineman and arcing LB and run right between them.

In actuality, the path of the LB is not that different in the dog or scrape off. The LB must square his shoulders to the line of scrimmage as soon as possible. It is a temptation for LBs to think they see a wide play developing and allow the ball carrier to cut back between them and the angling lineman.

Pass Rush

Pass rush can come off either the dog or scrape-off action. It is the LB's job to get to the QB. As he rushes, he must read backfield action and the QB. If it is a pass, he must watch the QB and adjust his course depending on whether it is drop back, sprint out, or play action. The pass rusher cannot expect to get through without being hit, so he must go through under control with his forearms ready to ward off blockers.

Pass Defense

With more teams throwing the football more often, LBs are being called on to be a crucial part of pass defense schemes. They usually are assigned to a hook zone but can be given a flat, man-to-man coverage, or even a deep third. This is one reason why LBs must always know the down and distance. If it's a passing situation, they must think pass first. Once a pass shows, yell it out to alert the secondary. Either back pedalling or cross-stepping footwork can be used in getting to a zone. LBs should not turn their backs on the QB unless they have lost their man on man-to-man coverage. Good peripheral vision is important. As the LB drops, he must watch the QB and at the same time anticipate which receivers are likely to enter his zone. Once the QB has released the football, the LB must run directly to the interception spot and attempt to take the ball at its highest point.

Read

In a read defense, the LB must key the offensive linemen in front of him and see backfield action *through* them. A LB on a 5–2 must watch the guard over him to see if he leads on the MG, comes out at him, or pulls. Each action suggests possible plays. A 4–3 MLB must watch the guards and center. If the center fires out at him, he must shiver and disengage. If the center blocks a defensive guard, the MLB must step up and look for an inside fold block or trap play. If the center moves to cut off the MLB, he must fight through the cut off block or spin out and get to the play.

FUNDAMENTAL SKILLS FOR SECONDARY

Stance

The stance is very similar to the "breakdown" position described for the LB. The outside foot is generally behind the inside foot unless the defender gets near the side line. Since secondary personnel must be ready to move in *any* direction, the weight should be centered over the base of support.

Alignments

Alignments vary greatly depending on the offensive formation, the defensive call, down, distance, position on the field, time left in the half, and the abilities of the defensive personnel. The following distances can be used only as a guide.

When there is a tight end and the secondary is using a revolving rotation to flow, a cornerback can play three yards outside the OE and three yards off the line of scrimmage. If he has man-to-man coverage on a tight end, the back obviously must play deeper. Inside safeties should be six to seven yards off the line. A strong safety should play up a little closer if the offense has a good strong side attack, and he has contain responsibility.

Against wide receivers HBs have the outside foot back and play the receiver slightly to the outside unless he gets within eight yards of the sideline. They should be at a depth of 8–10 yards. On zone defenses defenders normally line up slightly deeper.

Pass Defense

Zone. When pass shows, secondary personnel must sprint to the middle of their zone and play the ball. If the defender's zone is deep middle, he must be as deep as the deepest potential receiver. If his zone is an outside third, he must be as wide and as deep as the most dangerous receiver.

When rotating to zone coverage it is absolutely essential that the three deep men read their keys correctly, take the proper angle of movement, and then "take a picture" of the QB's actions as they scan potential receivers entering their zone.

Secondary personnel who revolve on the snap of the ball must know what dictates flow. There can be no mistake on this. In addition, HBs can key the offensive HB through the OE. If there is a wide receiver to his side, the HB should key the ball and locate the deepest man near his zone.

Angle of movement is crucial. A common error of a revolving secondary is to begin movement to their third on too shallow a path. When this is done, and a receiver goes deep, the defender may get tangled in his own feet trying to realign his route.

When the defensive pass coverage requires a secondary person to cover the backside two-thirds, the back must get depth quickly. He cannot allow the long throw-back pass. The exact route to take will depend on his location in relation to the sideline.

Man-to-Man. Few teams today can get by using zone pass defense exclusively. Man-to-man is popular when there are two wide receivers on each side or a double wing, but it can be used anytime. It has some advantages. A defender is not wasted in an empty zone. He can come up immediately for run support if his man blocks on the line of scrimmage. Also, covering man-to-man can help a primary zone pass defender to be tougher and develop confidence in his ability to play receivers tighter. Man coverage relieves the reading of any keys and lets the defense put their best defender on the best receiver.

The defender must know the receiver's favorite routes and take these away from him. If a receiver has caught eighty percent of his passes with a down-and-out pattern, the defender should play a little more to the outside. If he runs a lot of short hooks, the defender should play tighter. Give the 9.6 sprinter a little more room!

As the defender drops, he should stay low and take short steps. If he is dropping straight back, a back-pedaling action is best. If he is angling, a diagonal cross-step is most effective. The defender should keep a position approximately two to three yards away from the receiver and watch his "belt buckle." He cannot afford to be fooled by head and shoulder fakes.

At the end of his drop, the defender should be in a position two to three yards away from the receiver, but not between him and the QB. Ideally, he should be able to see the QB through the receiver.

Interception

The ultimate objective for the secondary is to intercept the football. This cannot be done if the defender is in an incorrect position. Most coaches stress going through the receiver's head and attempting to grab the football at the highest point possible. The defender must charge the football. He cannot allow the receiver to slip in front of him and catch it.

Tackling

Tackling was covered as a general skill at the beginning of this chapter, but a few additional points will be noted here. If the defender is not attempting an interception, he should time his hit to dislodge the ball from the receiver before he has control of it. If the receiver has gone high into the air to receive the pass, the defender should hit him low and as hard as possible. When this happens, most receivers will look for a soft landing and forget about the football! If the defender is on the same level as the receiver, he should rake his arms across the receiver's arms as he hits him in an attempt to dislodge the ball.

The defender must always be aware of the game situation. He probably should not intercept a fourth down pass. He should not be going for a dangerous interception if he is the last man between the receiver, the goal line, and a winning touchdown.

Run Support

Not only must defensive backs know how to revolve and keep correct angles on potential receivers, they must also be taught how to come up to the line of scrimmage at the proper angle on running plays.

Containment. The defensive back coming up for contain must never let a blocker hook him or get into his legs. The hand shiver explained under general defensive skills is the best block protection technique. When the back reaches the contain position, he must maintain leverage from the outside in. He cannot, however, get too deep into the offensive backfield and allow the ball carrier an alley to the sideline.

Inside Support. Safety men coming up from the inside use inside-out leverage, but should be ready to slide outside if containment breaks down. They must anticipate the ball carrier's route and set their course accordingly.

Backside Support. Defenders in the back two-thirds advance with caution once they are certain that the play is not a pass. They must be certain that their route does not overrun the ball carrier.

Pursuit. Proper pursuit angles are just as important for the defensive secondary as they are for defensive linemen and linebackers.

14

Elements of a Successful Defense

In Chapter 7, eighteen elements of successful offense were discussed. Some of these were: a competent coaching staff, stress on the fundamentals, development of team strength (physically), consistency, knowledge of each opponent, player evaluation, terminology, incentives, and goals. All of these contribute to a successful defense as well. Thirteen additional elements will be developed in this chapter.

HAVE A BASIC PHILOSOPHY

There are two differing philosophies of defense. Phrases such as "bend but don't break" and "give them three" reflect a different view of defense than a phrase like "penetrate and disrupt." Coaches that use the first two phrases maintain that "first downs don't show up on the scoreboard." They feel that eventually the offense will make a mistake (fumble, interception, penalty, broken play); it is the job of the defense to be patient and then capitalize when the opportunity comes. These defenses are often quite loose, with linemen and linebackers several yards off the ball. They key flow, pursue, and gang tackle with reckless abandon.

Other coaches attack with their defensive front. The "2nd and 13" situation is their goal on each series of downs. They feel that this situation disrupts the offense's game plan and limits their options. Offensive gaps are attacked. This can be especially effective against teams that run and pass in a predictable fashion.

USE VARIED ALIGNMENTS, NOT DEFENSES

Using varied alignments is different from using several defenses. The former is a good idea, the latter is not. If a team runs the 5–2 angle defense, it should be primarily a 5–2 angle team. It would be a mistake to try and master the 5–2 read and also the wide tackle six defenses. Varying alignments from a basic defense is a good idea. This can be done easily without altering individual techniques. A 5–2 angle team could use the same techniques, yet adjust alignments to force the offense to make adjustments.

USE DIFFERENT CORNER COVERAGES

The double and triple options are effective offenses in modern football. There are offensive coaches who maintain that defensive planning must begin at the corner and only after decisions have been made there should the other aspects of defense be considered. The QB should not know in advance who on the defense has what assignment. Various corner coverages are outlined at the end of Chapter 15.

VARY THE SECONDARY COVERAGES

If a QB can anticipate the rotations and coverages in the defensive secondary, his job is greatly simplified. Interceptions occur when he can't. There are times when a predominantly zone oriented team will utilize man-to-man or a combination of the two.

RECOGNIZE FORMATIONS

Most teams that run from several offensive formations do so for a reason. They like to pass from one formation or run from another formation. If defensive personnel can be taught to recognize each formation and the tendencies from each, they will defend more effectively.

ADJUST FOR EACH OPPONENT

An entire section of Chapter 4 dealt with scouting. The defense can use scouting reports to obtain much information on offensive tendencies, and should do so. A defense that doesn't alter its emphasis from game to game is an inefficient one. A team cannot learn a new defense for each ball game, but it certainly should alter alignments and emphasis.

OFFENSE DICTATES DEFENSE

Just as the offense must take into consideration the strength of its own defense, the defense must consider the strength of its own offense. If a team has a very explosive offense, the defense can afford to take more chances to get them the ball. If it appears that the offense will have to struggle to put seven points on the board, the defense had better be more cautious.

HAVE A SHORT-YARDAGE DEFENSE

The basic defense should be sound enough for most situations, but there are times that call for a special unit, and the defensive coaching staff must be ready for these situations.

HAVE A GOOD SCOUT TEAM

How is it possible to build esprit de corps in the "hamburger" squad? Every coach realizes the importance of the scout team. A coach should be assigned to them, even if it means sacrificing one from the defense. Maybe the team can be given special jerseys with "hamburger" or a "skull and crossbones" on them! The scout team should come out early during specialty work and go over the plays with a coach. They can't run the plays just by looking at them on an index card!

TRAIN THE DEFENSIVE SIGNAL CALLER

If a coach doesn't call the defenses from the sideline, he must make time to go over all situations with his signal caller. Tactical factors that must be considered before the defense is called are: score, time, field position, down, distance, wind, weather, key offensive personnel, and the general game plan.

DON'T GIVE UP THE BIG PLAY

A great defense can't give up the big play. Each player on the defensive unit has to know his assignment and execute it correctly. If an offensive lineman misses his assignment, it may result in a two-yard loss. If a defensive assignment breaks down, it can cost a touchdown. Since players are human and make mistakes, other defensive players must never give up in their relentless pursuit of a back who is running free or a QB who has broken contain.

PLAY THE HITTERS

Everyone on the defense must have a burning desire to get in on every tackle. Pursuit and gang tackling are hallmarks of great defenses. If a boy shies away from contact, he can't play on a defensive unit.

AWARDS

Many teams do a lot with individual awards. These awards include helmet decals, tackling charts, and hit of the week awards. Other coaches shy away from individual awards feeling that they can be divisive. They stress the successful accomplishment of team goals such as: 1) keeping the opponent under 100 yards rushing, 2) keeping the opponent under 100 yards passing, 3) allowing no touchdowns, 4) permitting no more than eight first downs, and so forth.

15

Defenses and Secondary Coverages

In many ways the history of American football has been one of ebb and flow between offensive movement and defensive stalemate. For a period of time defensive units hold offenses down and most games are rather low scoring contests. Then a new offensive idea is developed and contests tilt in favor of the offense. In Chapter 10 we saw how the T-formation, pro formation, and triple option attacks breathed new life into offensive football. Each demanded defensive adjustments.

The earliest defenses were more a mirror of the offensive formation than a creative attempt to stop a particular attack. The seven offensive linemen flopped over and became seven defensive linemen. The ends generally played a little wider, and it was their responsibility to box in the end run.

The offensive fullback backed up the linemen, and linebackers were initially called fullbacks. It was the fullback's job to clean up on any runner who got through the front seven. The fleetest offensive back played a deep safety position, often twenty-five yards off the line of scrimmage. He was the last line of defense and received punts and quick kicks. The two halfbacks watched for runners slipping outside or for occasional passes. Yardage was so difficult to make, it all boiled down to one admonition—when in doubt, punt. Most coaches preferred to wait for their opponent to drop the ball rather than try to push it down the field themselves.

One of the first adjustments from this basic 7–1 look was the 6–2. The center was pulled out of the line and became a linebacker. This gave more mobility to the defense. Linebackers could move laterally more easily than linemen and this was the reason behind the defensive adjustment. As was mentioned in the chapter on offensive systems, the legendary Don Hutson and "slinging" Sammy Baugh forced defenses to loosen up in the late 1930s. There was just no way that the ponderous defenses then in existence could cover all potential receivers, even on paper, much less on the field.

With the advent of the T-formation, some teams went with a 5–3 defense. Linebackers were in a better position than linemen to observe the faking inherent in the T-formation offense. The formation, however, was still weak against the pass since it only had three men in the secondary.

One of the first four-deep secondary defenses to be used was the "Eagle." It had a 5–2 front, but the two linebackers aligned over the ends. The four-deep secondary was better able to cover potential pass receivers and the linebackers could hold up the ends at the line of scrimmage and help in pass defense.

The flats were still vulnerable to the pass and a 6–1 defense emerged, but with the defensive ends ready to drop off. The MLB also could drop off, so the defense had the look of an umbrella and became known as the "umbrella defense." In many ways it was the forerunner of today's pro 4–3 defense.

One of the most noticeable changes in football from the 1930s to the present is not so much in the formations, but in the football players themselves. Size and strength were adequate in those early days. Mobility and speed are trademarks of today's football player, regardless of the position he plays. Defensive linemen have to be strong enough to stop the run but quick enough to get the passer. Nowhere is this mobility more noticeable than at the linebacker position. Linebackers must be strong enough to take on the charge of offensive linemen and quick enough to bump and run with swift pass receivers. The secondary personnel are no longer offensive cast-offs. They are considered by many knowledgeable coaches to be the most gifted athletes on the entire team.

Teams also began experimenting with reading versus stunting defenses. Linemen playing a read defense do not attempt to follow all the QB fakes and follow the ball carrier as much as they attempt to react to the direction and intensity of the movement and the force of the linemen they are facing. The defensive linemen, and even linebackers and secondary personnel, key their actions on the movement of the offensive linemen as much as the backs. A pulling, trapping, pass protecting, or drive blocking lineman can tip off a play more accurately and more quickly than backfield action with its increased amount of deception.

Stunting defenses follow a completely different philosophy. Rather than read the offense's intentions and then pursue and gang tackle, they explode men through gaps in the offensive lineup on the snap of the ball. In essence, the defense goes on the offense.

If an offensive team has a split end, the remaining six linemen leave seven gaps to be covered: outside right, LT-LG gap, LG-C gap, C-RG gap, RG-RT gap, RT-TE gap, and outside left. The creative defensive coach can design hundreds of ways to position and stunt his front seven to fill these gaps and confuse the blocking schemes of the offense. Several of these stunts are shown later in the chapter.

A more recent innovation has been to delay the stunt momentarily until the offense has made some indication of flow. In this way the value of the stunt can be maximized. This is the idea behind the very popular 5–2 angle defense.

Many coaches fail to develop their defensive strategies in a logical, consistent manner. They will teach their team a 5–2 read defense for one game and think that the 5–2 angle defense can be taught in one week for another game. The major differences are between read and angle (stunted) defenses, not between odd and even fronts. A 5–2 read and 5–2 angle defense are far more different theoretically and in practice than a 5–2 read and a wide tackle six.

In the remainder of this chapter several defenses will be developed. Many books have been written on each defense and the reader is encouraged to use this limited information as a springboard for further reading.

5–2 READ

In a read defense defenders usually watch blockers instead of the ball, on the theory that the blockers' actions will lead them to the ball. Each defender "keys" certain offensive personnel. Linemen must be both strong and quick since once they have read their keys, they must be able to pursue and chase down the ball carrier.

The 5–2 read defense requires a lot of teaching and drilling in the reading of keys. Each individual along the defensive front must react to what happens offensively *after* the snap of the ball. In this it differs from a 5–2 stunted defense where each person has his job to do *on* the snap of the ball, regardless of what the offense does.

The LBs playing over the guards should watch the guard in front of them and see the near back *through* the guard. If the guard post-leads on the MG, a trap or isolation is probably developing. In either case the LB should step up into the hole ready to deliver a shoulder or forearm shiver and tackle the ball carrier.

If the guard pulls behind the center, the LB should move quickly behind the MG and become a middle linebacker. He must not overrun a quick trap. Once he is sure that no play is coming back, the defender is free to continue to the other side of the center. Backside LBs who overreact too quickly leave the defense vulnerable if a ball carrier cuts back against the grain.

If the guard pass protect blocks or pass shows, the LB must get back to his hook zone or rush the passer, depending on the call. The MG must hit the C and watch the guards and backfield action. If a post-lead block develops, he must fight through it or spin out. If pass develops, the MG must get to the passer. If the guard pulls, he must beat the center's block and get to the play.

Tackles must hit the OTs and get to the play. If the OEs come down on them, they must fight the block and plug the off-tackle hole. If the guards come out on them, tackles must stop their charge. If the offensive tackles come out to block them, they must look at the backfield action, determine the play, and react accordingly.

Defensive ends generally have a variety of tasks. If the offensive ends attempt to hook them, they must stay on their feet and string the play out. If they are not blocked and an option develops, they must execute their assignment. This can vary from immediately hitting the QB, to stringing the QB out, to containing the pitch back. If a pass develops, they usually rush the passer with outside leverage.

Assignments of all the front seven obviously can vary from this. The point being made is that a 5–2 read defense demands disciplined athletes who have been drilled over and over again in their responsibilities, so that when they are presented with a given situation the response is automatic. Beginning coaches sometimes erroneously think that this is an easy defense to teach and run effectively. It is one of the most difficult.

5–2 ANGLE (STUNTED)

The 5–2 angle defense is as different from the 5–2 read as it is from a 6–2. It requires completely different skills from all the front seven men.

The basic concept of the 5–2 angle is that it becomes a six-man line on the snap of the ball, but with four men in the direction of offensive flow and two men away. The MG is considered one of the four men in the direction of flow. He obviously must be an agile, quick athlete capable of looping in one direction, but coming back quickly.

LBs must fill at the line of scrimmage when flow comes in their direction. Defensive ends have one basic responsibility: to be tough at the off-tackle hole. The tackles are either angling down or looping out and must be able to accelerate rapidly on the snap of the ball. Whereas strength may be more important than quickness in the 5–2 read, quickness is certainly more important in the 5–2 angle.

Linebackers must master four basic techniques covered in Chapter 13. They are: 1) dog, 2) scape off, 3) becoming a MLB, and 4) pass protection. The 5–2 angle is especially demanding on the LBs because they cannot know ahead of time which of these four techniques to use. It is determined by backfield action (flow), as indicated in Figure 15.1.

The MG must master the loop technique and be able to help on plays both toward and away from the direction of the loop. If he doesn't fight back when flow goes away from his initial loop, the MG leaves too large a gap between him and the tackle coming down.

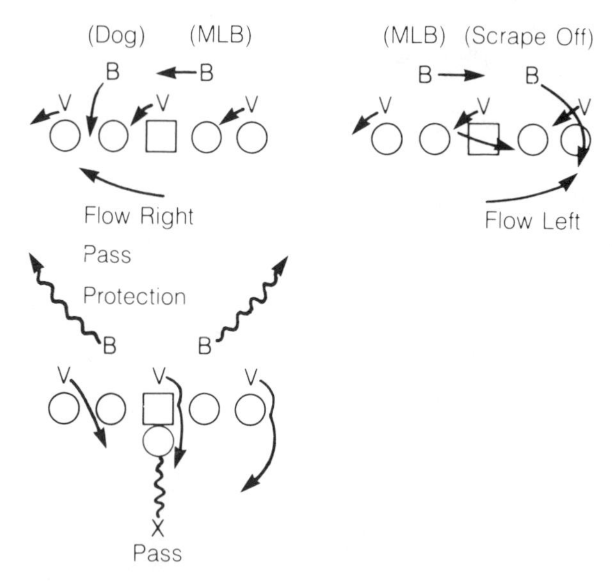

Figure 15.1 Linebacker Actions on 5-2 Angle Defense

Figure 15.2 illustrates the basic movements of the front seven. Notice that the movements of the down five remain the same regardless of flow, whereas the LBs' movements depend on the direction of flow. The direction of the angle would be called in the defensive huddle.

Tom Landry, for many years the highly successful coach of the Dallas Cowboys, developed the "Doomsday Defense." The defense was developed around the idea of filling every gap between offensive linemen and covering the flats. From whatever defensive formation the linemen and linebackers line up, they are assigned to a gap on the snap of the ball. The natural instincts of a football player are to go after the football. This cannot happen until the player is certain that the ball carrier is not coming to his gap.

A 5–2 stunted defense appears to be very similar to a 5–2 angle. The basic difference is that the LBs execute their stunts *on the snap of the ball without regard for flow.* Because of this fact, it is not always possible to get four men in the direction of the flow, since a LB will obviously stunt away from the flow on occasion. Many of the stunts mirror the 5–2 angle except that the LB involved dogs or scrapes off on the snap of the ball. A few additional stunts are shown in Figure 15.3.

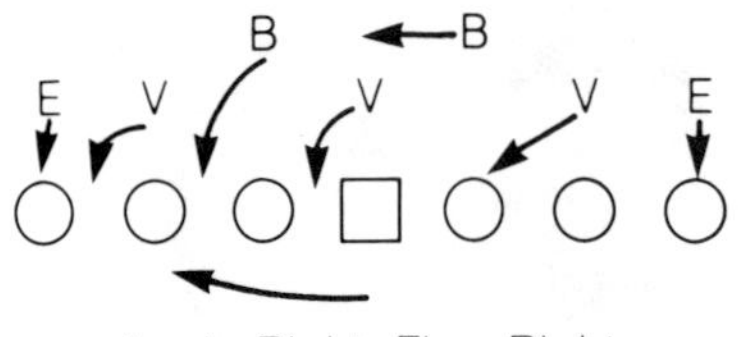

Angle Right, Flow Right

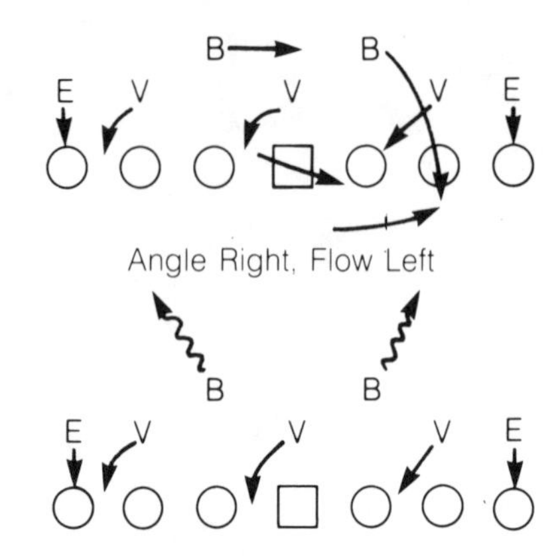

Angle Right, Flow Left

Angle Right, Drop Back Pass

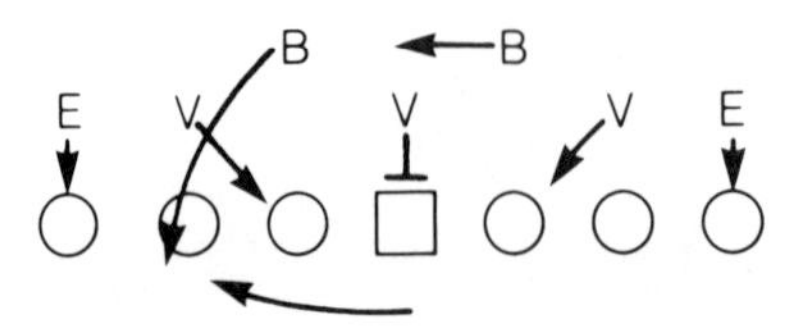

Angle In, MG Read, Flow Right

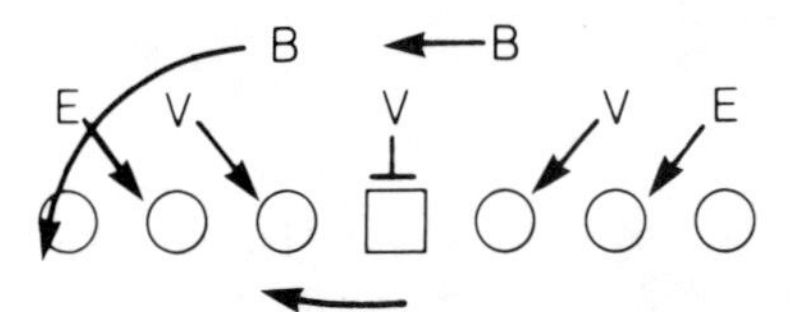

T's and E's In, Flow Right

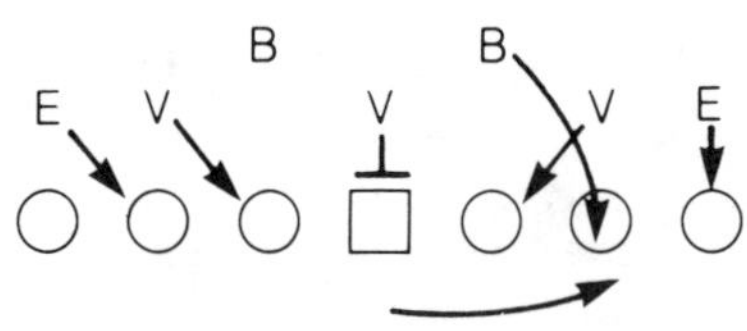

T's and RE In, Flow Left

▶ **Figure 15.2** Movements of Front Seven on 5-2 Angle Defense

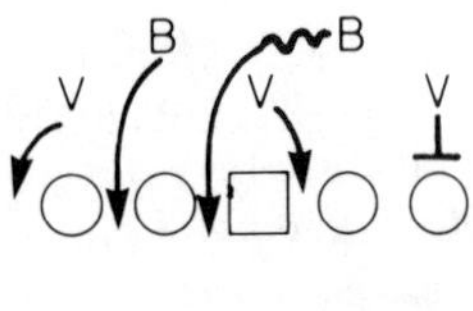

Sting Right

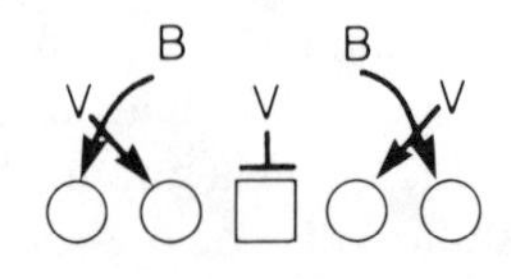

Double Scrape Off

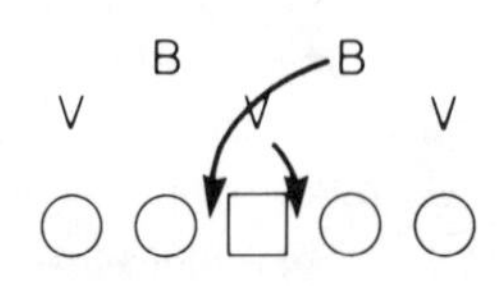

X

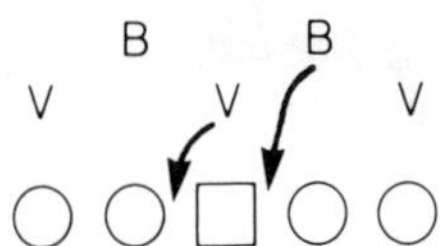

Chase

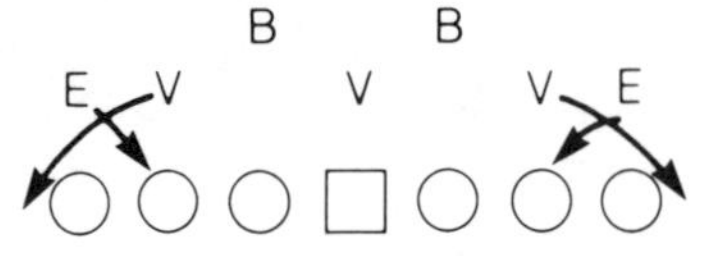

Tackle Cross

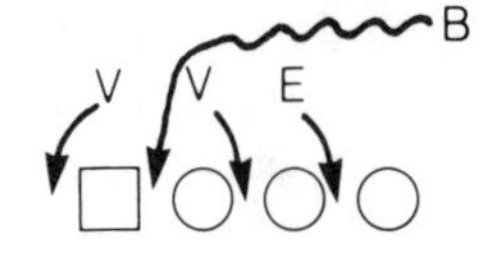

Close, Chase

▶ **Figure 15.3** Stunts from 5-2 Stunted Defense

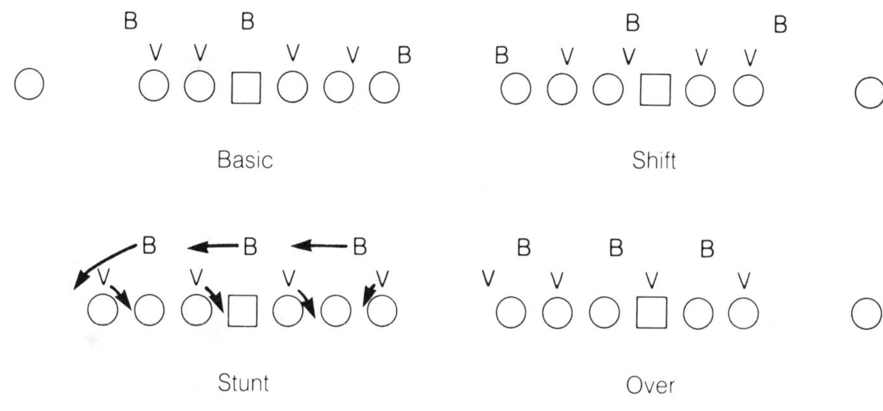

▶ **Figure 15.4** Various Looks Off the 4-3

4–3 (PRO) AND 4–4

The 4–3 is a flexible defense that can easily adjust to varying offensive strengths and sets. Figure 15.4 shows four different 4–3 alignments. Notice that one outside linebacker usually is placed on the line of scrimmage or stunts on the snap of the ball. The front seven can read offensive techniques, read flow, or stunt much like the front of a 5–2 defense.

The keys for reading are similar. The down linemen should be over offensive linemen and usually slightly off the ball. They must react and move, depending on their keys. On pass rushes the inside linemen usually take an inside rush route while the outside linemen take an outside pass route.

Some of the stunts and maneuvers that the front four can utilize are diagrammed in Figure 15.5. The terminology is that utilized in Ralston and White's text.[1]

The MLB must be able to read his keys, scrape off, dog, and pass protect much like the LBs in the 5–2.

Outside LBs in the 4–3 must be gifted athletes. They must be tough enough to hit linemen head on, quick enough to cover a fleet receiver, and smart enough to be doing the right thing at the right time. Some defenses do a lot with stunts of the 4–4 OLBs and DEs. See Figure 15.6.

The variations of the 5–2 and 4–3 involve the coordinated action of a seven man defensive front. The 4–4 involves a coordinated action of four down linemen and four linebackers. Several potential alignments are shown in Figure 15.7.

[1]Ralston, *Coaching Today's Athlete,* 352.

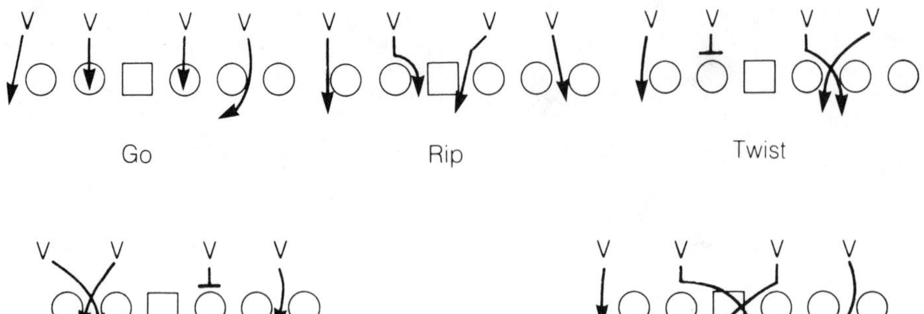

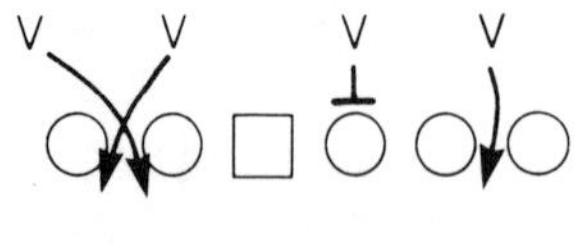

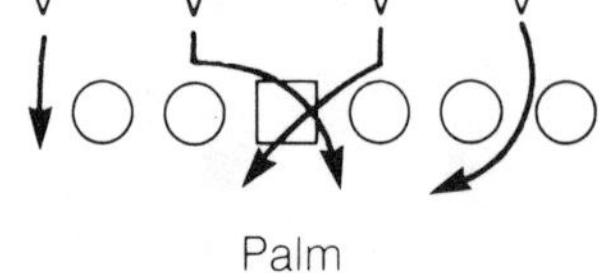

▶ **Figure 15.5** Stunts of Front Four on the 4-3

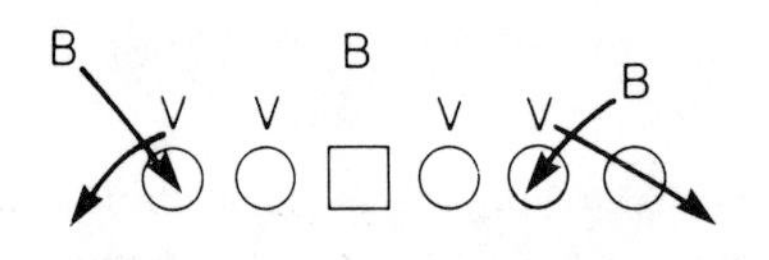

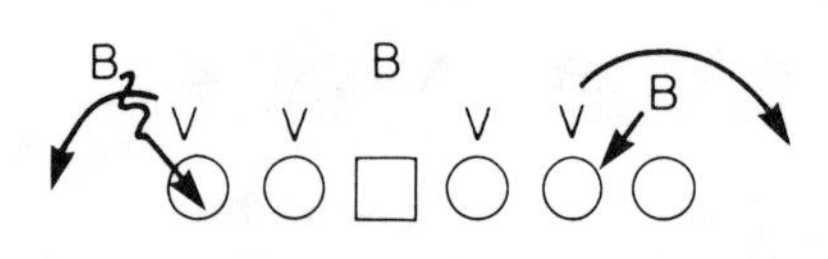

▶ **Figure 15.6** Stunts of Ends and Outside Linebackers (OLB) on the 4-3

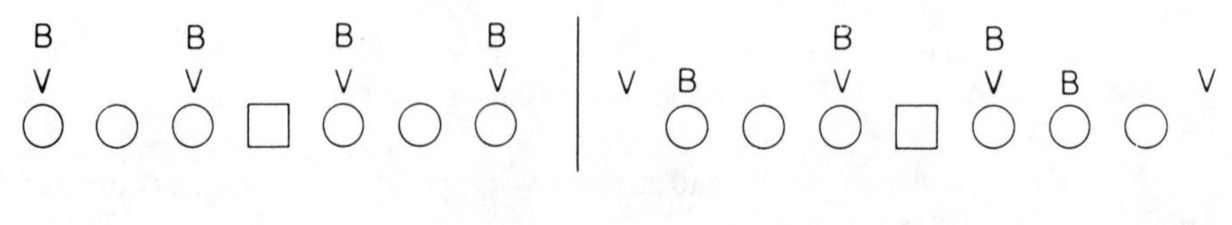

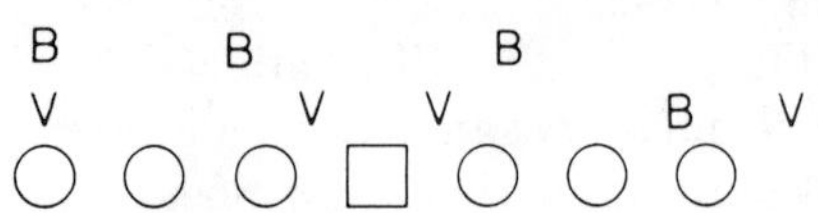

▶ **Figure 15.7** Various Looks Off the 4-4

The position of the down four varies. The inside linemen can play head up (2 technique), inside shoulder, or outside shoulder of the guards (3 technique). Sometimes they line up in the G-T gap (B technique), pointing at the G. Sometimes they line up in the G-C gap (A technique) and hit the center on the snap of the ball.

The ILBs can be stacked behind the inside linemen or on their inside foot. On the snap of the ball they can read or stunt much like LBs in the 5–2 or 4–3 defenses.

The OLBs and DEs vary their alignments also. They can align themselves in tandem and stunt. The OLB can line up on the OE (6 technique), chug him or play him man-to-man while the end lines up outside and plays contain.

WIDE TACKLE SIX

The wide tackle six is so named because the tackles generally play wider than in a regular 6–2. In many ways the alignment of personnel can be similar to the 4–4 but there are two differences. The LBs are not stacked behind linemen, and there is a tackle in the vicinity of the OE rather than a LB. The tackles can angle down and hit the offensive tackles or fire through the offensive ends. The defensive guards can read or stunt like the inside linemen in the 4–4. If an end splits out, the defensive end can move to a walk-away position, and the defensive HB can move out on the SE and play him man-to-man. Against a tight slot, the defensive tackle can shoot the tackle-slot back gap while the defensive end hits the offensive end before sliding outside.

The guards or inside tackles normally line up on the offensive guards in a 2 technique. Their primary assignment is to control the offensive guards. They should be looking through the offensive guard to the fullback as they play the guard's block.

The defensive tackles normally line up on the offensive end if he is tight and hit him immediately upon the snap of the ball. He should not be allowed to get into his pattern undisturbed. He will have off-tackle responsibility if a run develops. If a pass develops, he rushes the passer, but with outside-in leverage. Like the guards they must strike a blow, not get penetration, and look through the block of the offensive end to the backfield action.

The ends in a wide-tackle six defense are more like cornerbacks. Their normal alignment is two yards outside the defensive tackles and off the line of scrimmage, but this is varied. Their feet and shoulders should be square to the line of scrimmage. On the snap of the ball they should be looking through the offensive end and reading the action of the back nearest them. If an option develops, they are normally responsible for the pitch man. The defensive ends must not be knocked off their feet when blocked. The basic formation is shown in Figure 15.8.

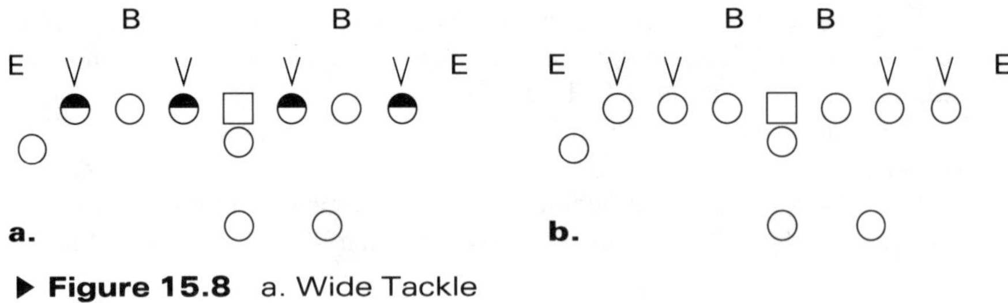

▶ **Figure 15.8** a. Wide Tackle Six; b. Split Six

SPLIT SIX

The only change in the split six is between defensive guards and ILBs. The ILBs are aligned next to each other and the defensive guards are split farther apart. The LBs can line up anywhere from the head on the tackle to the C-G gap. The basic formation is also shown in Figure 15.8.

THE DEFENSIVE SECONDARY

Corner Coverages—Four Deep

There are only four people that realistically can have contain responsibility. They are the corner back (HB), safety (SS) (WS), end, or outside linebacker. Three areas of responsibility must be covered. They are the off-tackle hole and QB on an option, the wide sweep and pitch back on the option, and the front-third deep zone of the field. These responsibilities are diagrammed in Figure 15.9.

Figure 15.9a shows the coverage used most often. The HB has the deep third, the SS contains, and the end takes the off-tackle hole. In 15.9b, the HB and SS switch assignments. The SS will have to slide over a little to meet his responsibility of deep third coverage. In 15.9c, the end takes contain and the SS comes up inside to cover the off-tackle hole. In 15.9d, the defensive end has reduced down over the offensive tackle and the LB has lined up over the end to take contain responsibility. This can be effective on a split-end side.

Corner Coverages—Three Deep

In an eight man front, the three deep men have to think "pass" first. When a running play develops, they must be ready to come up and assist on the tackle. Contain responsibility usually will be assigned to a defensive end or OLB.

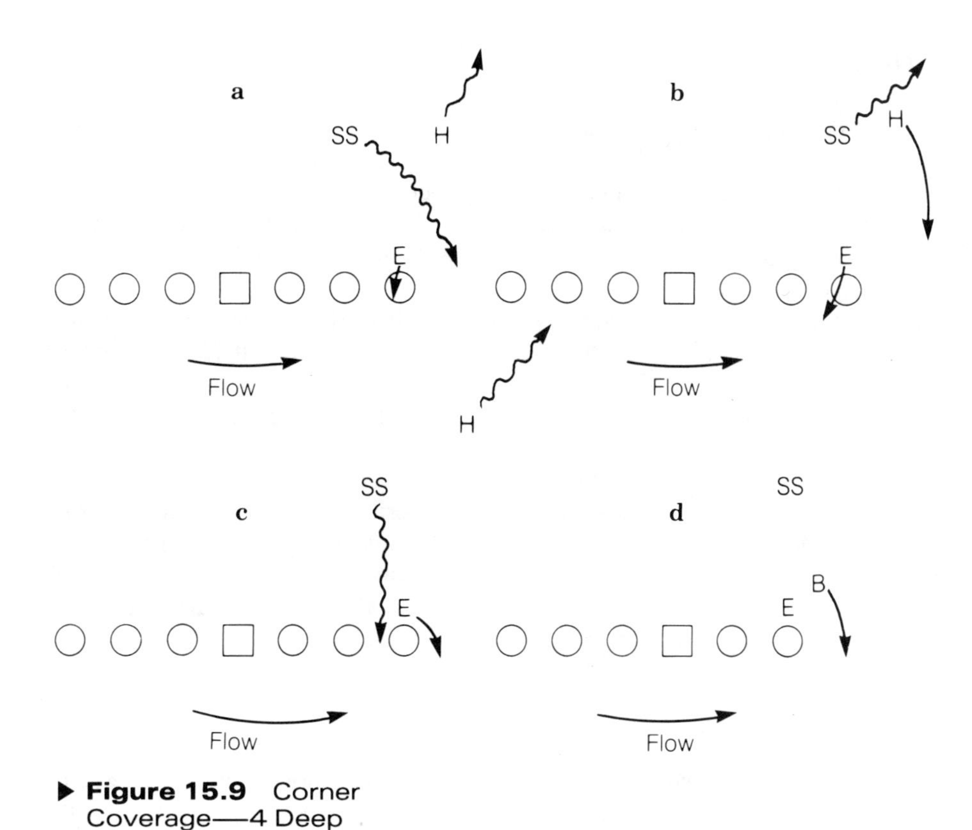

▶ **Figure 15.9** Corner Coverage—4 Deep

It is possible to revolve the secondary and have a HB come up for contain when flow comes in his direction. If this is called, a LB will have to cover deep middle or back third.

Run Support of Non-Contain Backs—Four Deep

When the outside corner or HB has contain responsibility and a sweep develops, the outside safety must approach the ball carrier with inside-out leverage. If containment breaks down, he must be ready to flatten out and adjust his angle of pursuit.

The backside safety should not come up too quickly. He keys the playside offensive end and makes sure no pass play is developing, including a HB pass. The safety's route to the ball carrier should prevent the ball carrier from cutting back against the grain. The backside HB should gain depth and width as soon as possible. He must be ready for a reverse, counter, or throwback pass.

Run Support—Three Deep

Against running plays between the tackles, the safety should meet the ball carrier head on. The HBs should converge on the ball carrier from an outside-in angle.

On running plays off tackle, the playside HB approaches the ball carrier from the outside-in, the safety meets the runner from the inside-out, and the far HB checks for a possible reverse or counter before taking a deep pursuit angle in case the runner breaks loose.

On the sweep, the playside HB approaches from the outside-in and the safety from the inside-out. The HB should not get too deep and make it easy for a pulling guard to kick him out. If a ball carrier breaks outside the contain man, all defensive personnel must immediately adjust their pursuit routes to prevent the touchdown.

More books have been written on various pass defenses than any other single aspect of football. It is almost foolhardy, as a result, to attempt to cover the subject in a few pages. Yet it is surprising that many young coaches who were offensive or defensive linemen know absolutely nothing about this aspect of football. The following sections explain a few variations in pass defense that can be implemented from three-deep or four-deep coverages.

Three-Deep Secondary

The three-deep secondary with an eight man front is primarily a zone pass defense. It depends on a strong rush and the holding up of receivers to disrupt the timing of pass patterns.

The simplest breakdown of the field, and the one most frequently used, is to divide the field into three deep zones and four short zones. The deep zones are covered by the three backs and the four short zones by the four LBs in the 4–4 or by two LBs and two ends in the five- or six-man line.

When the QB sprints or rolls out to one side, the arrangement becomes a bit vulnerable if the lineman assigned to outside rush allows the QB to go wide. When this develops, the OLB can rush, forcing the QB to hold up. The secondary can revolve in several ways. Two examples are diagrammed in Figure 15.10.

Although the three-deep secondary is generally a zone defense, man-to-man coverage is certainly a possibility. One man-to-man alignment against a pro set is diagrammed in Figure 15.11.

A combination ("combo") of zone and man-to-man defense can also be used, as in Figure 15.12.

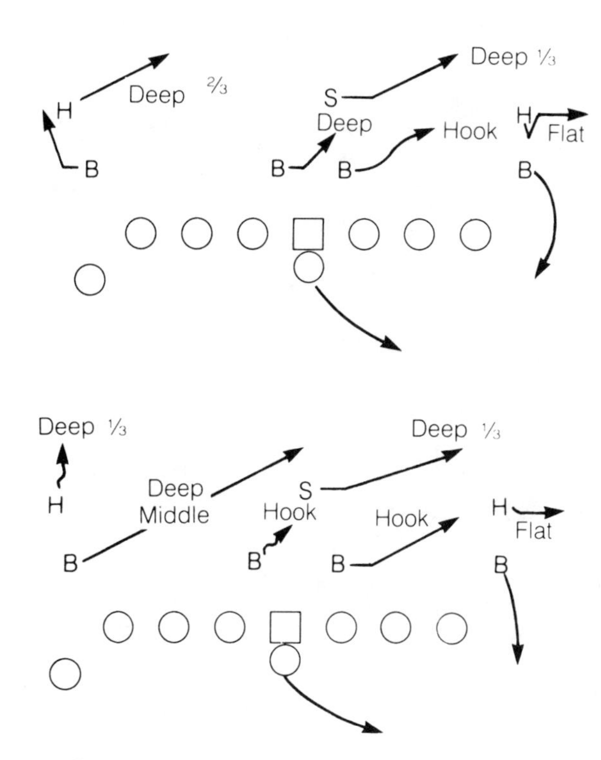

▶ **Figure 15.10** Secondary Rotations

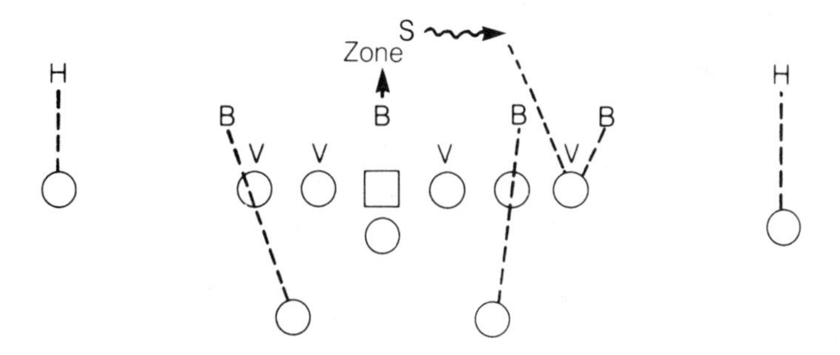

▶ **Figure 15.11** Man-to-Man Coverage from 3-Deep Secondary

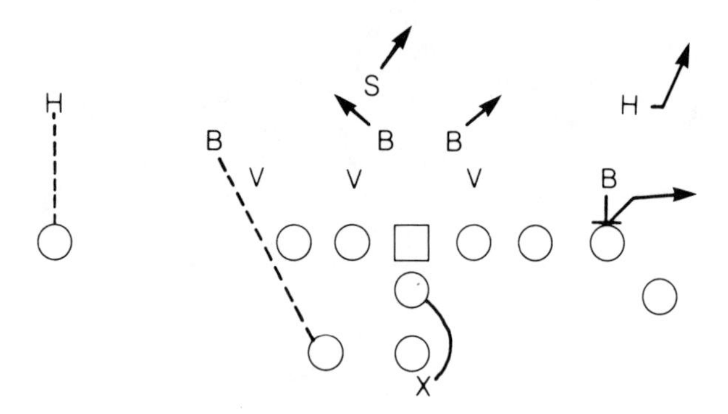

▶ **Figure 15.12** "Combo" Coverage

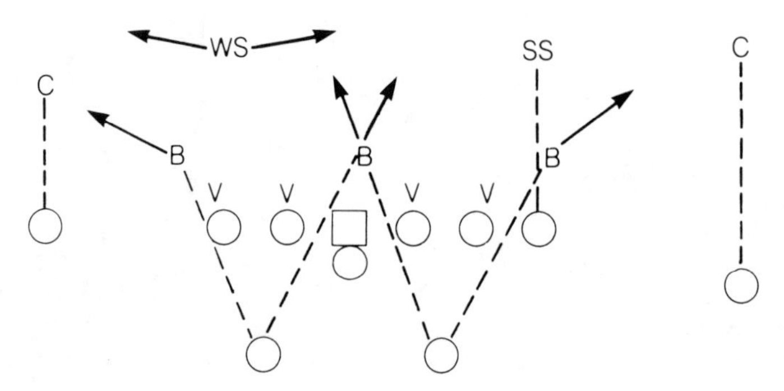

▶ **Figure 15.13** Free Safety

Four-Deep Secondary

The following defensive alignments can be used against the pro formation. They will be shown from the 4–3 defense, but with minor modifications the defensive end in a 5–2 could assume an OLB's responsibilities.

A popular pro defensive look is to leave the WS "free" and cover the five potential receivers, as diagrammed in Figure 15.13.

A basic adjustment to this man-to-man look is to have the WS move over and, with the SS and CB (HB), play "3 on 2" on the TE and FL in "combo" (note Figure 15.14).

A three deep and four short zone coverage can be executed easily. If the QB sprints out to the strong side, the most logical manner to assume this coverage is diagrammed in Figure 15.15.

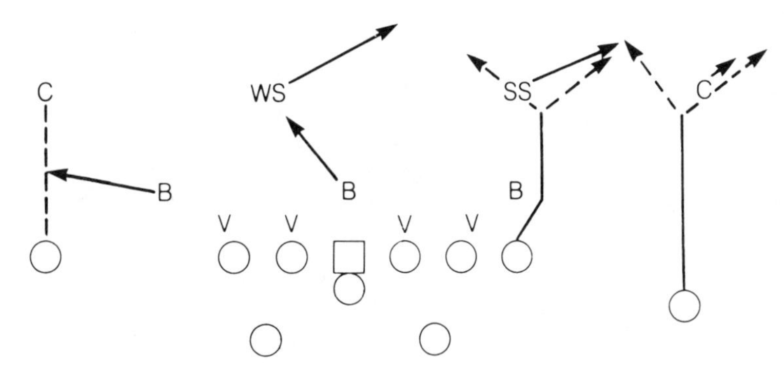

▶ **Figure 15.14** 3-on-2 ("Combo") Coverage

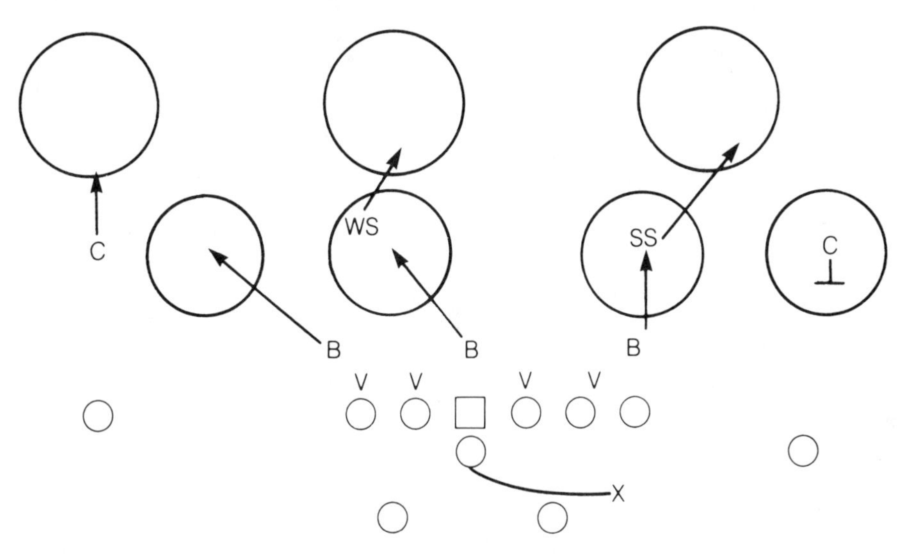

▶ **Figure 15.15** 3-Deep, 4-Short Zone Coverage (Cover 3)

The field can also be divided into two deep halves and five short zones ("cover 2"). This is an ideal arrangement if the offense is connecting on short hook and sideline patterns. It also allows the defense to double cover the FL and SE with the outside HBs and safeties, while the LBs cover the TE and running backs.

A team also can go to a four-deep zone coverage, giving each back a deep quarter of the field to cover. The three LBs or two LBs and an end would then divide the short zones into thirds.

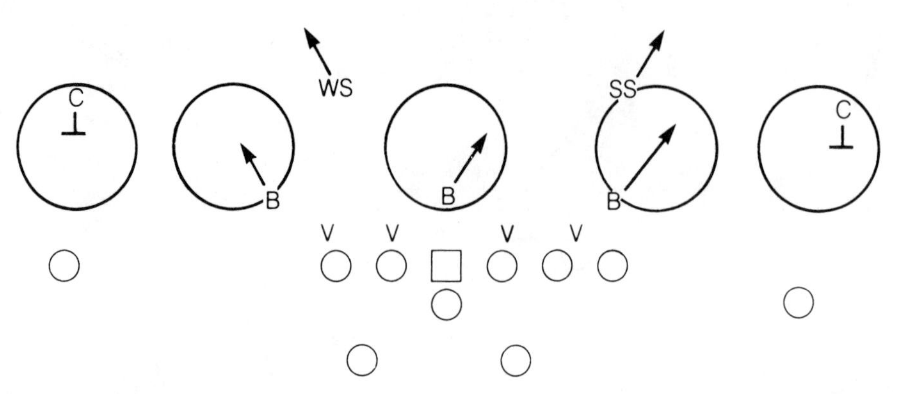

▶ **Figure 15.16** 2-Deep, 5-Short Zone Coverage (Cover 2)

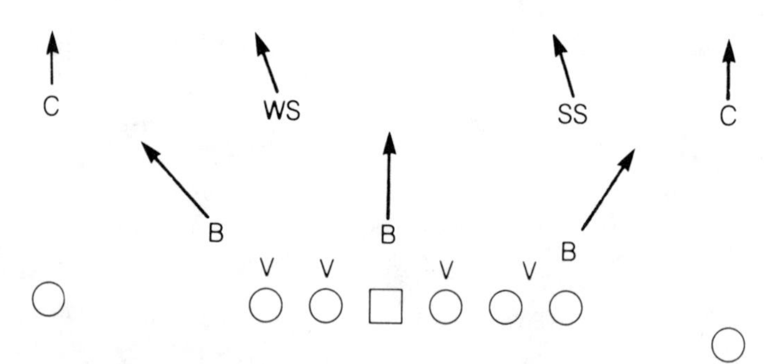

▶ **Figure 15.17** 4-Deep, 3-Short Zone Coverage (Cover 4)

16

Special Defenses

One characteristic of modern football is the explosive nature of offensive attacks. Offenses are much more willing to throw the football on second and goal from the one yard line or march down the field with a perfectly executed two minute drill at the end of a half. Coaches, as a result, have become more wary about going into short yardage or prevent defenses. Yet there are times when short-yardage defenses are necessary.

GOAL LINE AND SHORT YARDAGE DEFENSES

The 6–5 and 8–3 are the most common goal line defenses. The 8–3 is more vulnerable to the pass and thus is used much less frequently. It is easy to teach and, therefore, is still used at lower levels.

6–5 Defense

Many teams that split an end will go to a double tight end formation on the goal line. The defense will be presented against this formation.

The basic defense, possible man-to-man pass coverage assignments, and initial routes of the defensive linemen appear in Figure 16.1.

It is the job of the down linemen on either side of the center to fire through the C-G gaps as soon as the ball moves. They must penetrate at least three feet beyond the line of scrimmage. A low, four-point stance is probably best for this purpose. An offensive guard pulling from the opposite side of the center should hit the down lineman and be unable to lead a power play, as shown in Figure 16.1.

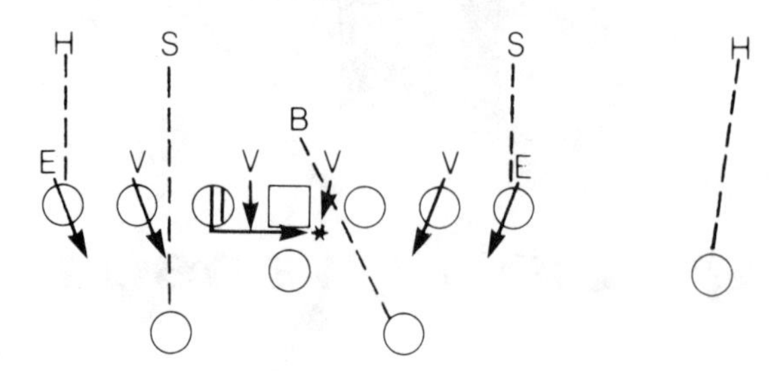

▶ **Figure 16.1** 6-5 Defense

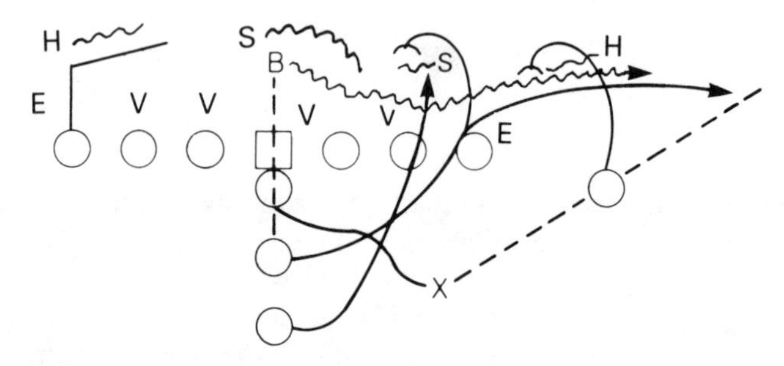

▶ **Figure 16.2** Fullback Flat

The DTs and DEs line up on the outside shoulder of the OTs and OEs and explode *through* their head as they angle down. It is important that their angle of attack be the same. If the end goes too deep it creates a running lane that the offense can capitalize on.

In theory, the MLB should be untouched and, therefore, in on every tackle. Misdirection plays, which are effective against a 6–5, don't allow this to always happen.

The secondary can use a man-to-man defense, a "combo," or a straight zone. In man-to-man, the MLB is generally assigned a halfback. A running fake with the FB slipping into the flat is a tough assignment for any LB. This is a popular goal line play against the 6–5. It is diagrammed in Figure 16.2.

Man-to-man coverage allows a defensive back to come up as soon as his man blocks. Secondary defenders coming up for contain must know the necessary yardage needed by the offense. If only one yard is needed, they may have to abandon outside-in leverage and gamble on a direct hit.

Gap Eight

The gap eight is no longer a popular defense. At the lower levels, however, it has some advantages. It is easy to teach. If a team uses a defense with an eight-man front (6–2, 4–4, wide tackle six), it leaves the linemen's assignments and positions almost unchanged. Once linemen are brought in for the ILBs, a team is ready to run the gap eight defense.

Its major weakness is that not all possible receivers are covered. A team that uses the gap eight must count on a hard pass rush as its best pass defense. The basic philosophy of the defense is to fire every gap and throw the offense for a loss. A low, four-point stance is used as the defensive linemen "submarine" through. Once they are through, the linemen must reach and grab for any legs that look like they belong to a ball carrier!

Because the rushing linemen are in an overextended position as they explode through the gaps, they are vulnerable to a trap block. Even though it might appear to be a poor place to run, a quick trap up the middle can be an effective play against a gap eight defense. The gap eight should only be used as a short yardage defense when a team is certain that the offense is going to run and not pass.

LONG YARDAGE PASS DEFENSE

In sure passing situations, more teams are going with five defensive backs. One possible deployment of personnel is shown in Figure 16.3. From this alignment any number of zone, man-to-man, and combination coverages can be used.

Figure 16.4 illustrates another way in which a team with a basic 5–2 look can go to an almost prevent defense.

PREVENT DEFENSES

Prevent defenses differ from long yardage defenses in that their main objective is to prevent a score rather than a first down. Obviously, the defense is only used at the end of a half. Today's offenses have worked on two-minute drills, so a coach must be careful about adopting a defensive posture too early.

One popular prevent defense that incorporates man-to-man and zone coverage is the 3–5–3 shown in Figure 16.5.

There is only a three-man rush. The two outside rushers must put *outside* leverage on the QB, while the middle rusher watches for the draw.

If a team wants to put more pressure on the QB, the 4–5–2 or 4–4–3 provides a four-man rush.

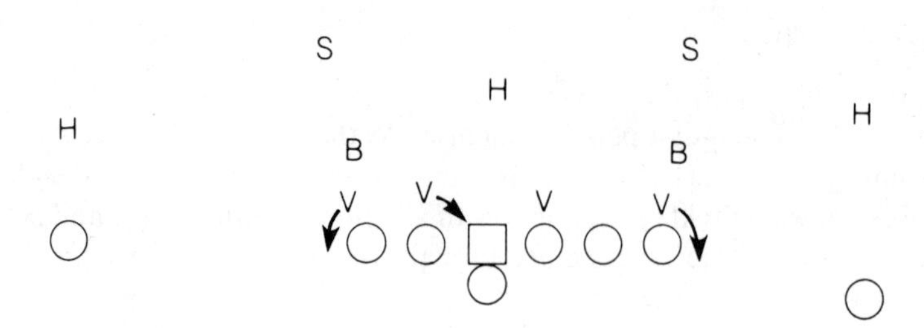

▶ **Figure 16.3** Long Yardage Pass Defense (4 Rushers)

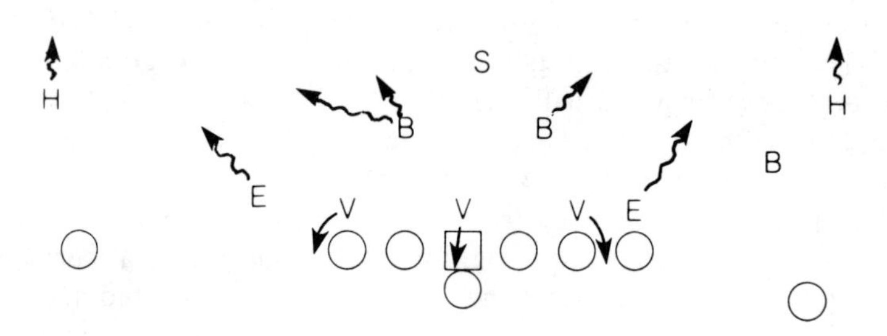

▶ **Figure 16.4** Long Yardage Pass Defense (3 Rushers)

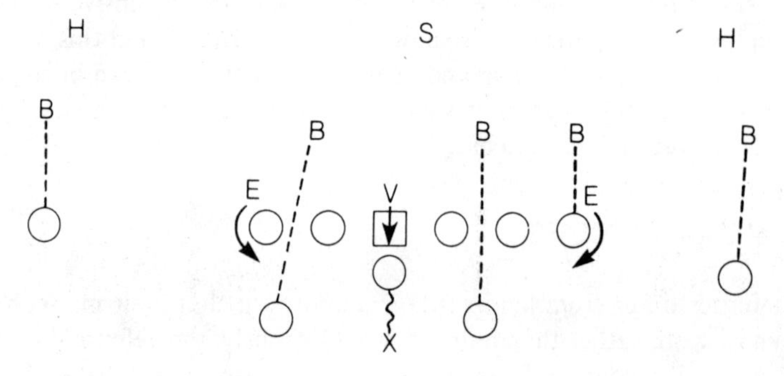

▶ **Figure 16.5** Prevent Defense

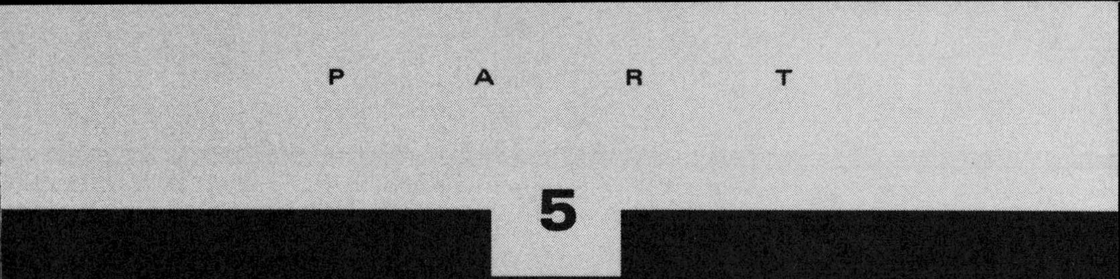

PART 5

17

Individual Skills

Only recently has the importance of the kicking game and the pivotal nature of its components been fully realized and appreciated by many coaches. The outcome of key games often hinges on the kicking game.

The dropped fair catch, a bad snap from center, or a punt block are obvious to everyone. Other aspects are not so readily noticeable. Defensive struggles are often decided in favor of the team that creeps down the field on the leg of the superior punter. Ball games have been lost when a team successfully executes an onside kick. A field goal block team can preserve a key win. The team that prepares for all of these situations by devoting quality practice time to them will be ready when the game situation calls for them.

Oftentimes, a coaching staff must look outside the football team to find good kickers. Kickers may not be among the players that like the traditional elements of football such as blocking and tackling. The day of the burly lineman with a big foot and a lot of beef getting stuck with the job is over. The soccer field, if a school has a soccer team, is an obvious place to look for kickers. Some gifted basketball players, even though the sport involves no kicking, possess the necessary coordination and leg explosion to develop into excellent punters. The coaching staff should assure these athletes that they need not go through all the blocking and tackling drills if they want to play football.

Football, more than any sport in the world, has become a game of specialists. A team is better off when the QB doesn't have to hold for field goal (FG) attempts, much less double as the punter. Once the coaching staff has found the kickers, they should explain to the entire team their essential role in the program. When the team also realizes just how crucial the kicking game is, they will be supportive of these individuals who often seem to be getting out of the tough parts of practice.

Kickers must have the proverbial nerves of steel. The punter who is kicking out of his own end zone while the team is nursing a one point lead must be oblivious to the rush of hostile jerseys. The FG kicker, who watches the clock tick down to four seconds before a time out is called, and he goes in for one attempt, knows that cheers or jeers await him depending on the outcome.

This unit consists of four chapters. They are: 1) Individual Skills, 2) The Punting Game, 3) Kick-off Coverage and Return, and 4) Field Goal and Point After Touchdown.

PUNTING

Deep Snap

Since single-wing offenses are almost nonexistent, a snap to anyone other than a QB standing directly behind the center has become a lost art. A coach has to teach someone to deep snap. Yet most coaches know little about the skill and published materials are rare.

Both hands should be used to snap the ball. The hand that is placed closest to the line of scrimmage is the power hand, and the other hand acts as a guide. Snapping with one hand is dangerous. One-hand snappers often lift the ball up and then snap it. This can prove costly since a quick middle guard might deflect the ball prior to release. It is also illegal. In inclement weather the second hand provides a surer grip.

The center's legs should be spread apart wide enough to allow the arms to snap through a maximum distance, thereby increasing the potential velocity. The arms should reach forward and grasp the ball without placing an excessive amount of weight on it. The power hand grasps the ball with the index finger close to the tip and the rest of the hand wraps alongside and slightly under the ball. The guide hand is placed along the left side of the ball. It keeps the point of the ball directed to the punter as the power hand drives through.

The center looks at the punter's hands between his legs and keeps his eyes focused on them as he snaps the ball. Only after the snap does he look upfield. His main job is to get the ball, on target, to the punter. In most offenses, the punter indicates when he is ready to punt by extending his hands to the center. The center, when he is ready, vigorously thrusts his power hand in an extended sweeping motion to the punter. The velocity of the power hand at the instant of release indicates the velocity of the ball. The ball must be given some spin, since spin is what gives an object stability in flight and prevents wobble. This happens quite naturally. The power hand flexes and comes up slightly while the guide hand remains slightly underneath. This action rotates the ball on its long axis.

If the snap is done correctly, the snapper will complete the motion with the palms rotated outward (pronated) and with the arms hitting the inside of the thighs so vigorously that it causes him to jump back.

Most punters like to receive the ball at waist height. Some punting coaches insist that knee height is more effective. A good center will get the ball to the punter standing at 13 yards in not more than .9 seconds.

Punter's Stance

Most coaches align the punter directly behind the center at a depth of thirteen yards. The kicking foot is generally placed six to twelve inches in front of the other foot. The arms are extended in front of the body with the palms of the hands down and no higher than the punter's waist, giving the center a good target.

Catch

The punter should always expect a bad snap and be ready to move to the ball. As the ball approaches, his arms are almost fully extended. When the ball contacts the hands, the arms absorb the force with a smooth recoil. This recoil action of the arms will bring the ball in close to the "hip pocket."

Steps

Punters must learn to take two steps. A three-step approach takes too long and brings the punter too close to the line of scrimmage. The only alternative is to receive the ball at fifteen yards and begin the steps well in advance of receiving the ball. This can be dangerous if the snap is not on target.

As the punter is receiving the football, he should be stepping forward with the kicking foot. The length of this initial stride varies greatly. Some punting experts stress forward acceleration of the total body. Other coaches recommend a longer initial stride. Still other coaches stress the angular velocity of the kicking leg as the key ingredient and recommend a shorter initial stride. Ball velocity will be determined by the linear velocity of the body and the angular velocity generated at the hip and knee joint. It would seem advantageous, therefore, to maximize stride length and speed of leg rotation.

The second step must be longer than the first and executed more quickly as the punting foot begins driving through. The steps must be made *directly in line* with the intended flight of the ball.

Ball Drop

Most experts agree that this phase of the punting sequence causes the most problems. The drop must be exactly the same every time. Some punters drop the ball with two hands while others make the final release with only the hand of the kicking foot. The drop that enables the kicker to be consistent is the drop that should be used. The ball should be guided down and released at as low a point as possible, since this provides less distance for its trajectory to vary.

Foot Contact

In order for the ball to have a consistent trajectory it must contact the foot at the same location every time. It should contact the foot virtually directly in the middle of the instep. Many punters drop the ball too far to the outside of the foot. This will give the ball increased spin and stability in flight but at the expense of height and distance. A ball does not need much rotation on its longitudinal axis to maintain stability. The normal unexaggerated movement of the kicking leg to the center of the body will give the ball the rotation it needs. Another controversial point is whether the ball should be dropped parallel to the ground or parallel to the instep of the kicking foot at the moment of contact.

The instep of the foot is angled slightly downward at the moment of contact; therefore, the ball must be angled slightly downward also. If the ball is not placed parallel to the instep of the kicking foot, the front or back end of the ball will make contact first and a good spiral will not result.

The ball should contact a rigid surface. The loose foot that some coaches advocate is incorrect. Force that is lost by absorption into the foot and shoe is force that is not transferred to the ball. Punters should not wear two pair of socks or do anything that will cut down on the rigidity of the foot surface.

Swing Leg

The key to height and distance in punting is the velocity that the kicking foot can generate at contact and the trajectory of the football. A 45 degree angle of release will provide maximum distance. A higher trajectory will provide greater hang time but less distance. Punters must work at generating foot velocity through a vigorous extension of the lower leg around the knee joint. It is a serious error for a punter to swing across the ball from the outside in. The leg will naturally roll slightly to the midline of the body, but an exaggerated movement will cause loss of height and distance.

Punters must work at getting the kick away in 1.3 to 1.5 seconds. The total time from the snap to the kick should not exceed 2.2 to 2.4 seconds.

Follow Through

Follow through is important in order to prevent injury and to insure maximum power through the point of contact. An ideal hang time is around four seconds.

Practice Tips

1. Punters should begin practice with a lot of stretching exercises because stretched muscles are less susceptible to injury and allow for greater range of motion of body parts.
2. Punters should start kicking slowly and not go for maximum height and distance until they are fully warmed up.
3. Punters must learn to "listen" to their bodies. They should let their legs be the judge of the number of kicks per day. It is impossible to set a specific number for every punter.
4. Kickers should continue weight work during the season. They cannot afford to lose strength in their legs.
5. Punters should simulate thèse game conditions:
   a. Kicking out-of-bounds (a punched, controlled line drive kick).
   b. Kicking into the wind (a low trajectory kick).
   c. Kicking out of the end zone (don't step on the end line; do get the kick off quickly).
   d. Kicking a wet ball (make sure the ball doesn't slip through one's hands).

THE KICKOFF

Traditional (Toe) Kickers

Most kickers do not place the ball at much of an angle on the kicking tee. The angle of the ball is not the key factor in height versus distance. If the foot contacts the ball through its center of gravity, a line drive will result. If the contact point is too far below the ball's center of gravity, the ball will go too high. If the ball is placed at too much of an angle on the tee, it provides the kicker with a smaller target and accuracy of foot placement on the ball becomes more difficult.

The laces on the football should be placed straight down the field. If they are to one side, it shifts the ball's center of mass to that side and will cause the ball to curve due to the creation of irregular air currents.

Kickers vary greatly in the distance that they travel prior to kicking the ball. Toe kickers usually take a longer approach since the creation of linear velocity by the body is more important than it is for the soccer-style kicker. A distance of approximately ten yards is common.

Regardless of the number of steps taken, the plant of the nonkicking foot should be about six inches behind and three inches to the side of the ball. This will allow the swing (kicking) foot to pass close to the plant foot and contact the ball with a slight upward angle to the foot. As the swing leg makes its final approach to the ball, it is bent greatly at the knee. This allows the leg to swing forward much more quickly. The ankle is locked. Just prior to contact, the lower leg is vigorously snapped forward by a forceful extension of the quadriceps (thigh muscles). The kicker should not try to kick the ball into the air. Foot contact point will determine that. He must concentrate on driving the kicking foot *through* the ball. Follow through is as important as it is in punting. It helps prevent injury and insures maximum foot velocity through the point of contact.

The kicking shoe should fit snugly. This gives the kicker a better feel for the ball. A firm, square kicking toe aids in both velocity and accuracy and must be worn by any serious kicker.

Soccer (Instep) Kickers

Since soccer-style kickers contact the ball high on the instep, it is more difficult for them to make contact close to the ground. This causes them to contact the ball closer to its center of mass, and a lower trajectory often results. Most toe kickers kick the ball at a 34–35 degree angle from the horizontal, while most instep kickers launch the ball between 29 and 30 degrees.

The approach angle varies, but a 30 degree variance from directly behind the ball is common. The distance of the approach also varies. Most soccer-style kickers use a shorter approach because more of the contributing force is from the leg swing and less from the linear velocity generated by the body.

The approach steps must be measured so that the nonkicking foot plants alongside the ball approximately one foot away. The toe is pointed only slightly toward the side of the kicking foot and will rotate away from it as the kicking leg sweeps through. The kicking leg is cocked back with the heel coming close to the buttocks.

As the nonkicking foot plants alongside the ball, the hips begin to rotate, the upper body straightens, and the kicking foot vigorously uncocks through knee extension as it sweeps through in an arc. The upper body almost leans back at contact. This is in direct contrast to the toe kicker, who drives his body as well as his foot *through* the ball.

PLACE KICKING: FIELD GOAL (F.G.) AND POINT AFTER TOUCHDOWN (P.A.T.)

Center

The center's first and foremost responsibility is to make a fast and accurate snap. The mechanics of a correct snap are the same as those covered for the deep snap. The holder on a place kick, however, is only seven yards deep and must bring the ball down and put it on the tee. The center must keep the snap low, and keeping the buttocks down assists in this. He must not be intimidated by sudden movements of the defense. The snap should arrive in the holder's hands in .5 to .6 seconds.

Holder

The holder generally coordinates the attack. He counts to make sure that only eleven men are on the field, gets the offense set with a verbal command, and indicates to the center with a slight hand movement when he and the team are ready for the snap. Good holders must be individuals who are used to handling the football. They must have quick, "soft" hands. A QB in this capacity gives the team greater potential in a fake field goal situation.

The knee nearest the kicker is on the ground about six inches behind the point where the ball will be spotted. The ball should be placed almost vertically on the tee with the index finger of the hand closest to the line of scrimmage. The other hand spins the ball to insure that the laces intersect the plane of the crossbar. A good holder can position the ball on the tee in .5 to .6 seconds from the time he receives it.

Kicker

The basic mechanics covered under the kickoff apply. The obvious difference is the defensive pressure that places a time constraint on the kick. Because of this pressure, a good place kicker must have self-confidence and poise. Coaches should take care not to shake the beginning kicker's confidence by having him try long shots early in the season unless it is absolutely necessary. Nothing bolsters confidence like success.

Most place kickers take two steps. For some, the first step is a short rolling step, but with others it is longer. The kicker cannot wait until the ball is resting securely on the tee to begin his first step. He must begin this step while the ball is being placed on the tee. The toe kicker must generate a lot of total body momentum in a short period of time. A longer step enables him to do this.

Accuracy is often more crucial than distance. The place kicker must line himself up properly, make sure that the plant foot is straight to the target, and drive the kicking foot directly through the point of contact. When kicking an extra point, elevation is important. The plant foot should be positioned almost alongside the ball so that the kicking foot will make contact lower on the ball. Once the ball is on the tee, the kick should go off in .2 seconds or less.

On the follow through most place kickers will skip along with the plant foot before the kicking foot finally lands about two to three yards behind the center.

Many kickers feel that successful kicking is as much mental as it is physical. Kickers should review or visualize kicks over and over in their minds.

Practice Tips

1. Practice kicking from the hash marks. Some kickers have great difficulty making correct alignment when they have to kick at an angle. Make sure that kickers practice from varying angles at every practice.
2. Take advantage of adverse weather practice days. A kicker who takes a long stride onto the plant foot may slip on wet or icy turf and will have to shorten his last stride.
3. Use onrushing linemen in practice. Field goal practice should be realistic. Interrupt scrimmages occasionally and give the place kicker a *single* try.
4. Practice on windy days. The kicker must adjust to crosswinds. The only way he can learn their effect is through practicing under these conditions.
5. Develop leg strength. Kickers must spend time in the weight room during the season as well as in the off-season. The quadriceps (extensors of the knee) of the kicking leg are the single most important muscle group to develop.

THE KICKOFF AND PUNT RETURN

Fielding the Ball

Certain individuals possess the necessary physical attributes to gather in a punt or kickoff. Others seem to lack the necessary depth perception to position themselves in the proper location and must make dangerously quick adjustments at the last minute. Coaches must identify those individuals on the team that can catch a kicked football consistently and allow them to practice this skill.

Running in the Open Field

Not all successful runners from the line of scrimmage are as effective when initiating their run from the open field. The punt returner, especially, must be oblivious to movement around him. He must not let the ball hit the ground. This demands a confidence bordering on cockiness.

Blocking above the Waist

Open field blocking above the waist on kickoffs, punt returns, and after interceptions is a skill that most teams do not practice. The blocker must stay on his feet and approach the person he intends to block in a controlled manner. At the last moment he should coil and strike *up* and *through* the chest area of the man he is blocking.

BLOCKING THE PLACE KICK OR PUNT

Every coach should spot those players who aren't afraid to launch their bodies in the direction of an oncoming football. Oftentimes this is the same person who makes those jarring open field tackles on the other specialty teams. This person must have the quickness to get off on the snap of the ball, the speed to get to the contact point, and the agility to get by potential blockers. But all of these qualities are of no use if he is unwilling to have a hard kicked football hit him.

The blocker must have the common sense to not continue an incorrect route when he senses that it will cause him to hit the kicker. Bad judgment that results in a penalty and gives the opposition an automatic first down can be a very costly mistake.

18

The Punting Game

PUNT FORMATION, PROTECTION, AND COVERAGE

Punt Formations

A spread punt formation of some sort is used by almost every football team. The formation diagrammed in Figure 18.1 is the most common. Other formations have the upbacks on the line of scrimmage or back with personal protector creating a three-deep wall. In the latter instance, two protectors will be on the side of the punter's kicking foot.

The spread punt formation allows for a quicker release off the line of scrimmage since the punter is deeper. It also gives the punt team greater lateral coverage of the field since the splits are wider.

Punt Protection

Protection can either be by area or by person. In *person* protection, the upbacks and linemen use a counting process in determining who they block. Counting can be done from the *inside-out* or the *outside-in*. The center is generally not assigned anyone. His sole job is to deliver a good snap to the punter and get to the ball. Since a punt is blocked most frequently from the kicking foot side, the upback away from the kicking foot takes a man lined up on the center. It is a simple counting process with the upback taking the #1 man, the guard the #2 man, and so on. If the #4 man is outside the offensive end, he need not block him. If he is inside, he must not be allowed to take a direct path to the punter. Note Figure 18.1.

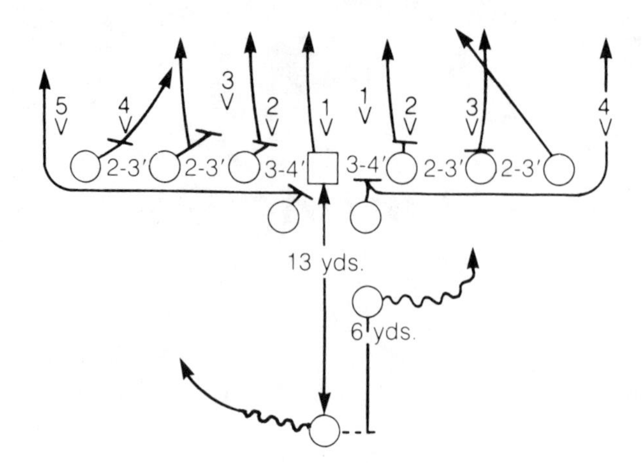

▶ **Figure 18.1** Punt Formation and Coverage

Other teams will number blocks from the *outside-in.* If a team rushes nine men, the offense will have nine men to block them since the center normally is not given a blocking assignment and the punter obviously can't block anyone. If a team rushes ten men, the center may have to stay in and the upbacks will have to spot where the rush is coming from and be ready to slide across and help immediately after the ball passes them. A verbal call like "red light right" or "red light left" can alert the upbacks to the direction from which the rush is coming.

In *area* blocking, the linemen recoil and the upbacks step up, thereby creating a wall of blockers. Each blocker blocks the man over him or to his outside unless the man inside of him yells "gap." In that case he must block down to the inside. Each blocker must watch for stunts and pick up any attacker that comes into his area. In both types of protection, the personal protector picks up the most dangerous man.

Another variation of area blocking is to have the linemen all block *out.* If a man is head up on him, he is blocked by the next person to the inside. Defensive players from the nose of the guards to the inside are blocked by the upbacks and the personal protector. In this type of protection these three people must be excellent blockers. If more than three defensive players are coming from the nose of the guards to the inside, "red light middle" is called and players block down.

Punt Coverage

Some coaches will send the center and ends on a direct path to the ball as recklessly and quickly as possible. The two upbacks swing wide to contain the ball carrier. The interior linemen release after their blocks and move down the field as a wide unit of four. They should converge on the ball carrier through their inside shoulder. Coaches with this philosophy will be less concerned about the height of the punt. They prefer a little more distance and will gamble on the center and ends getting to the return man.

Most coaches, however, look for good "hang time." In this way the protection can be better and return yardage is unlikely.

If the punt receiver calls for a fair catch, the first man should run straight past the receiver in case he lets it go over his head. The rest of the team should come to a balanced position five yards in front of the receiver and wait.

The kicker and personal protector are the safeties on the right and left sides of the field. The kicker also must yell "right," "left," "middle," and "short" to assist the men going down the field.

If teams know that the offensive ends are sent directly to the football, other personnel can be called in the huddle to perform this function. The upbacks or even the tackles could be sent, with the ends staying in to block.

PUNT RETURN

Several principles should be kept in mind as a team plans and practices its punt return. One person should be assigned to insure that the kicker kicks the ball and isn't allowed to wait until the offensive linemen can run under the kick. Some teams have two receivers back in tandem or side-by-side while others have three back. The number and positioning of the receivers depends on the effectiveness, accuracy, and strategy of the punting team. A final principle that is important is to bring the wall or picket to the ball. If a punt is to the receiving team's right and the wall is forming to the left, it should be brought over near the middle of the field.

Punt return formations differ considerably. Teams generally will attempt to disguise their intentions of a right, left, or middle return. In the right or left return when the ball is snapped, the linemen on the side of the return hit the offensive linemen over them and peel back to form a "picket." The linemen closest to the sideline of the return go the deepest. The depth of the picket will depend upon the anticipated distance of the punt. The outside lineman away from the side of the return will penetrate to the kicker, force the kick, and then swing around and form the farthest post of the picket. If the punting team sends its upbacks or ends down the field on the snap of the ball, they should be held up. Some teams will even assign two men to alternately hit an effective open field tackler. Backs who do not receive the punt must get in front of the ball carrier and block. Two possible punt returns are diagrammed in Figure 18.2.

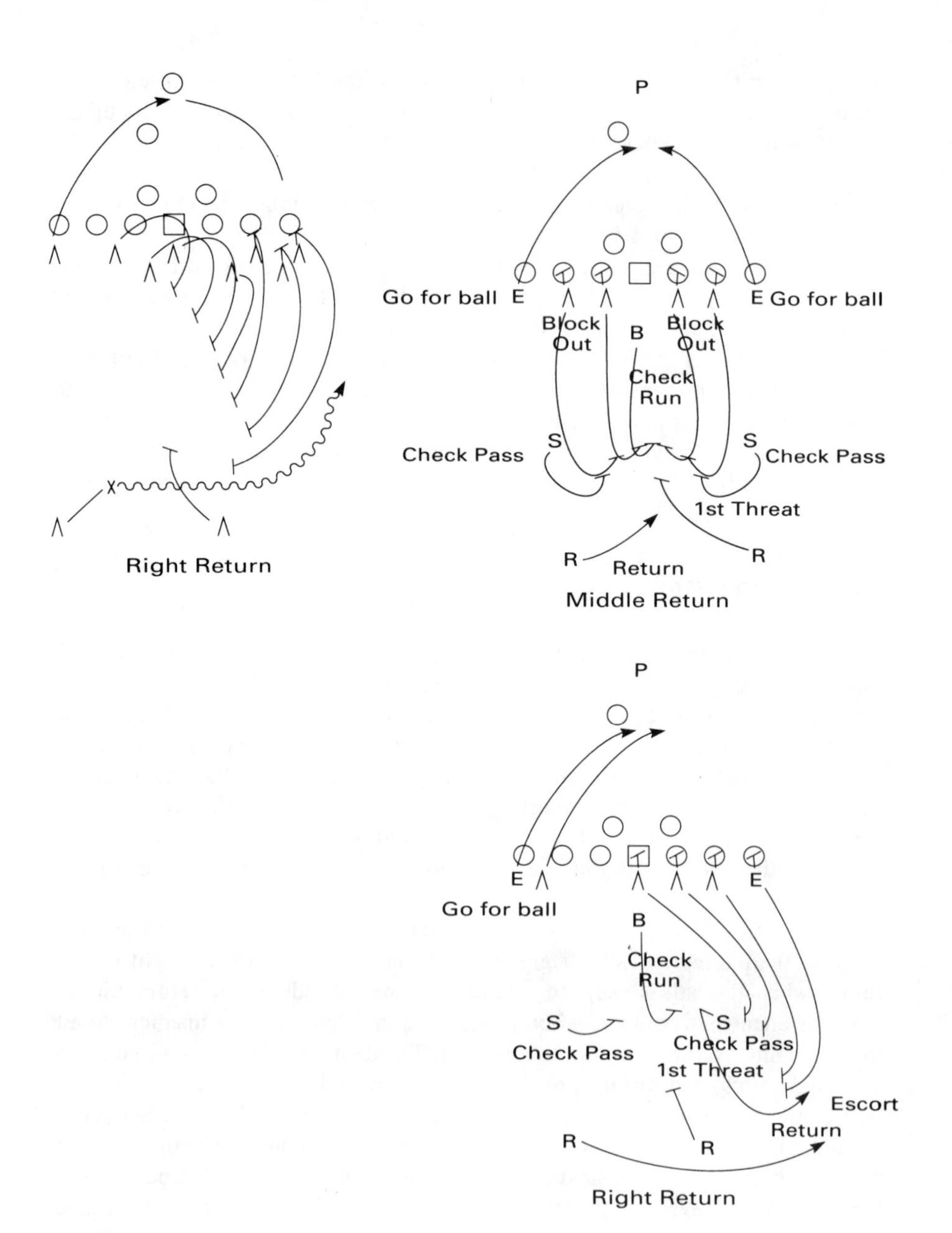

▶ **Figure 18.2** Punt Return

PUNT BLOCK

A punt block or even a near block early in a game can unnerve a team. The punter rushes subsequent kicks and the linemen block longer, thereby making their coverage less effective. When coaches are scouting a team, they should look for weakness in personnel, alignment, or technique. If the line splits are small, it may be best to attempt a block from the outside. If, on the other hand, they are wide, a block from the inside might be more effective. If the center doesn't have a lot of velocity on the ball or the punter takes slow, long steps, the punt block is in order. An inside block is more dangerous since the path of the punt blocker is more directly at the punter. For this reason it is better to plan the block with the key blocking lane outside the tackle.

The basic idea of most punt blocks is to create a seam for a defensive person to get through by overloading an offensive blocker. A roughing the kicker penalty is costly, so the blockers must be drilled in going to the point where the ball will be kicked rather than to the point where the kicker initially lines up.

Placing one's body over a football that has just left a kicker's foot is not a natural instinct and, therefore, needs to be practiced. Some athletes will not do it. Coaches need to identify players with this instinct and then allow them to actually experience the feeling in a controlled environment. Actually feeling the sensation of taking a ball off a punter's foot easily at first, and then with added velocity, will alleviate some of the fear that is associated with this unnatural skill.

Some teams make it very obvious whether they are attempting a run back or a block. Without too much work, the defense can be aligned so that their intentions are masked until the last moment.

FAKE PUNT

Every team should have a run and a pass from their basic punt formation. There will come the time in a ball game when these plays are needed, and if they haven't been practiced, they won't be as effective. A simple pass play is to have the punter or the personal protector, if the ball is snapped to him, pass the ball to either end as he fans out. The pass also can go to the upbacks as they slip into the hook zones. The most effective pass will depend on defensive tendencies as noted in the scouting report.

One of many fake punt run plays that a team can use has the personal protector getting the snap from the center and making a forward hand off to the far upback as he runs around end, with the other upback as a lead blocker.

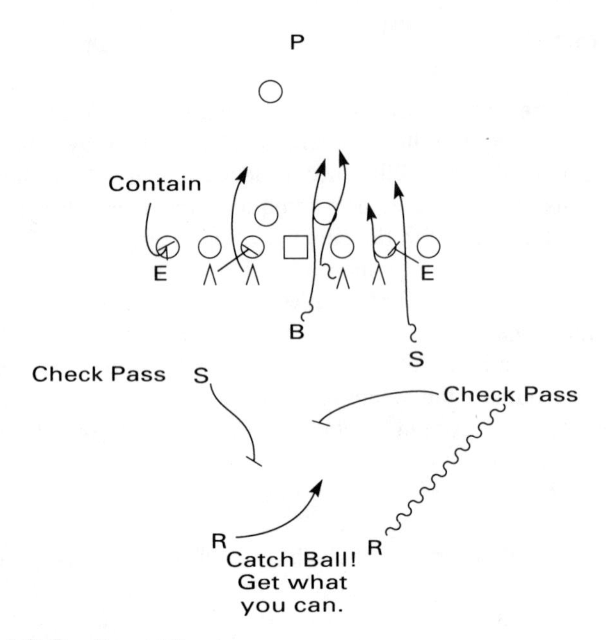

▶ **Figure 18.3** Punt Block

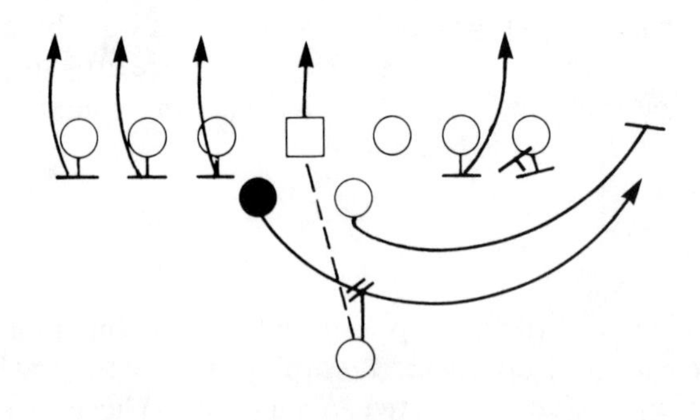

▶ **Figure 18.4** Fake Punt

QUICK KICK (PUNT)

There are times when it is advisable for a team to disguise its intentions to punt. If a team's offense isn't very effective, if the punter has a low trajectory to his punt, or if a team is backed up on its own goal line, surprising a team with a quick kick from a nonpunting formation can be effective strategy. When inclement weather is making the snapping and handling of the ball treacherous, a third down punt with the QB taking a direct snap from the center and pitching it to a back to punt may very well be the best and safest strategy.

Some creative coaches never line up in a traditional punting formation. They line up on fourth down in a formation from which they can run, pass, or punt. A triple threat back gets the ball and runs with the option to pass or kick from the run. If a team does not have a punting specialist, but has a QB who can do an adequate job, this may be an exciting possibility to explore.

SHORT PUNT

The short punt has also been called the squib, blooper, coffin-corner, and out-of-bounds punt. It is used when the kicking team wants to put the opposition inside its own ten yard line. The punter can either aim for a corner and attempt to direct the ball out-of-bounds inside the ten or put more loft on the ball and have it land inside the ten. The squib or blooper kick has the advantage of a potential fumble by the opposition. If, however, a team has a very accurate line drive type punter, they may have him aim at the corner flag. The blockers should be told the direction of the intended punt so that their protection can be stiffened in that direction. If a punter is going to kick at the corner flag to his right, the defensive left end obviously must be blocked. This should be the assignment of the personal protector.

INTENTIONAL SAFETY

There may be times when a coaching staff will decide to give the opposition a two-point safety. This might occur in the waning moments of a game when the offense is backed up against its own end zone and has more than a two point lead. When an intentional safety is called, the linemen should hold their blocks a little longer. The punter should take as much time off the clock as possible before stepping out the back of the end zone or dropping to one knee.

19

Kickoff Coverage and Return

THE KICKOFF

Coaches must work at developing an esprit de corps in the kicking team. Their role is crucial in determining where the opposition will begin its opening series of offensive plays.

Most teams tee the ball in the middle of the field and position five men on each side of the kicker. The initial alignment of the coverage men varies. Some teams line them up in a straight line on the 25- or 30-yard line. Other teams line up in a bowed formation with those close to the center of the field deeper and those on the sideline up with the ball. Still other teams will stagger the depth of various coverage men, depending on their assignments on the kickoff. Some teams have even explored the use of motion on the kickoff, with two players going in motion on a signal from the kicker and cutting upfield between players. This can confuse blocking assignments and be a very effective onside kick technique.

A kickoff team should consist of four types of people: containers, laners, sprinters, and safeties. The kicker could perform any of these functions, depending on his skills. Two people are containers. It is their job to see that the ball carrier does not get outside of them. They need not necessarily line up on the sideline. Some teams use two safeties, others use one. Three players usually are assigned to go directly to the ball and are encouraged to take any chances in their attempt to disrupt the opponent's return plan. The remaining men are laners that

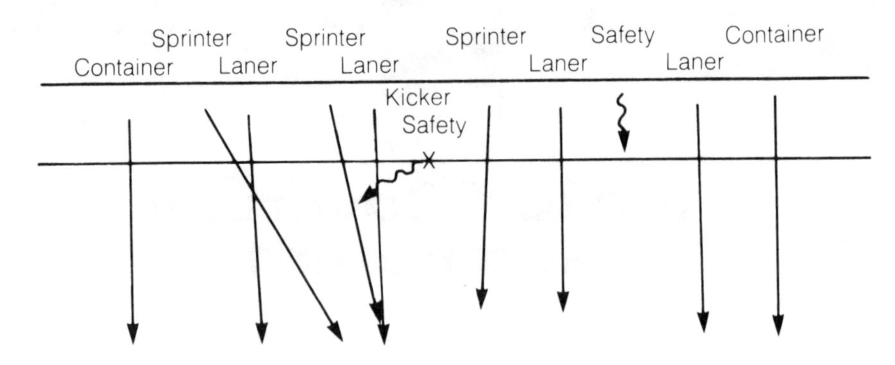

▶ Figure 19.1 KickOff Coverage

sprint down the field in their respective lanes until the return route is clearly determined. They should watch for reverse. Figure 19.1 illustrates how a kickoff team might look.

ONSIDE KICK

This is another example of a little thing sometimes overlooked in a coach's preparation that can become crucial in a given situation. Once the ball has gone ten yards, it becomes a free ball and can be recovered by the kicking team.

Some kickers kick the ball with a combination of top and sidespin by hitting the ball on the top right in an attempt to send it skidding to the left side just past ten yards. Others run at the ball from an angle and kick it near the top hoping for a high bounce just before the ball travels ten yards. The speedsters that have been placed on that side sprint to recover the ball.

Onside kicks have been returned for touchdowns, so the men on the opposite side of the ball should become safeties. Onside kicks can be kicked from the hash to give a team more field for coverage and less chance for the ball to go out of bounds.

Not many teams seriously consider using an onside kick unless they are behind in the late stages of a game. Some coaches, however, scout each opponent's alignment and drop to determine if the kick might be an effective surprise element at any point in the ball game. If a 15-yard penalty is assessed against the kickoff return team, it can be an excellent time for the kicking team to attempt an onside kick. This is another aspect of the kicking game, where the creative coach can have a little fun.

DEFENSING THE ONSIDE KICK

Coaches must be aware of the possibility of an onside kick. The front five men must always check the depth of the kick before setting up their return. They also must align themselves across the field so that they don't leave the sideline area vulnerable.

When the game situation calls for an onside kick, coaches on the receiving team must get men with sure hands up front and bring additional men up into any vulnerable areas.

KICKOFF RETURN

There are two schools of thought on returning kickoffs. Many coaches draw up plays with all eleven men assigned specific tasks. They will have a middle and a sideline return. This approach has the advantage of clearly assigning responsibilities. Diagrammed in Figure 19.2 is a common sideline return with the two most crucial men being double-teamed and Figure 19.3 diagrams a middle return.

Critics of this approach say that it is unrealistic. They contend that by the time the blockers and potential kickers reach the blocking zone, it may be better to have the blockers blocking someone else. Even though a team has been scouted carefully, it is difficult to know which individuals will become safeties or the route that each kickoff person will take. For these reasons, other coaches shy away from complicated kickoff return plays. They will attempt to form a picket or alley with the front five blockers and use the ends and backs as a wedge or personal escort for the ball carrier. No specific blocking assignments are made. An example of double wedge blocking is shown in Figure 19.4.

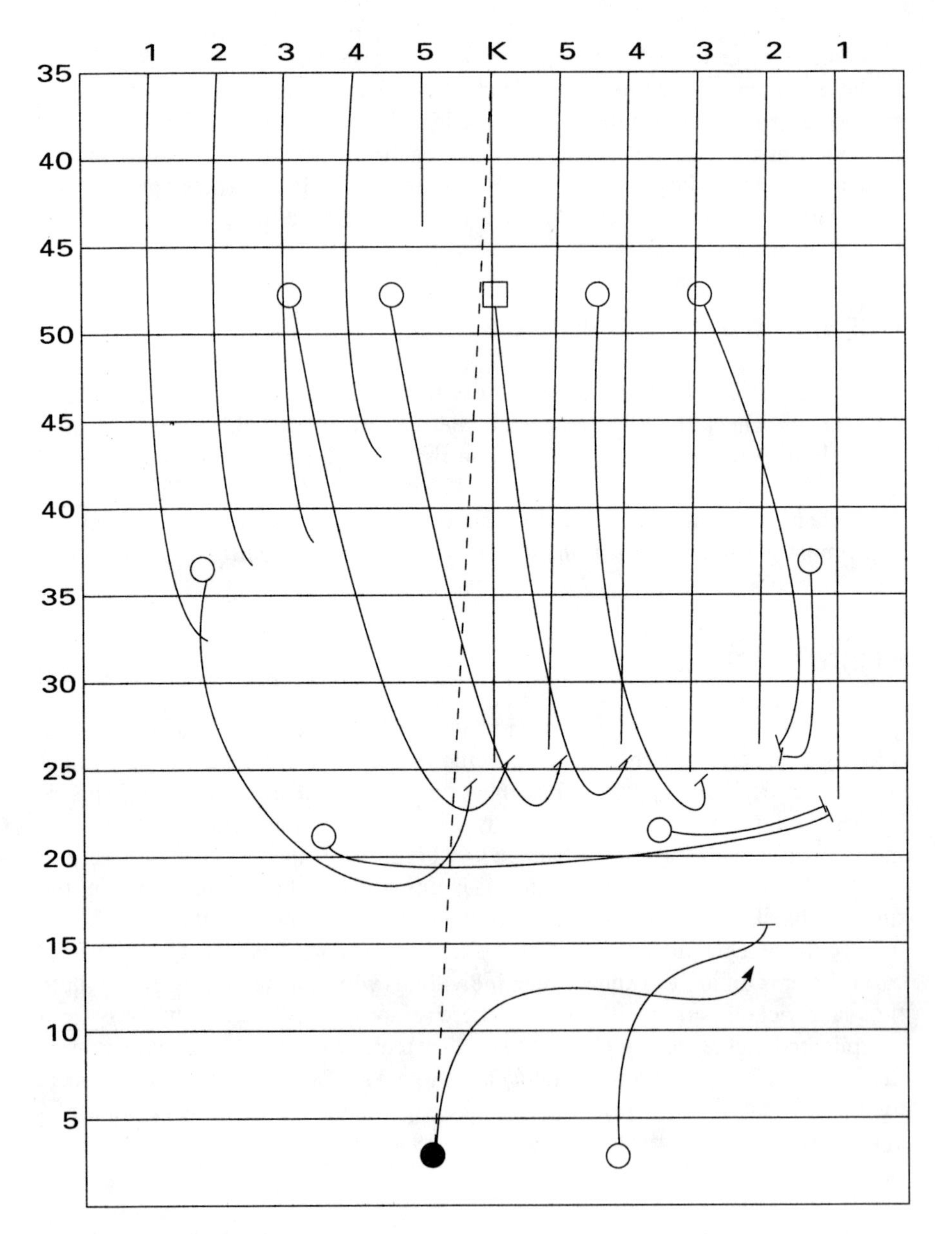

▶ **Figure 19.2** KickOff Return (Right-Left)

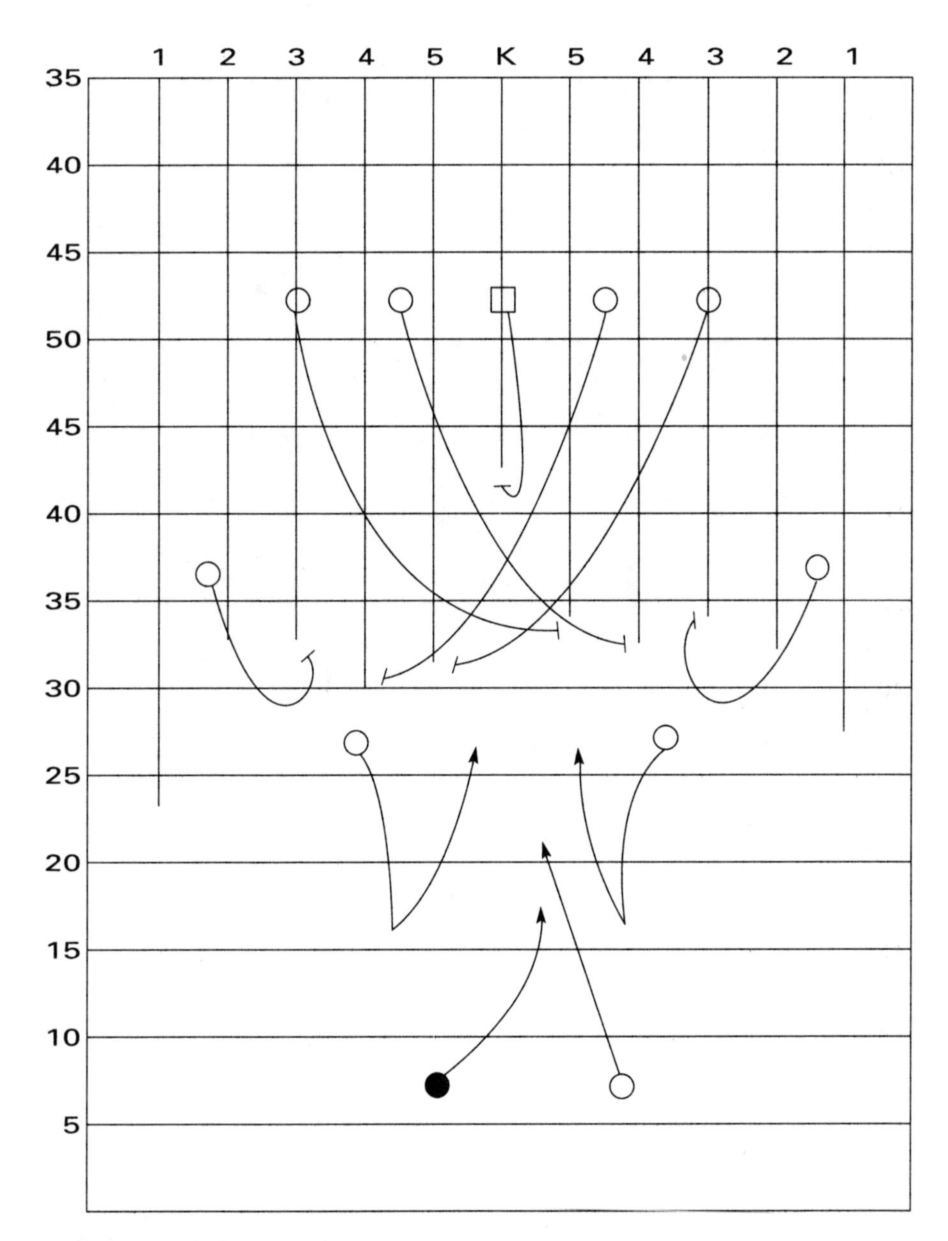

▶ **Figure 19.3** KickOff Return (Middle)

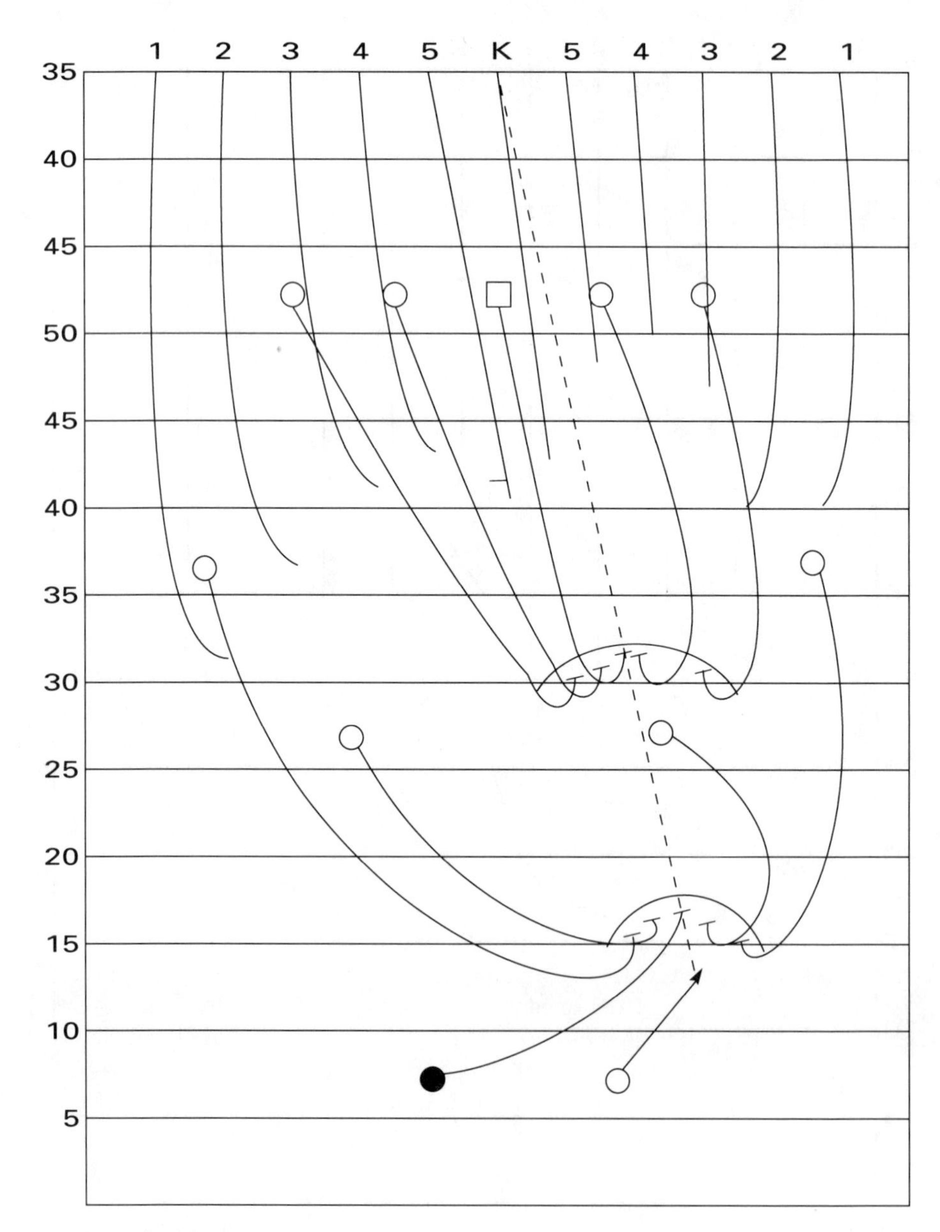

▶ **Figure 19.4** Double Wedge Return

20

Field Goal and Point After Touchdown

F.G. AND P.A.T.

The most common formation for the field goal (F.G.) and point after touchdown (P.A.T.) is diagrammed in Figure 20.1. Attempts are usually blocked by an outside rusher so the offensive unit must get blockers with as much width as possible along the front. Everyone along the front must understand that he is responsible for the gap to his *inside.* He has absolutely no outside responsibility.

When a F.G. is attempted, the two outside upbacks contain and the linemen fan out and advance down the field. The holder and kicker become safeties.

F.G. AND P.A.T. BLOCK

The most likely place from which the defense can block an attempt is from the outside. Men should be placed on either side of the outside upbacks. The inside rusher should try to force the upback to cave down as far as possible, thereby leaving as direct a route as possible for the outside rusher to literally hurtle his body to a point five feet in front of the holder.

Another possible location to block a F.G. attempt is over the center, if the two linemen on either side of him do not collapse to the middle as they should.

FAKE F.G. AND P.A.T.

The fake F.G is another play that coaches often don't practice. Yet it can turn the complexion of a ball game around. In a recent game, one professional football team known for its willingness to be creative broke a game open at the close of

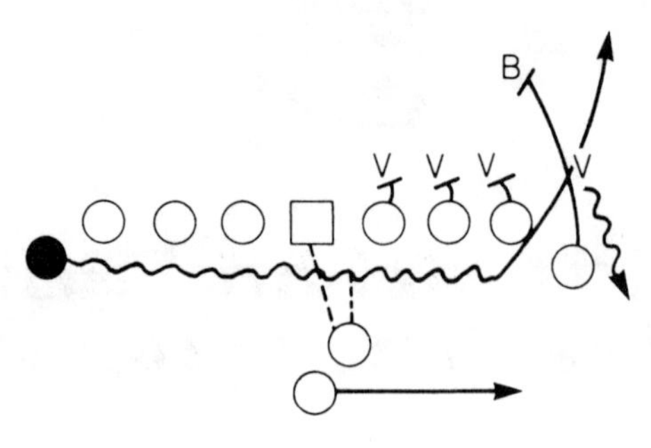

Figure 20.1 Field Goal (P.A.T.) Formation and Fake F.G. Run

the first half with a beautifully executed fake field goal. They had the kicker swing wide to his right, drawing the defensive left end with him. The offensive right end blocked the tackle down. The holder made a beautiful forward flick pass to the left upback as he scooted behind the line, took the flip, and raced upfield inside the defensive left end. He scored a fifteen yard touchdown and was not touched until he was at the three yard line! Note Figure 20.1.

Coaches can use their creativity and come up with other exciting but workable fake F.G. plays.

INDEX

C

D

E

F

G

H

O

P

Q

R

S

W